REGIONALISM AND NATIONAL UNITY IN NEPAL

FREDERICK H. GAIGE

REGIONALISM AND NATIONAL UNITY IN NEPAL

UNIVERSITY OF CALIFORNIA PRESS
BERKELEY · LOS ANGELES · LONDON

UNIVERSITY OF CALIFORNIA PRESS
Berkeley and Los Angeles, California

University of California Press, Ltd.
London, England

Copyright © 1975, by
The Regents of the University of California

ISBN 0–520–02728–0
Library of Congress Catalog Card Number: 74–76385

Photosetting by Thomson Press (India) Limited, New Delhi.

Printed in the United States of America.

Austra and I dedicate this book to
the memory of a beloved friend,
Gordon C. Roadarmel

*With appreciation to Davidson College
for subsidizing the publication of this book.*

CONTENTS

Preface	xv
I. Geopolitics of the Tarai	1
The Physical Setting	2
Religious Characteristics of the Population	12
Linguistic Characteristics of the Population	15
Caste Characteristics of the Population	17
Marriage Ties Between the People of the Tarai and Northern India	22
The Process of "Nepalization"	22
II. Economy of the Tarai	24
Notes on the Economic History of the Tarai	24
The Economic Importance of the Tarai	26
The Tarai, Nepal, and the Rice Trade	29
Trade Ties Between the Tarai and India	29
Communal Characteristics of Village Shopkeepers and Itinerant Village Traders	31
The Relationship of Tarai Industry to the Indian Economy	35
Communal Characteristics of Owners of Small-Scale Industry	38
Nepalese Attitudes Toward Indian Economic Domination	40
Extension of the Nepalese Currency System into the Tarai	43

III.	Nepal-India Border Problems	46
	Border-Demarcation Disputes	47
	Control of Crime Along the Border	48
	Smuggling	49
	Illegal Economic Activity and Cultural Stereotypes	55
	The Blurred Border	56
IV.	Migration into the Tarai	58
	Migration from Northern India into the Tarai	58
	Migration from the Hills into the Tarai	62
	The Tarai as a Population Vacuum	66
	The Scale of Migration	70
	Caste and Communal Characteristics of Migrants	73
	Previous Residence of Migrants	76
	Economic Status of Migrants	78
	Government-Sponsored Resettlement Projects	82
V.	The Politics of Citizenship	87
	Status of Tarai Subjects before 1951	87
	Citizenship Laws in the 1950s	89
	Citizenship Laws in the 1960s	91
	Citizenship Requirements for Various Types of Economic Activity	94
	Citizenship-Application Procedures	99
	Controversy over Citizenship	100
	Dual Citizenship	104
	The Specter of Migration	105
	Anti-Indian Sentiment and Citizenship Restrictions	106
VI.	The Politics of Language	108
	Government Language Policy and the Language Controversy, 1956–58	109
	Is Hindi the Predominant Language of	

	CONTENTS	
	the Tarai?	115
	To What Extent is Nepali Spoken in the Tarai?	119
	The Language Issue During the Period of the National Election Campaign and the Nepali Congress Government, 1958–60	121
	The Government's Language Policy since 1960	124
VII.	Language, Communication, and National Integration	126
	The Press and the Radio	126
	Government Officials' Contact with Villagers	130
	The Integrative Function of the Educational System	132
VIII.	Politics in the Nepalese Tradition	136
	Origin and Structure of the Panchayat System	136
	Politics at the Village Level	141
	Politics at the District Level	144
	Politics at the Zonal Level	156
	Politics at the National Level	158
IX.	Oppositional Politics in the Tarai	171
	The Land-Reform Program and Discontent in the Rural Areas	171
	Opposition Parties	181
	Support in India for Opposition Parties	191
X.	The Problem of National Integration	194
	Appendix. Methodology of the Field Survey Conducted in the Tarai, November 1967–March 1968	207
	Glossary	215
	Selected Bibliography	217
	Index	231

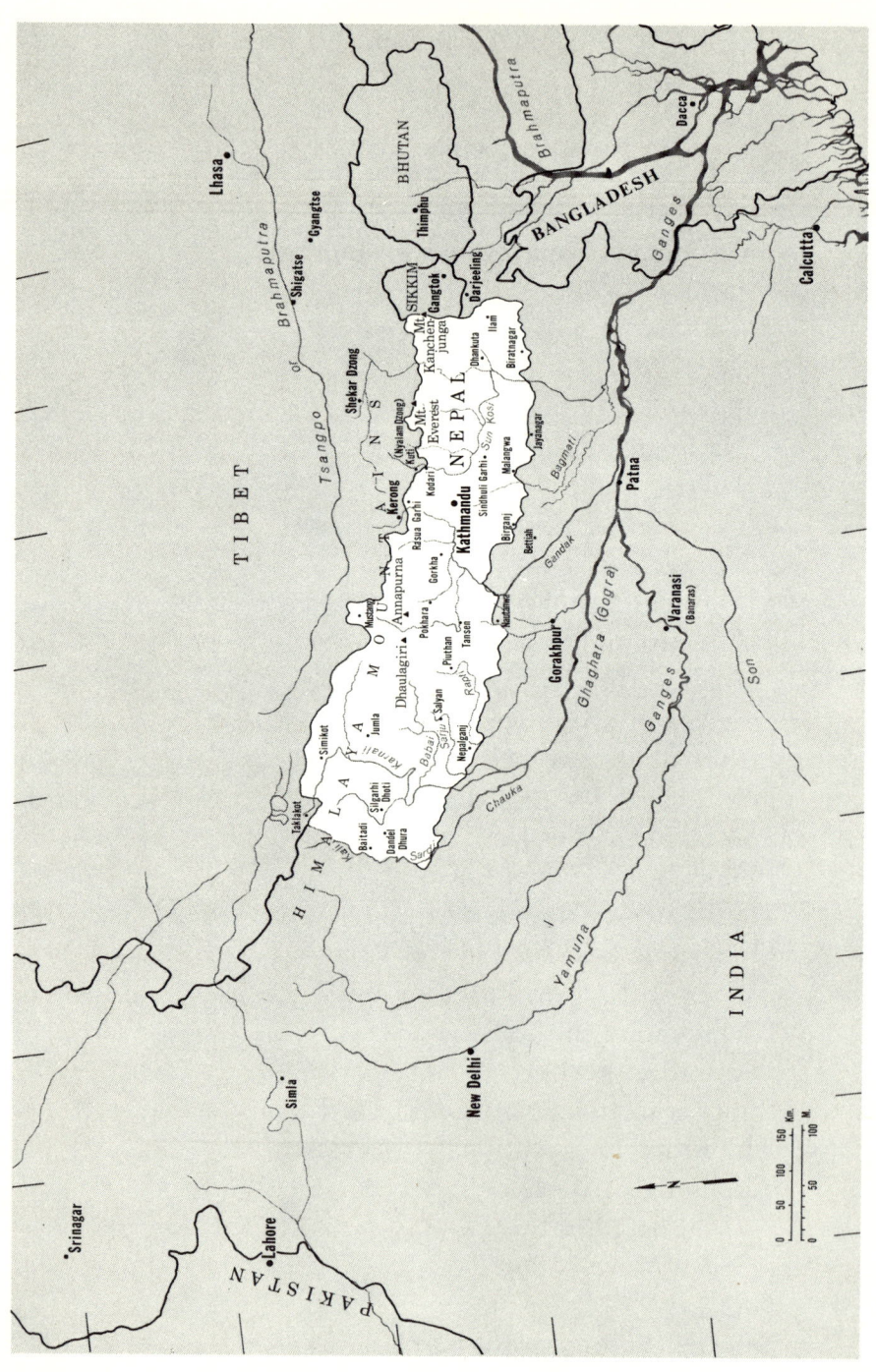

Outline map of central Himalayas. Source: Leo E. Rose, *Nepal: Strategy for Survival* (Berkeley and Los Angeles, 1971).

MAPS, TABLES, DIAGRAMS

MAPS

1.	Census regions and census districts of Nepal	6
2.	Development zones and development districts of Nepal	8
3.	Speakers of hill languages, plains languages and plains tribal languages as percentages of tarai district populations	18
4.	Commercial centers of the tarai at Indian railheads	36
5.	Population density in districts of Nepal and India's border districts	67
6.	Forested and cultivated areas of the tarai	69
7.	Linguistic subregions of the tarai	208
8.	Subregions of the tarai having similar religious characteristics	209
9.	Subregions of the tarai having similar population density characteristics	210

TABLES

1.	Religious Composition of the Population of Nepal	13
2.	Religious Composition of the Tarai Population	14
3.	Major Languages Spoken in the Tarai, 1961	16
4.	Population by Regional and Communal Grouping in Five Tarai Districts	21

5. Regional and Communal Affiliation of Shopkeepers in Sample Villages	32
6. Itinerant Traders in Sample Villages of Five Tarai Districts, by Regional and Communal Groupings	34
7. Small-Scale Industry in the Tarai, by District and Type of Industry	39
8. Owners of Small-Scale Industry in Five Tarai Districts, by Regional and Communal Groupings	40
9. Migrant Families as a Percentage of All Families in Sample and Nonsample Villages, by District and Subregion of District	71
10. Percentage of Migrant Families Settling Permanently in Sample Districts, by Region in Which Migrant Families Resided Previously	77
11. Migrant Families Settling Permanently, 1959–67, as a Percentage of Total Population in 1967, by District and Economic Status	79
12. National Panchayat Electorate	140
13. Jhapa District: Participation in Village- and District-Level Panchayat Bodies, by Caste, Tribal, and Regional Affiliation	148
14. Mahottari-Dhanusha: Participation in Village- and District-Level Panchayat Bodies, by Caste, Tribal, and Regional Affiliation	149
15. Bara District: Participation in Village- and District-Level Panchayat Bodies, by Caste, Tribal, and Regional Affiliation	150
16. Kapilabastu District: Participation in Village- and District-Level Panchayat Bodies, by Caste, Tribal, and Regional Affiliation	151

MAPS, TABLES, DIAGRAMS

17. Kailali District: Participation in Village- and District-Level Panchayat Bodies, by Caste, Tribal, and Regional Affiliation   152
18. Regional and Communal Groups within the 1959 Parliament and the 1967 National Panchayat   164
19. Regional and Communal Distribution of National-Level Administrators   166
20. Caste Breakdown of Senior Army Officers, 1967   167

DIAGRAM

1. Nepal's Panchayat System   138

PREFACE

The mountains of Nepal, or hills as they are called locally, and the "hill" people of Nepal have attracted the attention of adventurous travelers, mountain climbers, and scholars since Nepal was opened to the outside world in the early 1950s. In contrast, the plains region of Nepal—the tarai—has received comparatively little attention from either Nepalese or foreign scholars, perhaps because it is hot, dusty, topographically undramatic and, until recently, malarious. Consequently, little is known about the tarai's geographic, historic, economic, or cultural characteristics, despite the fact that it comprises 15 percent of Nepal's land area and is home to 31 percent of Nepal's population. This neglect is particularly striking because the tarai is the backbone of Nepal's economy, producing about 59 percent of the nation's gross domestic product and about 76 percent of the government's revenue.

Included in this volume are two studies, a regional study of the Nepal tarai and a study of the national-integration process in Nepal. The first two chapters provide a description of economic and cultural characteristics of the tarai population, based to a large extent upon data gathered in a field survey of selected villages during 1967 and 1968. This is the first systematic interdisciplinary study of the tarai region and provides an essential framework for the chapters which follow. In geographic terms, the tarai is the northern fringe of the Gangetic plain abutting the foothill range of the central Himalayas. In sociological terms, it is the northern fringe of the Indian plains cultural region into which large numbers of hill people are now migrating. The tarai is also the region in which Indian and Nepalese national interests meet and sometimes confront each other. Economic and political developments on one side of the border often have repercussions on the other side and, therefore, it is impossible to separate a study of the tarai's relationship with the rest of Nepal from interaction between Nepal and India. For this reason, the story of relations between the two nations weaves itself throughout the volume, although only in chapter III, which deals with Nepal-India border problems, does consideration of international relations take precedence over developments within Nepal.

The tarai is the one important region of Nepal that is geographically and culturally distinct from the hills and, for this reason, problems of national integration focus primarily on the relationship between the two regions. The economic importance of the tarai, the political restiveness of its population, and the growing sense of national purpose among members of the governing elite in Kathmandu have prompted the Nepalese government to seek ways to link the tarai more effectively to the hill region and at the same time to loosen the economic and cultural ties which the tarai population has shared with the population living across the border in northern India. Chapters IV through X focus upon the process of national integration, that is, upon the various government policies designed to link the tarai with the hills and upon the reaction of the tarai population to these policies.

What is meant by the term "integration"? Myron Weiner's definition provides us with a useful touchstone:

> The term "integration" thus covers a vast range of human relationships and attitudes—the integration of diverse and discrete cultural loyalties and the development of a sense of nationality; the integration of political units into a common territorial framework with a government which can exercise authority; the integration of the rulers and the ruled; the integration of the citizens into a common political process; and, finally, the integration of individuals into organizations for purposive activities.[1]

All facets of this definition are relevant to the Nepalese situation, but this study is primarily concerned with the integration of diverse and discrete geographic regions and the interaction of groups with diverse and discrete cultural loyalties. How can the plains people of the tarai be drawn into association with the people of the hill region in order to insure national stability and to mobilize support for the government's development policies? This is the critical problem studied here.

This volume was written for three groups of readers. The first comprises all who are interested in Nepal and seek more information about the country. The second group includes political scientists who are primarily concerned with the process of integration in developing nations and would find this type of interdisciplinary case study useful for their comparative and theoretical analyses. In the third

[1] "Political Integration and Political Development," *Annals of the American Academy of Political and Social Science*, vol. 358 (March 1965), 54.

group are Nepalese policy makers, the members of Kathmandu's governing elite who face the problems related to national integration. It is my hope that these individuals, some of whom are friends and acquaintances, will find the new data presented here helpful as they proceed with their difficult task.

This work grew out of my doctoral dissertation, and I would like to acknowledge the support I received for the doctoral research, an N.D.E.A.-related Fulbright-Hays Fellowship from the U.S. Office of Education and a Fulbright Fellowship from the Institute of International Education for eighteen months of data collecting in Nepal. While in Nepal, I was awarded a grant from Tribhuvan University which enabled me to hire a research assistant for the period of the field survey. A one-year appointment at the Institute of International Studies, University of California, Berkeley, allowed me to write a major part of the dissertation. Two summer grants from Davidson College made it possible for me to complete the dissertation and then to revise it for publication.

There are many individuals to whom I owe a great deal of gratitude for assistance with various aspects of this research. Many are Nepalis who, by their friendship and their interest in my work, made my stay in Nepal an unforgettable experience. They have added important dimensions to this work. I would like to acknowledge them by name, but refrain from doing so in the event that any of my conclusions may be objectionable to their government.

I have received generous support from members of the Department of South Asia Regional Studies at the University of Pennsylvania: Dr. Holden Furber, Dr. Alan Heston, Dr. Richard Lambert, Dr. Joseph Schwartzberg, and especially Dr. Norman Palmer and Dr. Dorothy Thomas. Since 1964, I have been in constant touch with Dr. Leo Rose and have spent three periods of study at the University of California to use materials he has collected and to obtain his advice with regard to my research. The time he has devoted to discussing my research with me and to reading and suggesting revisions of my work runs into countless days. It is difficult to imagine how this study could have been completed without his counsel and his concern.

Finally, I owe my wife, Austra, far more than gratitude for her involvement in all aspects of my work. Her incisive observations about Nepal and about my research, her companionship even in the most trying field conditions, her patient editing, and constant encouragement over the years since I began the research make this book not mine, but ours.

definition includes the long and narrow strip of plains abutting the Himalayan foothills all the way from Uttar Pradesh through Nepal, West Bengal, and Bhutan and into India's North East Frontier Agency, now called Arunachal Pradesh. The second definition, the one that will be used throughout this study, includes only the plains region adjacent to the foothills within Nepal's national boundaries. This foothill range is called the Siwaliks or sometimes the Churia range. As the crow flies, the Nepal tarai is approximately 500 miles long, from its western boundary, the Mahakali River, to its eastern boundary, the Mechi River. Of course, the actual boundary line between the Nepal tarai and the Indian states of Uttar Pradesh, Bihar, and West Bengal follows a circuitous route of considerably more than 500 miles. It wanders across the countryside, sometimes following a winding river bed and sometimes the seemingly arbitrary surveyor's line from one stone boundary pillar to the next. At its widest point, the tarai has a span of 33 miles and, at its narrowest, 2 or 3 miles. The estimated average width of the tarai along its entire east-west axis is 20 miles. Nepal does not control an uninterrupted strip of plains along the entire length of its southern border. For reasons not yet clear to historians, India controls sections of the tarai south of Dang-Deukhuri and Chitwan districts.[2]

The Siwaliks range was the last created by the mighty geological forces that produced the Himalayas. The youth of the Siwaliks is borne out by the frequent earthquakes in the region and by the geological action that continues to push up the level of the tarai closest to the Siwaliks, producing a gradual slope away to the south. The tarai has been created not only by this "orogenic activity,"[3] but also by alluvial action in the Siwaliks and the higher Himalayan ranges. Dozens of snow-fed rivers drain the Himalayas and literally thousands of smaller rivers and streams which flow only during the rainy season originate in the Siwaliks range itself. These rivers and streams deposit rocks, gravel, sand, and fertile topsoil on the tarai, accentuating its slope. During the dry months, from mid-September to mid-June, most of these river beds are no more than broad expanses of gray and bone-white rocks and gravel, with an occasional spring-fed trickle threading its way amid the alluvial debris. But during the rainy season, these rivers and streams become raging torrents, emptying out of the

[2]See map 2 for names of the tarai districts.
[3]O. H. K. Spate and A. T. A. Learmonth, *India and Pakistan: A General and Regional Geography*, 3d ed. (London, 1967), pp. 27, 30.

mountains, flowing south across the tarai into the major tributaries of the Ganges and the Brahmaputra. As they reach the tarai, they widen rapidly and slow down, depositing the materials they have carried down from the mountains. As they slow down, they deposit first the heavier material, the huge boulders, then smaller rocks and gravel, and finally the silt.

If, during the dry season, one were to follow one of these river or stream beds south across the tarai from the narrow gorge where it cuts through the Siwaliks, one would first have to pick his way carefully down a declining alluvial fan of boulders and rocks. The fan broadens and flattens out quickly to a width of several hundred yards if it is a small stream or to as much as a mile if it is one of the largest snow-fed rivers. When one reaches the end of the alluvial fan, he continues south over a broad expanse of parched gravel mounds and white sand bars, shining brilliantly in the intense tropical sun. Although the riverbed remains wide, the gravel deposits gradually become finer.

If the river is the product of monsoon rains, its bed may be completely dry, but if it is snow-fed, a rather large volume of water may be making its way around the boulders and gravel mounds and across the sandy expanses. Along the alluvial fans and for several miles downstream, dense hardwood forests of *sissoo* and *khair* will line the river bed. These deciduous hardwood trees thrive on the rocky terrain at the foot of the Siwaliks. Several miles farther down the riverbed where sand and silt begin to replace the coarser alluvial materials, the forest is dominated by other hardwood species such as *sal, siri, semal, karma* and *bot dongero*. These species, valuable as timber, thrive in less coarse soil. Still farther south, where the sand gives way to silt, the hardwoods are mixed with savannah grass and bamboo, and one begins to find forest clearings where crops are being cultivated. By the time one has walked 6 to 10 miles downstream from the Siwaliks, he reaches a point where the forest gives way completely to broad expanses of cultivated fields. From this point on there is little slope, and the river—if indeed there is water running in the river bed—begins to meander slowly between mud and grass banks. At this point, 10 to 20 miles south of the Siwaliks, the tarai merges imperceptively with the rest of the great Gangetic plain.

There are not only differences in the tarai vegetation closer to and farther from the foot of the Siwaliks, but also vegetation differences in the western and eastern reaches of the region. In the tarai of western Nepal, where the annual rainfall is 25 inches or less, the dry tropical

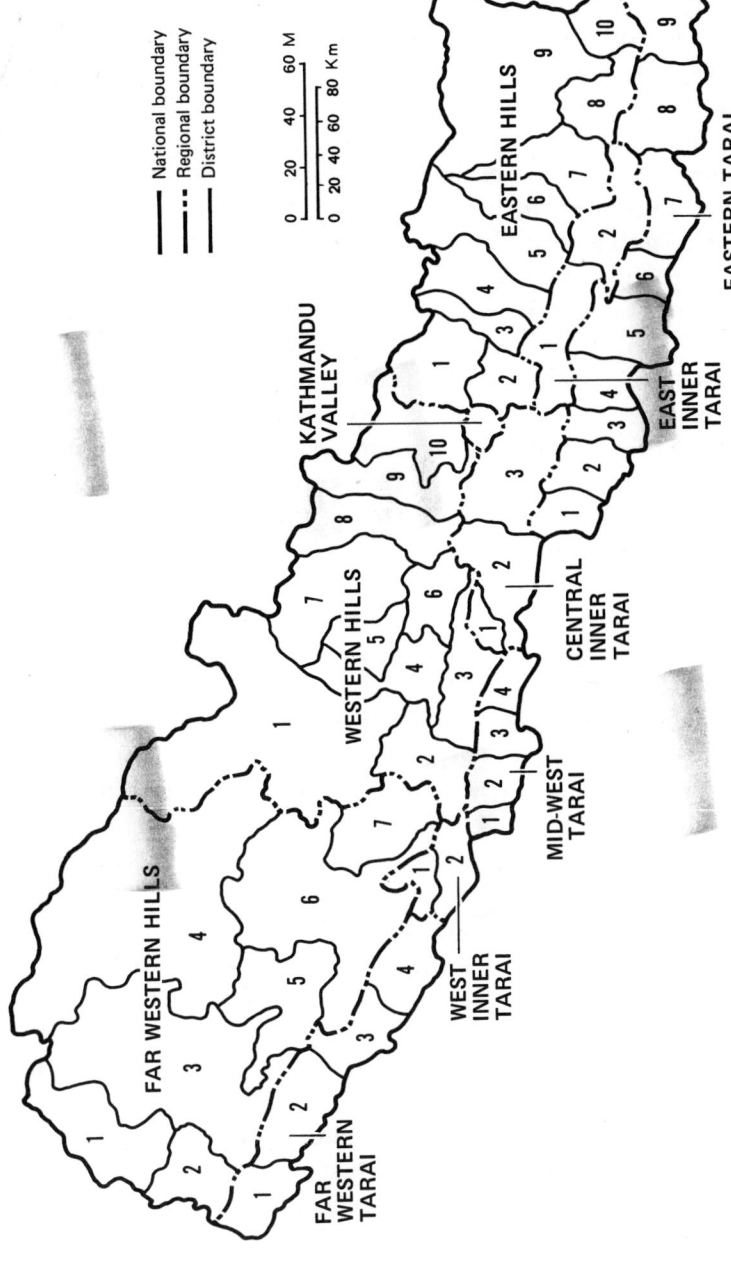

Map 1. Census regions and census districts of Nepal. See accompanying list of names of census regions and districts.
Sources: *Census of Nepal*, 1952/54 and 1961.

type of vegetation predominates—savannah grass and bamboo. In eastern Nepal, where the rainfall averages more than 100 inches a year, the vegetation is of the moist tropical type, mostly tall deciduous hardwoods. *Sal*, commercially the most valuable of the hardwoods, grows throughout most of the tarai.

Two geographical terms frequently used in Nepal, "inner tarai" and "outer tarai," must be introduced here. The three broad, low-lying river valleys north of the Siwaliks are referred to in Nepalese government publications as *vitri madhesh* or inner tarai. The outer tarai is the plains region within Nepal's border south of the Siwaliks. The term tarai as used in this study refers only to the outer tarai.

The term "hills" is used throughout this study to include all of Nepal from the Siwaliks foothill range north to the Tibetan border. This is a broader definition of the term than the Nepalese use. A fuller definition of this and other important terms such as "hill languages," "hill people," "plains," and "plains people" is given in the glossary.

To determine the square-mile area of the tarai, its territory can be defined in several ways: one, as the area of Nepal south of the Siwaliks or, two, as the area of the tarai districts established by the government as administrative units. Using the first of these definitions, the tarai has an area of 8,282 square miles or 15.2 percent of Nepal's total 54,363-square-mile area. If the tarai area is calculated on the basis of administrative districts, there will be two slightly different results, because there are two sets of districts, census and development districts. The area of the census districts is 8,921 square miles and the area of the development districts is 9,437 square miles, or 16.4 percent and 17.4 percent, respectively, of Nepal's total area. Both sets of administrative districts include some territory in the Siwaliks, particularly in Sunsari and Morang districts, hence the 8,282-square-mile calculation is the more accurate. The fact that Nepal now has two sets of district organizations, one for the census and the other for development and general administrative purposes, is likely to cause some confusion. Because it is necessary to refer to both sets of districts throughout this study, a map for each is included.

The ecology of the tarai has changed greatly during the past several hundred years, indeed, during the past several decades, and the pattern of change follows closely that which has taken place in other parts of the Gangetic plain. In the 16th and 17th centuries, the Mughal emperors hunted wild elephants, buffaloes, bison, rhinoceros, and tigers in the region between the Ganges and Jumna rivers. Until several

List of Census Regions and Districts for Map 1

I. Far-western hills[a]
 1. Baitadi
 2. Dandeldhura
 3. Doti[b]
 4. Jumla
 5. Dailekh
 6. Sallyan
 7. Piuthan

II. Far-western tarai
 1. Kanchanpur
 2. Kailali
 3. Bardia
 4. Banke

III. Western hills[a]
 1. Baglung
 2. Gulmi
 3. Palpa
 4. Syangja
 5. Kaski
 6. Tanahun
 7. Lamjung
 8. Gorkha
 9. Dhading
 10. Nawakot

IV. Western inner tarai
 1. Dang
 2. Deukhuri

V. Mid-western tarai
 1. Shivaraj
 2. Khajahani
 3. Majkhanda
 4. Palhi

VI. Kathmandu Valley
 1. Kathmandu
 2. Bhaktapur
 3. Lalitpur

VII. Central inner tarai
 1. Nawalpur
 2. Chitwan
 3. Chisapani

VIII. Eastern hills
 1. Sindhu Palchok
 2. Kabhre Palchok
 3. Dolakha
 4. Chisankhu (East No. 2)
 5. Chisankhu (East No. 3)
 6. Majh Kirat
 7. Bhojpur
 8. Chha Thum
 9. Terhathum
 10. Ilam

IX. Eastern inner tarai
 1. Sindhuli
 2. Udaipur

X. Eastern tarai
 1. Parsa
 2. Bara
 3. Rautahat
 4. Sarlahi
 5. Mahottari
 6. Siraha
 7. Saptari
 8. Biratnagar
 9. Jhapa

[a] In the 1952/54 census, the western and far-western hills are together in one region called the western hills.
[b] In the 1961 census, Doti is divided into two districts, Doti and Achham.

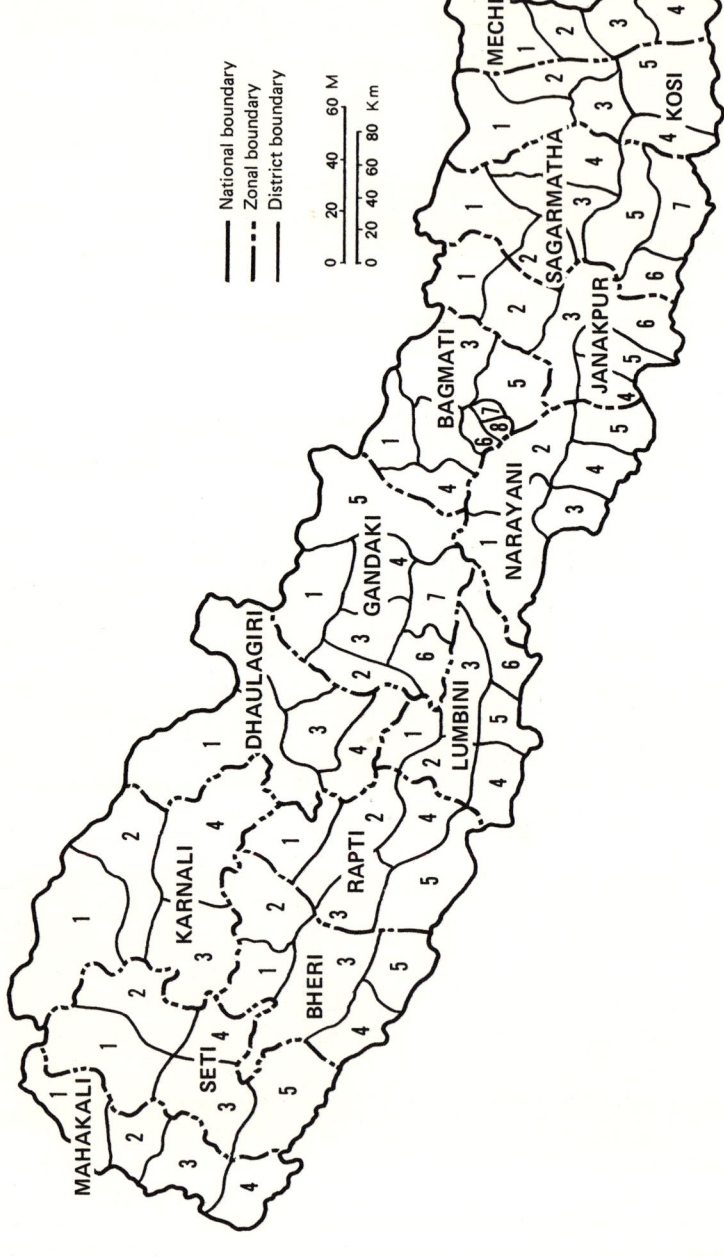

Map 2. Development zones and development districts of Nepal. See accompanying list of names of development zones and districts. Source: Map M. 301, April 1964, Communications Media Division U.S. Aid/Nepal.

List of Development Zones and Districts for Map 2[a]

I. Mahakali zone
  1. Darchula
  2. Baitadi
  3. Dandeldhura
  4. *Kanchanpur*

II. Seti zone
  1. Bajhang
  2. Bajura
  3. Doti
  4. Achham
  5. *Kailali*

III. Karnali zone
  1. Humla
  2. Mugu
  3. Jumla
  4. Tibrikot

IV. Bheri zone
  1. Dailekh
  2. Jajarkot
  3. Surkhet
  4. *Bardia*
  5. *Banke*

V. Rapti zone
  1. Rukum
  2. Rolpa
  3. Sallyan
  4. Piuthan
  5. Dang Deukhuri

VI. Dhaulagiri zone
  1. Dolpa
  2. Mustang
  3. Mygadi
  4. Baglung

VII. Lumbini zone
  1. Gulmi
  2. Argha
  3. Palpa
  4. *Kapilabastu*
  5. *Rupandehi*
  6. *Nawal Parasi*

VIII. Gandaki zone
  1. Manang
  2. Parbat
  3. Kaski
  4. Lamjung
  5. Gorkha
  6. Syangja
  7. Tanahu

IX. Narayani zone
  1. Chitwan
  2. Makwanpur
  3. *Parsa*
  4. *Bara*
  5. *Rautahat*

X. Bagmati zone
  1. Rasuwa
  2. Nuwakot
  3. Sindhu Palchok
  4. Dhading
  5. Kabhre Palchok
  6. Kathmandu
  7. Bhaktapur
  8. Lalitpur

XI. Janakpur zone
  1. Dolakha
  2. Ramechhap
  3. Sindhuli

[a] Tarai development districts are italicized. The three districts of Kathmandu Valley are districts 6, 7, and 8 of Bagmati zone.

       4. *Sarlahi*
       5. *Mahottari*
       6. *Dhanusha*

XII. Sagarmatha zone
       1. Solukhumbu
       2. Okhaldhunga
       3. Khotang
       4. Bhojpur
       5. Udaipur
       6. *Siraha*
       7. *Saptari*

XIII. Kosi zone
       1. Sankhuwasabha
       2. Terhathum
       3. Dhankuta
       4. *Sunsari*
       5. *Morang*

XIV. Mechi zone
       1. Taplejung
       2. Panchthar
       3. Ilam
       4. *Jhapa*

decades ago, the rulers of Nepal hunted these same animals throughout the tarai. However, the same population pressure that resulted in deforestation and extinction of wild animals in other parts of the Gangetic plain in the course of the past few hundred years[4] has also occurred much more recently in the tarai.

The last large stands of hardwood timber are rapidly being felled by settlers and, in the process, the last sanctuaries for wild animals are being destroyed. For example, the central inner tarai is one of the few remaining places in Asia where wild rhinoceros survive. Despite protection by forest guards, however, their number has dwindled to less than one hundred. In the eastern tarai, where rainfall is comparatively heavy, the cleared forest land becomes dry grass land, but in the drier western tarai, deforested land dries out rapidly, turning to scrub thorn. In the more densely populated parts of the Gangetic plain, where the land has suffered decades of overcultivation and overgrazing, it is becoming a dusty, arid waste. Such conditions await the tarai, if the same pattern of ecological desiccation is not interrupted.

For those who have lived or travelled on the Gangetic plain, the settled areas of the tarai will look very familiar. There are 6,258 nucleated villages in the tarai, most of them no more than several hundred mud and thatch huts clustered around large shady *pipal*, *pakari* or *bargad* trees. Occasionally one will find a two-storey brick house built by a large landowner. The village water is drawn from open hand-dug wells, and the villages' links with the outside world consist of rutted bullock-cart tracks, generally impassable during the monsoon season.

The similarities between tarai villages and those located elsewhere

[4] *Ibid.*, pp. 92–95.

on the Gangetic plain are so numerous that it is more informative to point out a few significant dissimilarities. From almost any tarai village one can look north on a clear day to see the forest fringe, often quite near at hand and, beyond, the Siwaliks. For several months after the monsoon rains of June, July, and August have washed the dust out of the air, it is often possible to see the majestic snow-capped peaks of the Himalayas reaching up behind the Siwaliks.

Modernization has only begun to have its effects upon the villages and bazaar towns of the tarai. The nearly ubiquitous macadam roads, buses and electric-power lines of rural areas across the Indian border in Uttar Pradesh and Bihar have not yet reached tarai villages. These are just now being introduced to the few commercial towns of the tarai. Without bridges or hard-surface roads, life comes almost completely to a standstill during the rainy season. The hundreds of tame streams and rivers that can be forded by foot during the dry season swell dangerously, often flooding cultivated areas along their banks and cutting off one village from the next.

Aside from the lack of modernization, the most obvious difference between the tarai and the rest of the Gangetic plain is the presence, still in relatively small numbers, of hill people. Particularly evident in the commercial centers, mingling with the dhoti-clad and sari-clad plains people, are hill men dressed in pants which are tight below the knee and baggy around the middle, vest-like jackets and distinctive peaked caps. The hill women wear long skirts with layered cloth belts and long-sleeved blouses. Unlike the plains people who carry their goods on their heads or in bullock carts, the hill people, adjusting to the demands of their mountain terrain, carry goods in cone-shaped wicker backpacks. Settlers from the hills often construct their houses in the distinctive architectural style of the hill region. The houses have two floors, the ground floor generally designed as shelter for animals and storage of tools and supplies, the upper storey as living quarters for the family. As one travels through the villages of the tarai, one can easily distinguish these houses by their overhanging upper-storey construction.

Thus, the tarai is geographically and culturally a transitional region between the hills and the plains. The plains features predominate, but the hill features make their impact. The transitional nature of the tarai creates for Nepal problems associated with integration of the region into a national economic and political framework. This study is an analysis of these problems. But the tarai also provides Nepal with promise in the form of abundant resources that can be tapped for development of the whole nation. This aspect should be kept in mind as the problems are analyzed.

Familiarity with some of the most important cultural characteristics of the tarai population, of both its plains and hill components, is essential if the problem and promise of national integration are to be properly understood. Most tarai inhabitants are plains people. Their religious traditions, languages and the caste system, their food, style of clothes, forms of entertainment and even personal mannerisms are cultural characteristics they share with people who live across the Indian border in Uttar Pradesh and Bihar. During the past decade, hill people have begun to settle in the tarai in significant numbers, carrying their own traditions with them and bringing about a perceptible change in the cultural equation of the region. Let us consider three important cultural characteristics, religion, language, and social structure, in order to measure the extent to which the north Indian plains culture predominates in the tarai and the extent to which the Nepalese hill culture is penetrating the region.

RELIGIOUS CHARACTERISTICS OF THE POPULATION

According to the 1961 census of Nepal, 88 percent of Nepal's total population is Hindu. This percentage is about the same for both the tarai and hill regions. The percentage is actually somewhat lower in both regions, because Nepal's census enumerators categorized the tribal people of both the plains and the hills as Hindus despite the fact that many of them are only nominally Hinduized. Many of the hill tribal groups are still primarily influenced by religions they practiced before the advance of Hinduism into the region. The hill tribals' religions are Mahayana Buddhism, a Tibetan religion called Bon, and local variants of animism. Many of the plains tribals continue to practice their own forms of animism. Table 1 gives statistics on the religious composition of Nepal's population.

Hinduism represents a bond between the plains and hill people as well as a barrier to interaction between them. The Hinduism of both regions has many features in common, for example, worship of many of the same gods, celebration of many common festivals, and recitation of religious stories involving many shared myths and legends. The Brahmin priests of both regions share a common body of Sanskrit literature and ritual. The orthodox Hindus in both Nepal and India

TABLE 1
Religious Composition of the Population of Nepal

Region	Hinduism	Buddhism	Islam
All Nepal	87.7	9.3	3.0
Eastern Hills	81.9	18.1	.0
Kathmandu Valley	80.7	18.8	.3
Western Hills	84.6	15.1	.3
Far-western Hills	99.1	.9	.0
Eastern Tarai	89.8	1.1	8.9
Mid-western Tarai	87.1	.1	12.7
Far-western Tarai	91.5	.0	8.5

Source: *Census of Nepal*, 1961, vol. II, pp. 16–17.

take satisfaction from the fact that the King of Nepal is a Hindu and stands at the head of the only government in the world in which Hinduism enjoys special status.

On the other hand, Hindu practices in the hills differ from those in the plains in a number of respects. Hinduism in its orthodox form has never been accepted by many hill people. Strict vegetarianism is practiced by few of those people; some hill Brahmins even eat meat such as chicken and goat. Upper-caste plains people observe the dietary restrictions of Hinduism much more carefully. Although by no means common, intercaste marriages sometimes take place among hill people; such marriages are considered taboo among the plains people. The more flexible social traditions of Hinduism as practiced in the hills result largely from the interaction between Hinduism and the less rigid social traditions of Tibetan Buddhism. In the plains, Hinduism has been affected by interaction with Islam, from which it has adopted practices such as *purdha*, the keeping of women in a state of seclusion. This is a widespread practice among nonurbanized upper-caste plains Hindus.

Table 2 provides more detailed information about the religious composition of the tarai population. The concentration of Muslims in some tarai districts and their almost total absence from other districts provides the major religious variation in the subregions of the tarai.

Almost no Muslims live in Bardia, Kailali, and Kanchanpur, three districts of the far-western tarai. Large tracts of dense forest just south

TABLE 2
Religious Composition of the Tarai Population

Regions and districts of the tarai	Hinduism	Islam	Buddhism
Eastern tarai:	89.8	8.9	1.1
Jhapa	95.6	3.4	.9
Biratnagar	91.0	7.0	1.1
Hanuman Nagar	93.0	6.8	.0
Siraha	93.1	5.6	.8
Mahottari	89.2	9.0	1.8
Sarlahi	87.8	7.8	4.4
Rautahat	83.4	16.9	.0
Bara	88.2	11.4	.2
Parsa	87.3	12.6	.0
Mid-western tarai:	87.1	12.7	.1
Palhi	91.7	8.3	.0
Majkhanda	88.9	10.7	.3
Khajahani	83.1	16.9	.0
Shivaraj	82.3	17.7	.0
Far-western tarai:	91.5	8.5	.0
Banke	78.0	21.9	.0
Bardia	97.0	3.0	.0
Kailali	99.8	.2	.0
Kanchanpur	99.9	.1	.0

Source: *Census of Nepal,* 1961, vol. II, pp. 16–17.

of these districts have discouraged migration into them from the heavily populated areas of northern Uttar Pradesh to the south. The inhabitants of these three sparsely populated districts are almost exclusively Tharus, plains tribals who have lived isolated in the forest for countless generations. They are only now beginning to experience the process of Hinduization.

The next district to the east, Banke, has the largest Muslim concentration of any tarai district. This seemingly contradictory situation results from the fact that there is no forest south of Banke to discourage migration from the areas of Muslim concentration in northern Uttar Pradesh. Although there is some fluctuation, a general decline in the percentage of Muslims is evident as one moves through tarai districts east of Banke, the lowest percentage (with the exception of those districts mentioned above) being in Jhapa, the most easterly tarai district. This follows the same pattern of decline in the percentage of the Muslim population that one finds while moving from west to east across northern Uttar Pradesh and Bihar. This correspondence in the Hindu-Muslim ratio on both sides of the border is one measure of the cultural affinity between the tarai and northern India.

LINGUISTIC CHARACTERISTICS OF THE POPULATION

In this discussion, the languages of Nepal are categorized as "hill languages" and "plains languages." The hill-language category includes all the languages spoken as "mother tongues" or "first languages" by the hill people of Nepal. They include Nepali, Newari, Magar, Gurung, Rai, Limbu, Tamang, Sunwar, and several Tibetan dialects spoken chiefly in Nepal, e.g., Thakali and Sherpa. The plains-language category includes languages spoken as mother tongues by plains people living in the tarai. These include Hindi, Urdu, Maithili, Bhojpuri, Bengali, dialects of these such as Awadhi and the Morang Pradesh dialects, and some languages spoken by relatively few people—languages such as Jhangar, Marwari, and Raji.

The most important language of the hill region is Nepali. According to the 1961 census of Nepal, this language is the mother tongue of 51 percent of Nepal's total population. In the western and far-western subregions of the hills, the census reports that 76 and 96 percent of the population speaks Nepali as a first language. Perhaps even more important, Nepali is spoken as a second language by a great many other hill people, making it the *lingua franca* of the hill region. In Kathmandu Valley, the language of the majority is Newari and in the eastern subregion of the hills a large minority, 43 percent of the population, speaks Tibetan-related tribal languages, Tamang, Rai/Kirati, Limbu, and Sherpa.

A great majority of tarai inhabitants speak languages spoken elsewhere on the Gangetic plain. As documented in table 3, Maithili is spoken by more than 85 percent of the population in four eastern tarai districts and Bhojpuri by more than 92 percent of the population in three other eastern tarai districts. Awadhi is the first language of 87 percent or more in four mid-western tarai districts and Tharu dialects of plains languages predominate in three districts of the far-western tarai.

Maithili and Bhojpuri are the predominant languages of the nor-

TABLE 3
Major Languages Spoken in the Tarai, 1961

Region and district	Total population	Maithili		Bhojpuri		Awadhi		Tharu	
		Numbers	%	Numbers	%	Numbers	%	Numbers	%
Nepal	9,412,996	1,130,401	12.0	577,357	6.1	447,090	4.8	406,907	4.3
Eastern tarai:	2,213,282	1,129,576	51.0	576,546	26.1	340		88,663	4.0
Jhapa	119,700	1,773	2.0	963	.8	319	.3	2,713	2.3
Biratnagar	325,645	70,255	21.6	1,994	.6	2		64,070	19.7
Hanuman Nagar	299,869	284,653	94.9					2,134	.7
Siraha	210,532	187,962	89.3					7,105	3.4
Mahottari	488,218	439,883	90.1	47		24		1,287	.3
Sarlahi	162,979	139,743	85.1	20				3,366	2.1
Rautahat	218,661	5,272	2.5	205,847	94.1			2,407	1.1
Bara	250,054	898	.4	231,560	92.6	5		5,300	2.1
Parsa	137,357	137	.1	136,115	98.9			281	
Mid-western tarai:	400,357	644		75		360,279	90.0	23,704	5.9
Palhi	96,227			56		92,502	96.1	177	
Majkhanda	141,627	583		16		123,438	87.2	8,215	5.8
Khajahani	125,036	61		3		109,417	87.5	13,857	11.1
Shivaraj	37,467					34,932	93.2	1,455	3.9
Far-western tarai:	271,551	35				86,460	31.8	170,604	62.8
Banke	95,148	25				73,580	77.3	15,240	16.0
Bardia	67,731	5				11,715	17.3	53,274	78.7
Kailali	89,795	4				791	.9	84,266	93.8
Kanchanpur	18,877	1				374	.2	17,824	94.4

Source: *Census of Nepal*, 1961, vol. II, pp. 18–21.

thern Bihar districts contiguous to the tarai districts where these languages are spoken. Hindi is the predominant language spoken in the northern Uttar Pradesh districts contiguous to the mid-western tarai districts where Hindi is the major language, but for political reasons discussed in the section on Hindi in chapter VI, Nepalese census enumerators have preferred to call the Hindi speakers of the mid-western tarai Awadhi speakers. Tharu, although categorized by the census as a separate language for simplicity's sake, is not a single language. Tharus appear to speak dialects of the languages spoken around them. Many Tharus who live in the inner tarai valleys north of the Siwaliks have developed dialects of Nepali and those south of the Siwaliks speak dialects of Hindi, Maithili, and Bhojpuri. The correspondence between the predominance of various plains languages spoken in the tarai and in northern India is another measure of the cultural affinity between the people on both sides of the Nepal-India border. The predominance of speakers of plains languages in the tarai is presented graphically in map 3.

CASTE CHARACTERISTICS OF THE POPULATION

Caste as a system of social organization is peculiar to Hindu societies. Since the hill culture of Nepal as well as the plains culture of northern India are included under this broader cultural umbrella of Hinduism, the social structure of both regional cultures is organized along hierarchical caste lines. The two cultures share interlinking but significantly different caste systems.

To anyone familiar with the caste system as it exists in most of Uttar Pradesh and Bihar, the caste system of the tarai plains people will be familiar. There are a great many castes arranged hierachically according to the extent of their purity, and purity is expressed ritualistically in terms of pollution, interdining and intermarriage. Although the occupational dimension of the caste system is slowly breaking down under the impact of modernization, at least theoretically, most castes have traditional occupations which caste members practice. Because the caste system of the Nepali hill culture is significantly different in a number of ways, caste, like religion and language, is an important yardstick with which to measure the degree to which the plains culture dominates the tarai and the extent to which the hill culture is beginning to create a new cultural configuration in the region.

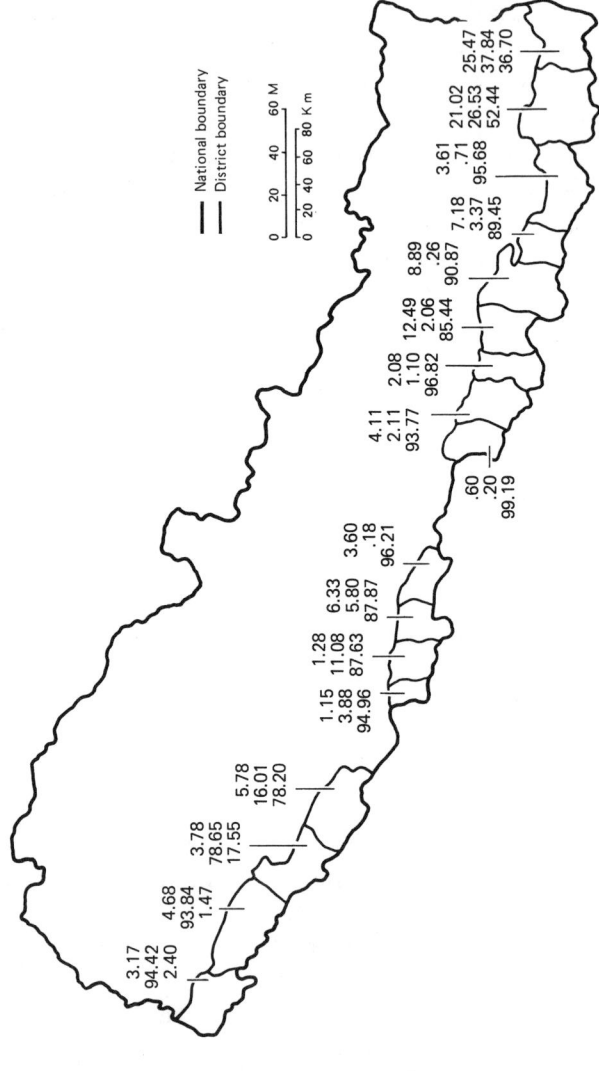

Map 3. Speakers of hill languages, plains languages and plains tribal languages as percentages of tarai district populations. Note: For each district there is a set of three percentages. The upper figure represents speakers of hill languages, the middle figure represents plains tribal dialect speakers (Tharus, Rajbanshis, Tajpurias, Dhimals, and Mechis), and the lower figure represents speakers of plains languages. See glossary for definitions of hill and plains languages. Source: *Census of Nepal*, 1961, vol. II, pp. 18–25. Base map: Survey of India 1:2,534,400, 3d edition, 1959.

There are some obvious similarities in the two caste systems. The traditional priest caste of Brahmins remains fixed at the apex of both systems, and both have a number of the same occupationally defined castes which differ only in name. For example, both caste systems have a traditional warrior caste often called the Rajput or Thakur caste in the plains and the Chetri[5] caste in the hills of Nepal. The Kumhales of the hills and the Kumhars or Kohars of the plains are traditionally makers of clay pots. The Kamis of the hills and the Lohars of the plains are blacksmiths. The Sarkis of the hills and the Chamars of the plains are leather workers.

However, there are more significant differences. Similar occupational castes have different ranking within their respective systems. For example, the Sunars of the hills and the Sonars of the plains are makers of gold and silver ornaments. In the plains, as might be expected, the Sonars have the highest status among the various craft castes. However, the Sunars of the hills are untouchables, ranked even below the blacksmiths.

An even more striking difference is the number of castes in each of the systems. During a 1967–68 survey of tarai villages, fifty-nine Hindu castes were encountered. There appear to be no more than a dozen castes among the Hindus in the hills.[6] The considerably greater number of plains castes, resulting in a more complex social system, is at least partly the result of the more complex economic order that has developed on the plains over the past millennium, continually splitting occupational castes into more specialized categories.

There is one interesting caste in the hills which has no counterpart in the plains—the Gharti caste, whose members are descendants of ex-slaves. Slavery, an institution that never developed widely in India, was not abolished in Nepal until the 1920s. Members of all castes, except presumably Brahmins, could be bound over to slavery for various crimes, and since slavery became fairly common in the hills, members of the Gharti caste are often encountered in the hills today.

The tribal groups of the hills and the tarai were not included among the large number of plains castes and the smaller number of hill castes referred to above, despite the fact that they are really tribal castes or castes in the making. The absorption of tribal groups into the caste system has been proceeding for thousands of years in northern India

[5]Chetri is a corruption of the word Kshatriya.
[6]See, for example, Dor Bahadur Bista, *The People of Nepal* (Kathmandu, 1967), p. 1. See the appendix for the methodology used in the 1967–68 field survey.

and for a considerably shorter time in the hills of Nepal. The manner in which tribal groups are being absorbed into the two caste systems is another factor that differentiates the two. In the hills, the Magars, Gurungs, Rais, Limbus, and others are still undergoing the slow process of absorption, but already there is a discernible hierarchy among them. Those which have become the most Hinduized, that is, those having the longest and most intense interaction with the caste Hindus, tend to be ranked by caste Hindus above those who are less Hinduized. Some of these tribal groups are ranked considerably above the lowest untouchable castes.

Tribal groups in the tarai—the Tharus, Rajbanshis, Tajpurias, Gangais, Mechis, and other smaller tribes—are also gradually being absorbed into the caste system of their region. Unlike the hill tribals, however, the tribals of the tarai are relegated to the very bottom of the hierarchy, even below many of the untouchable castes. Until recently, the tribal people have been able to find isolation from the subcontinent's more advanced economic society in the forests of the tarai and other geographically peripheral regions. The surge of population into the peripheral regions and the clearing of forests to provide additional farm land have confronted the tribal people with the need to adjust to a new and essentially hostile society. Relegated as they are to the lowest rungs of the caste ladder, without the experience needed to compete for scarce economic resources, they have generally found the adjustment process confusing and painful. Indeed, in many cases, it has been a struggle for survival.

Table 4 has been compiled to give a more complete picture of the distribution of caste and tribal characteristics in the tarai population. The data indicate that the caste Hindus of plains origin predominate in Mahottari-Dhanusha, Bara, Kapilabastu, and neighboring districts of the eastern and mid-western tarai. They also represent a sizable minority in Jhapa district. In Kailali and neighboring far-western tarai districts, the plains tribal people predominate, and they also constitute a large minority of Jhapa's population. Although not in large numbers, the Muslims have significant representation in Bara and Kapilabastu districts. Only in Jhapa district are the hill people represented in significant numbers, and most of them are caste Hindus rather than tribals. In the other four districts and the tarai subregions they represent, hill people are present in considerably smaller numbers.

The caste data therefore support the religion and language data presented earlier in the chapter. Until recently, the tarai was totally

TABLE 4

Population by Regional and Communal Groupings in Five Tarai Districts

Regional and communal groupings	Jhapa		Mahottari-Dhanusha		Bara		Kapilabastu		Kailali	
	1961 census data	Sample survey data	1961 census data	Sample survey data	1961 census data	Sample survey data	1961 census data	Sample survey data	1961 census data	Sample survey data
Hill castes	20.4	14.1	6.3	6.4	2.9	1.2	1.1	8.5	4.7	9.6
Hill tribals	5.0	2.0	2.6	7.4	1.2	.4	.2	.5	.0	.0
Hill people (subtotal)	25.4	16.1	8.9	13.8	4.1	1.6	1.3	9.0	4.7	9.6
Plains Hindus	33.3	18.1	81.9	77.9	82.4	79.4	70.8	66.4	1.3	.9
Muslims	3.4	4.3	9.0	7.1	11.4	13.7	16.9	18.0	.2	1.2
Plains tribals	37.8	56.2	.3	1.2	2.1	5.4	11.1	6.6	93.8	88.3
Plains people (subtotal)	74.5	78.6	91.2	86.2	95.9	98.5	98.8	91.0	95.3	90.4
Caste not identified		5.3								
Total	100.0	100.0	100.0	100.0	100.0	100.0	100.0	100.0	100.0	100.0

Sources: *Census of Nepal*, 1961, vol. II, pp. 16–17, 18–21.

The following is a description of the method used for compiling the census data for this table. It was assumed that the hill caste people were the speakers of Nepali and the hill tribals were the speakers of hill-tribal languages. As mentioned earlier in this chapter, some hill tribals are beginning to speak Nepali as a mother tongue. Therefore, the hill tribals are somewhat underrepresented when language data are used in this manner. Next, the number of speakers of hill languages was subtracted from the population totals for the districts. This left the number of plains people living in the districts. From this figure the number of Muslims was subtracted, using figures for Muslims given in the religion tables of the census. The number of speakers of plains-tribal languages was also subtracted from the number of plains people. It was assumed that the number remaining are plains caste Hindus.

The second source is the 1967–68 survey of tarai villages. As indicated in the appendix, the five tarai districts were selected because they represented fairly accurately the five subregions of the tarai in which they are located.

The two independent sources of data make it possible to evaluate both with some degree of accuracy. Naturally, there are some differences in the two sets of data, but they are relatively small. Some of the differences are normal, given the small size of the sample in the survey.

a part of what may be called the northern Indian plains cultural sphere, but settlers from north of the Siwaliks are now introducing the Nepalese hill culture into the region.

MARRIAGE TIES BETWEEN THE PEOPLE OF THE TARAI AND NORTHERN INDIA

Brief mention of marriage patterns needs to be made here because they are indicators of broader cultural ties between the tarai and the hills on the one hand and the tarai and northern India on the other. Marriage patterns are also significant because they are generally associated with patterns of business and political activity.

In the tarai, and presumably in other regions of the subcontinent, low caste and tribal people tend to marry their children to others living in neighboring villages. Marriages rarely take place between families living more than a few miles apart. However, among the upper- and business-caste people, marriages are not infrequently arranged between families living many hundreds of miles from each other. This pattern results at least partly from the fact that there are generally fewer families of these castes living in nearby villages.

There is another factor. All the caste Hindus and Muslims are migrants into the tarai or descendants of migrants. The upper- and business-caste people tend to maintain closer ties to their ancestral villages than do the low-caste migrants. Marriage arrangements continue to be made in the region of the ancestral village, even if the ancestral village is a long journey from the tarai. In addition, the higher-caste marriage pattern is also a function of relatively higher levels of education, greater mobility, and more extended communications systems.

Many of the hill Brahmin, Chetri, and Newar settlers in the tarai arrange marriages for their children in Kathmandu Valley and other parts of the hill region. The plains Brahmins, Rajputs, and members of the various business castes often arrange marriages all over northern India. These marriage patterns represent a continual and active reinforcement of the cultural ties that are shared by the tarai population with the hills of Nepal and the plains region of northern India.

THE PROCESS OF "NEPALIZATION"

Over the past several hundred years, the hill tribal people have been undergoing cultural change. This includes the introduction of Nepali, a Sanskrit-based language, as well as of Hindu practices. Scholars have called the process one of Sanskritization or Hinduization, but it actually extends beyond linguistic and religious changes to include a whole complex of interrelated cultural changes, ranging from the adoption of different values to that of different clothing styles and food preferences. Nepalization is therefore a broader and more appropriate term for the process by which hill tribal people absorb the values and customs of the hill Brahmins and Chetris.

In fact, the Chetris more than the Brahmins have been the sturdy and flexible people responsible for Nepalization. Overwhelmed by the Muslim invasions of the 12th, 13th and 14th centuries, these Kshatriya warriors fled to the mountains with their Brahmin advisors and established principalities throughout the hill region. At that time, they accommodated aspects of the various hill tribal cultures to their own. Thus, the Nepal hill culture of today, in contrast to the Hindu culture of the plains or the Buddhist culture of Tibet, has evolved fairly recently. Nevertheless, it is a vital and expansive culture.

The process of Nepalization is beginning in the tarai, now that hill people are settling in the region. Some of the plains tribal people will undoubtedly respond readily to Nepalization as their own tribal cultures prove unable to withstand the disintegrative pressures of the more complex and aggressive hill culture. However, it must be remembered that the tarai culture is simultaneously being merged into that of the north Indian plains as a result of migration from Uttar Pradesh and Bihar. The plains tribals living closest to settlements of caste Hindus of plains origin have been undergoing assimilation into the north Indian plains culture for many centuries.

The caste Hindus of plains origin are not as susceptible to cultural assimilation as the tribals of either the hills or plains because the Hindu culture of the plains is an ancient and rich one, as vital and expansive as the Nepalese hill culture. As later chapters will document, the Nepalese government has taken various steps to encourage the Nepalization process in the tarai, but it is clear that the plains people will resist the government's more obvious efforts to transform their cultural patterns.

Some assimilation will take place slowly and naturally as hill people interact with plains people in the tarai. However, cultural homogeneity is not a necessary precondition for national unity. Certainly the plains people of the tarai could be brought into a participating relationship with the hill people without adopting the hill culture.

Chapter II

ECONOMY OF THE TARAI

Nepal's location on the southern side of the Himalayas places it on the periphery of the greater Indian economic sphere. More than 90 percent of Nepal's trade is with India. The country's major lines of transportation and communication are with India, and it is dependent upon India for the supply of many essential commodities such as cloth, sugar, kerosene, and most metallic articles. Because it borders directly on India, the tarai is even more closely linked with the greater Indian economic sphere than is the hill region. Blessed with rich agricultural resources and stimulated by the economic activity of northern India, the tarai has become the most productive agricultural and industrial region of Nepal. For this reason, it generates much of Nepal's national wealth and most of the government's revenue. This chapter will survey the historical and contemporary reasons for the hill region's economic dependency upon the tarai and the various economic links that have been established between the tarai and northern India.

NOTES ON THE ECONOMIC HISTORY OF THE TARAI

The hill kings of Nepal have cast covetous eyes on the tarai for centuries. In the 16th century, the Sen kings of Makwanpur in the central hill region of Nepal conquered the eastern tarai from kings of plains origin whose locus of power was in what is now Bihar. When hill kings were not strong enough to wrest parts of the tarai away from kings living in the plains, they sought the tarai as zamindaris.[1] In the 18th century, the kings of Palpa in the western hills received the districts of Kapilabastu, Rupandehi and part of Nawal Parasi as a zamindari from the Nawab Wazir of Oudh, at that time one of northern India's most powerful rulers. In the early 1770s, after the conquest of Kathmandu Valley, Prithvi Narayan Shah, founder of the present ruling dynasty

[1] A zamindar is a nonofficial tax-collecting functionary, and a zamindari is the land holding of such a functionary.

and unifier of modern Nepal, turned his attention to the conquest of eastern Nepal. His aim was to control the eastern tarai. In a letter to his generals in the field he commented that little was to be gained from control of the low-revenue-yielding hill region without also appropriating the high-revenue-yielding tarai region.[2] Subsequently, revenue derived from the eastern tarai became a major source of income for the government of the Shah kings.

The Nepalese expansion along the Himalayas in the late 18th and early 19th centuries paralleled the expansion of British power on the Gangetic plain. Inevitably there was conflict between the two powers in the region where their administrators and soldiers came face to face. This region was the tarai, and the struggle for control of Butwal and Shivaraj (modern Kapilabastu and Rupandehi districts) in the mid-western tarai ultimately led to the Anglo-Nepali War of 1814–16. When, after valiant resistance by the Nepalese, the British finally demonstrated the superiority of their military technology, the British considered annexing the Nepal tarai as a means of cutting off this valuable source of revenue and thereby financially crippling the government in Kathmandu. By the terms of the treaty of Sugauli, December 1816, the British took over the entire tarai. A year later, the eastern and central tarai from the Mechi River to the western Rapti River was returned to Nepal and in 1858, after the Nepalese aided the British during the Indian Mutiny, the western tarai was returned.

During the period when the Rana prime ministers held sway in Kathmandu, tarai lands were liberally distributed to family members and loyal retainers. The income from these lands accumulated into fortunes for these land-grant holders. Particularly after the beginning of World War I, when India's industrial economy was expanding rapidly, it was possible for these people to exploit their forest reserves with great profit. Prime Minister Chandra Shamsher in Morang and Bara during the 1920s, and Prime Minister Juddha Shamsher in Mahottari in the 1930s, had their forests logged by Indian timber contractors and hill-tribal laborers in order to supply the demand of the Indian railroads for ties (sleepers) and that of Indian industry for construction materials. To increase land revenue, the Rana government also encouraged the settling of tarai lands. Because the

[2]Yogi Narahari Nath, ed., *A Collection of Treaties in the Illumination on History*, vol. II (published on the occasion of the Spiritual Conference convened at Dang on 2022 B. S. [1966]), p. 42. (Trans. by Regmi Research Project, 1967.)

land shortage was more acute in northern India than in the hills during the late 19th century and the early 20th, and because the hill people found the tarai climate hot and living conditions strange, the Ranas could not persuade hill people to settle in the tarai. Indian zamindars were encouraged to take tarai land and induce tenant cultivators of plains origin to settle it. The mid-western tarai was settled largely in this manner between the 1890s and the 1930s.

THE ECONOMIC IMPORTANCE OF THE TARAI

By the 1960s the tarai had become the economic backbone of the nation. In order to put this economic importance into quantitative terms, let us look at the tarai's contribution to Nepal's gross domestic product and to the government's revenue.

Nepal's gross domestic product (GDP)[3] accumulates primarily from agricultural activity. Ninety-four percent of Nepal's economically active population is dependent on agriculture for a living, and 65 percent of the GDP for the fiscal year 1964–65 was estimated by the Nepal Rastra (National) Bank to come from the agricultural sector.[4] On the basis of crop-production data gathered by the Ministry of Agriculture,[5] tarai districts' production of 11 major crops alone accounts for 48 percent of Nepal's total agricultural product. Allowances have to be made for the fact that the Rastra Bank's figure for the total agricultural product is an underestimate by about 15 percent, because of the tarai's agricultural contribution beyond the 11 major crops, that is, contribution from minor crops, animal husbandry, and forestry.[6] The tarai's contribution to the nation's agricultural product therefore, is approximately 55 percent.

The Nepal Rastra Bank has estimated that in 1964–65, 11 percent of the GDP was generated by manufacturing.[7] In 1962, 72 percent of Nepal's 1,686 privately owned smaller industries were situated

[3] The Nepalis use the term gross domestic product rather than gross national product in order to indicate that foreign-aid contributions are not included.

[4] Nepal Rastra Bank, *Report of the Board of Directors to His Majesty's Government for the Fiscal Year* 1961/62, 1962/63, 1963/64, *and* 1964/65, p. 5. The Bank quotes as its source the National Planning Council.

[5] Unpublished data obtained from HMG/Nepal, Ministry of Land Reform, Agriculture and Food, Agricultural Economics Section.

[6] At present, no figures are available on the percentage of agricultural product from minor crops, animal husbandry, or forestry; however, the tarai generates most of the product from minor crops and forestry.

[7] Nepal Rastra Bank, *op. cit.*

in the tarai, which probably accounted for more than 72 percent of industrial production because the largest industries, some of which are publicly owned, are also located in the tarai.[8] The Rastra Bank has also estimated that commerce, transport, communications, construction activity, financial institutions, private housing, public administration, and utilities make up the remaining 24 percent of the GDP. It should be assumed that the tarai's share of the GDP generated from these sources is slightly less than its share of manufacturing, because most of the public administration and utilities are centered in Kathmandu Valley. Sixty-five percent as the tarai's share should be a reasonably accurate estimate.

55% of Rs. 3,959,000,000 GDP for agriculture[9]	= Rs. 2,177,450,000
72% of Rs. 594,000,000 GDP for manufacturing	= Rs. 427,680,000
65% of Rs. 1,248,000,000 GDP for commerce and services	= Rs. 811,200,000
Total GDP from the tarai in 1964–65	= Rs. 3,416,330,000

This is 59 percent of Nepal's total GDP of Rs. 5,801,000,000 in 1964–65.

Let us now estimate the contributions the tarai makes to government revenue. The government's total revenue for the fiscal year 1965–66 was Rs. 391,798,000. Of this, 55 percent was derived from domestic sources; the rest was received as foreign aid. Rs. 176,124,000 or 81 percent of the domestically generated revenue for that year came from four major sources: 1) taxes on timber operation, 2) excise or industrial taxes, 3) land taxes, and 4) customs duties.[10]

Because Nepal's most valuable stands of timber are located in tarai districts and because roads are available to transport the timber to Indian markets, 87 percent of timber revenue comes from this region. Of the remaining timber revenue, the inner tarai valleys produce

---

[8]Badri Prasad Shreshtha, *The Economy of Nepal* (Bombay, 1967), p. 155.

[9]Fifteen percent has been added to the Rastra Bank's estimate of Nepal's total agricultural product in order to bring it into line with Ministry of Agriculture data. The manufacturing, commerce, and service estimates are those made by the Bank. It is assumed that the percentage of industry in the tarai is the same in 1964/65 as it was in 1962.

[10]Nepal, Ministry of Finance, *Budget Speech of the Fiscal Year* 1967–68 (Delivered by the Honourable Finance Minister, Surya Bahadur Thapa, July 9, 1967), appendixes A and D.

9 percent and the western hills 4 percent.[11] Ninety-three percent of the government's excise revenue flows from sugar and jute processing, and from cigarette and match manufacturing in tarai towns. Most of the remaining excise revenue is contributed by Kathmandu Valley. Revenue from land tax is the second largest source of domestic revenue; 75 percent comes from tarai districts, 3 percent from Kathmandu Valley, and the remaining 22 percent from the inner tarai valleys and the hills.[12] The government's largest source of revenue is the duties levied on imported and exported goods. Almost all of this revenue is collected at 118 customs posts along the tarai border with India, for more than 90 percent of Nepal's trade is carried on with India. It is very difficult to make a regional breakdown of customs revenues because some of the goods that pass through tarai customs posts have their origin or destination north of the Siwaliks. It is therefore necessary to estimate that about 70 percent of customs revenues are generated by economic activity in the tarai. This is a reasonable estimate, perhaps even a low one, when one considers the high percentage of the nation's industry located in the tarai and the large exportable surplus of rice and other agricultural produce grown there.

87% of Rs. 18,029,000 timber revenue	=	Rs.	15,685,230
93% of Rs. 20,062,000 excise revenue	=	Rs.	18,657,660
75% of Rs. 44,518,000 land revenue	=	Rs.	33,388,500
70% of Rs. 93,515,000 customs revenue	=	Rs.	65,460,000
Total revenue generated by the tarai, fiscal year 1965–66	=	Rs.	133,191,890

This is 76 percent of the total domestically generated revenue of Rs. 176,124,000 from the four sources given above.[13] It can be assumed that the tarai contributes approximately the same percentage of the other Rs. 40,372,000 revenue collected by the government from a multitude of less important sources.

To sum up, although the tarai accounts for only 17 percent[14] of Nepal's land area and 31 percent of its population, it contributes approximately 59 percent of Nepal's GDP and 76 percent of the revenue.[15]

[11]Unpublished data obtained from HMG/Nepal, Office of the Chief Conservator of Forests.
[12]Unpublished data obtained from HMG/Nepal, Ministry of Finance.
[13]*Budget Speech*, 1967–68, *op. cit.* appendix D.
[14]Area of the tarai census districts.
[15]A word of caution is required about comparing these figures. The population figure is for 1961, the GDP figures for 1964–65, and the revenue figures for 1965–66. The percentages are likely to vary slightly each year.

THE TARAI, NEPAL, AND THE RICE TRADE

The economic importance of the tarai is further underscored by the volume of the agricultural surplus it produces. Statistical documentation of these surpluses is published elsewhere.[16] Most important is the tarai's surplus rice production. Not only does the food-deficit hill region of Nepal depend upon substantial yearly imports of rice from the tarai, but the tarai also sends large amounts of rice to India. In 1965 an estimated 348,000 metric tons of rice were exported from the tarai to India, making Nepal the fifth largest rice exporter in the world that year. The importance of this large-scale rice export to Nepal's economic development can not be overstated. It is estimated that Nepal earned 237,772,685 Indian rupees from its rice exports in 1965. Other agricultural surpluses exported from the tarai, particularly raw jute and oil seeds, have added lesser but still substantial Indian-currency earnings to the nation's financial ledger.

The Nepalese government levies duties on these exports, and revenue raised by this means contributes to government income from the tarai. In the private sector, the major beneficiaries of the export business are the large-scale farmers, rice-mill owners and various middlemen. Some of the Indian-currency earnings are invested in India, because many of those who profit from the trade have family and business connections in India. Some of the earnings are plowed back into the land in the form of seeds, fertilizer, repair or improvement of farm tools, irrigation facilities, etc. or for rice-mill maintenance. However, a large share of the profits accumulates as capital for consumer or development purposes; for example, the construction of a new house in Kathmandu or another rice mill in the tarai. Inasmuch as most of the manufactured items needed in such construction must be imported from India, and can not be purchased with Nepalese currency, the Indian-rupee balances earned from the export of the tarai's agricultural surpluses become the key to much of the private sector's economic vitality.

TRADE TIES BETWEEN THE TARAI AND INDIA

Aside from rice, the tarai produces surpluses of jute, tobacco, oil seeds, sugar cane, herbs, spices, timber, hides, and many other agricultural

[16]See Frederick H. Gaige, "The Role of the Tarai in Nepal's Economic Development," *Vasudha* (Kathmandu), II (June 1968), 53–61, 71.

items in smaller quantities. Trading networks have developed for each of these items, flowing from the villages to the tarai towns and from there to the major cities of India. Some of these networks are overlapping, with the same businessmen buying and selling several different items. In order to present a more graphic description of how one of these trading networks operates, let us follow one, the rice network, since it is the most important, from the village southward across the border into India.

Despite the fact that the tarai is a food-surplus region, many of its farmers live at a subsistence level. They have no surplus food or money and often fall into debt before the end of the economic year, which arrives in October, just before the harvest of their main crop, generally rice. Farmers who find themselves in this situation are forced to sell their rice as soon as it is harvested, when the rice prices are at their lowest. Even before the harvest season, they are occasionally forced to promise the sale of their rice at prices below the harvest-season price level in return for loans to tide them over until the harvest season.

The poorer villagers usually sell their rice to village shopkeepers, often on a barter basis in return for goods such as salt and matches, or to commission agents who tour the villages periodically as rice buyers. The few more wealthy farmers can afford to hold their rice until after the end of the harvest season, when prices rise. They also own bullock carts and can transport their rice to markets where prices are higher, thus bypassing the set of middlemen represented by the shopkeepers and commission agents.

The shopkeepers, if they can afford to tie up capital, hold rice until prices rise and then sell to stockists, large grain dealers in tarai towns and Indian border towns. Usually, the shopkeepers and commission agents have little capital. In fact, they often borrow money from the stockists with which to buy rice in the villages. Their profit is small, the difference between the price at which they buy from the villagers and sell to the stockists, minus interest on loans they may have taken.

Each of the five tarai districts in the 1967–68 field survey had half a dozen trading centers at which stockists maintained their storehouses. These centers ranged in size from large towns to small villages. The stockists sometimes store hundreds of tons of rice until the harvest season is well over and rice prices have mounted in India. Then they sell to rice-mill owners in the tarai or India or to much larger Indian wholesalers, who distribute rice to major Indian cities. The price of rice is influenced and often manipulated by the Indian wholesalers, who can create artificial scarcities by withholding it from the market.

The rice-mill owners often act as their own stockists, sending out commission agents to the villages. They mill unhusked rice and sell polished rice to the wholesalers; their profit comes from the difference between the price of the unhusked and that of polished rice. If the harvest in India is good, the Nepalis generally go to India to make their contacts with wholesalers. If the Indian harvest is poor, the Indian wholesalers visit the tarai. Whether the Indian harvest is good or poor, Indian market prices determine prices in the tarai and other parts of Nepal. This is true not only for rice but also for all the tarai's agricultural surpluses except jute, which has an overseas market.

Economic ties are reinforced by the trade in manufactured goods, which follows the same network, but in the opposite direction, from the urban centers of India through the towns on the Nepal-India border and into tarai villages. The goods are purchased with earnings from the sale of agricultural surpluses. The trading network has extensions into the hills as well. The hill region has little to export except its people, who seek work in the tarai and India. Except for the salaries and pensions Gurkha soldiers earn in the British and Indian armies and the wages earned by hill people working as laborers and gatekeepers in the plains, the hill people have little with which to purchase Indian goods. Consequently, the economic ties between India and the tarai are stronger than the ties between India and the hill region.

COMMUNAL CHARACTERISTICS OF VILLAGE SHOPKEEPERS AND ITINERANT VILLAGE TRADERS

In the preceding chapter, caste and other communal characteristics of the total tarai population were surveyed in order to assess the strength of the hill and plains cultural influences. In order to make a more complete assessment, it is necessary to know the communal affiliations of economically and politically important people in the region. Chapter VIII deals with the communal affiliations of politically important people; this chapter focuses upon those having economic importance.

As indicated in table 5, in Mahottari-Dhanusha, Bara, and Kapilabastu districts, which represent the tarai subregions in which they are located, the percentage of plains Hindu shopkeepers in the shopkeeper population exceeds the percentage of plains Hindus in the

TABLE 5
Regional and Communal Affiliation of Shopkeepers in Sample Villages

Regional and communal groupings	Jhapa		Mahottari-Dhanusha		Bara		Kapilabastu		Kailali	
	Village population	Shopkeepers	Village population	Shopkeepers	Village population	Shopkeepers	Village population	Shopkeepers	Village population	Shopkeepers
Hill people	16.1	17.8	13.8	7.5	1.6	1.1	9.0		9.6	16.7
Plains Hindus	18.1	71.2	77.9	88.4	79.4	75.0	66.4	80.0	.9	33.3
Muslims	4.3	1.4	7.1	4.1	13.7	15.9	18.0	12.0	1.2	50.0
Plains tribals	56.2	8.2	1.3		5.4	7.9	6.6	6.0	88.3	
Cooperative		1.4						2.0		
Total	100.0	100.0	100.0	100.0	100.0	100.0	100.0	100.0	100.0	

Source: Field survey of 81 villages, 1967–68.

general population, verifying the high degree to which they have become commercialized. This fact is underscored in Jhapa, where only 18 percent of the population is plains Hindu but 71 percent of the shopkeepers are individuals whose castes are included in this communal category. Generally, Muslims throughout northern India have developed a fairly high degree of commercialization, particularly at the level of the small-scale trader and shopkeeper. This seems to be less the case in the tarai, except in the far-western tarai district, Kailali, where practically all the Muslims are businessmen. From the survey data gathered, it appears that the percentage of hill people who are shopkeepers corresponds fairly closely to the percentage of hill people in the total tarai population. With the exception of the Sherpas and Thakalis, hill tribals appear to have relatively little interest in business. Almost all hill people pursuing business in the tarai, whether shopkeeping, itinerant trade, or small-scale industry, were Brahmins, Chetris, or Newars. As one would anticipate, the plains tribals are the least commercialized. This fact is underscored by the data collected in Jhapa and Kailali districts.

The upper-caste plains people do not seem reluctant to enter business, even though business is traditionally a middle-caste occupation. Among the hill people there are no traditional business castes, except among the Newars and, therefore, no preconceived attitudes about the rank of businessmen in the caste system. In any case, the caste system has not been able to force its regime of occupational rigidity upon the hill people to the extent that it has until recently upon the plains people. Also, economic resources having always been more limited in the hills than in the plains, hill people have been forced to retain a flexibility that permits them to take advantage of whatever economic opportunities present themselves.

Like shopkeepers, itinerant traders play important economic roles in tarai villages. They often act as commission agents, buying agricultural surpluses, and occasionally sell light provisions and knickknacks. In 48 of 81 villages surveyed, the headmen responded that most of the villagers sold their surplus crops to traders who came to the village. In another 18 villages, a significant number, if not the majority, of villagers sold to these traders. There are several reasons for the importance of this type of businessman. First, in many of the smaller villages, there are no shopkeepers to fill the traders' functions. Second, traders, like the shopkeepers, sometimes function as moneylenders. When villagers borrow from these individuals, they obligate themselves to pay very high interest rates, and thus form dependency relationships with these businessmen.

TABLE 6
Itinerant Traders in Sample Villages of Five Tarai Districts, by Regional and Communal Groupings

Regional and communal groupings	Jhapa	Mahottari Dhanusha	Bara	Kapila-bastu	Kailali
Hill people	36.8			1.7	44.4
Plains Hindus	36.8	89.1	90.0	70.7	11.1
Muslims		7.3	10.0	27.6	22.2
Plains tribals	21.1	3.6			22.2
Unknown	5.3				
Total	100.0	100.0	100.0	100.0	100.0

Source: Data collected in field survey of 81 villages, 1967–68.

As the data in table 6 indicate, the hill people are well represented among the traders of Jhapa and Kailali districts, where there are significant numbers of hill settlers. The plains tribals are better represented among the traders than among the shopkeepers of these two districts. In Mahottari-Dhanusha, Bara, and Kapilabastu districts, the plains Hindus dominate the itinerant trading class as they do the shopkeeper class, with the Muslims holding their own in the competition.

Except in the western and eastern ends of the tarai, the evidence indicates that the plains people, particularly the plains Hindus, hold a dominant commercial position throughout the region. Most of them were businessmen when they migrated to the tarai. They were looking for new business opportunities, and it appears that many of them maintain marriage and business ties with extended-family and caste members in the Indian villages and towns from which they or their families migrated, sometimes as long as three or four generations ago.

Probably nothing persuades people to cross caste and communal lines faster than the prospect of economic gain. For this reason, it is unwise to weigh too heavily generalizations about the relationships between family, caste, and economic activity. Nevertheless, these informal and often invisible ties do exist and tend to reinforce the network of buying and selling that links the tarai and northern India.

THE RELATIONSHIP OF TARAI INDUSTRY TO THE INDIAN ECONOMY

The development of industry in the tarai is a response to the expansion of Indian economic activity. The construction of the Indian railroad system to the Nepal-India border in the late 19th century and the establishment of railheads along the border is a graphic example of the northward expansion of the Indian economy. Around the railheads sprang up typical northern Indian towns: a few unplanned, sun-baked mud streets lined with dark and cluttered one-room shops crowded in upon each other, streets bustling with heavily loaded porters, squeaking bullock carts, animated buyers and sellers, cows, goats, and dogs. In the days before such towns were established on the Nepal side of the border, the tarai's agricultural surpluses flowed directly to these railhead settlements for shipment to Indian cities. Map 4 indicates the points of termination for the railroads along the border. Note the close proximity of major tarai towns just north of the railheads.

According to B. P. Shreshtha, one of Nepal's leading economists, 88 percent of Nepal's industrial investment is in the tarai, as is nearly 100 percent of the nation's industrial labor force.[17] Unpublished records of the government's Industry Department list 28 public limited companies operating in 1967—seventeen in the tarai, nine in Kathmandu Valley, and two in the western hills. Public limited companies are among the largest industries in Nepal. As already mentioned, an estimated 72 percent of Nepal's smaller industries are also located in the tarai.

The availability of the Indian transportation system, now macadam roads as well as the railroads, is a key factor in the development of industry in the tarai and a primary reason for the lack of such development in the hill region. Only two roads connect India with the hill region, one from Birganj to Kathmandu, completed in the late 1950s, and one from Bhairawa to Pokhara, completed in 1972. There is also a hard-surface road from the Tibetan border at Kodari to Kathmandu. Most hill people must transport what they need by backpack over foot trails from tarai markets to their homes. They can not carry much and, in any case, they can seldom afford to buy much. Therefore, tarai farmers and small-scale industrialists are dependent upon the Indian market to absorb their goods.

[17] *An Introduction to Nepalese Economy*, p. 147.

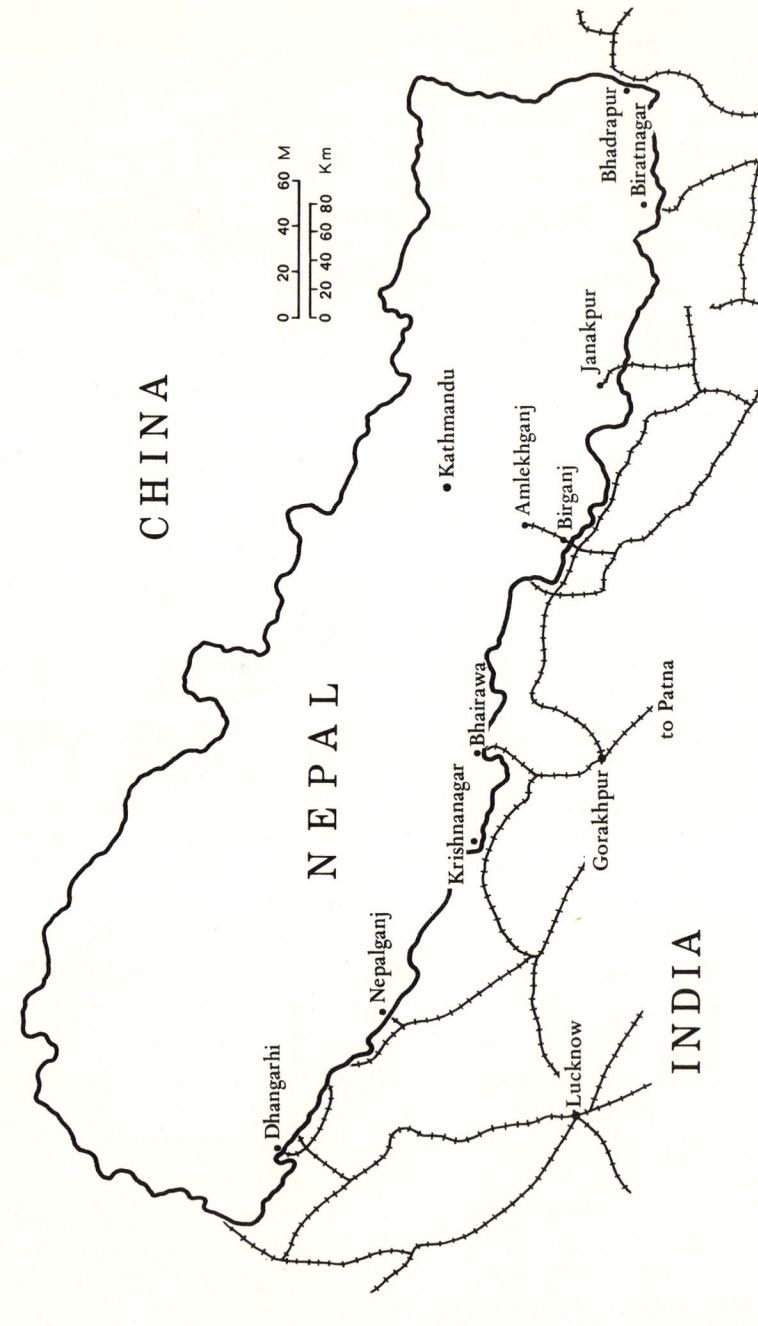

Map 4. Commercial centers of the tarai at Indian railheads. Source: Elaboration of inset map made by P. P. Karan, *Nepal: A Cultural and Physical Geography* (Lexington, Ky., 1960), p. 88.

Indian capital is also instrumental in the development of tarai industry. The Indians who invest in the tarai are often involved in a similar business across the border. For example, Radha Kissen Chamaria, a Marwari important in Calcutta's jute processing and exporting business, was chiefly responsible for the establishment of Nepal's largest jute mill in 1936. Chamaria had already built a jute mill at Katihar, a town in Bihar about 75 miles south of Biratnagar. The tarai area around Biratnagar had become a major jute-growing area by the 1930s, and the price of jute was high. Chamaria persuaded his friend, Juddha Shamsher, Rana Prime Minister of Nepal at the time, to set up a holding company financed jointly by the two of them. Aish Narayan Singhania, Chamaria's brother-in-law and manager of Chamaria's mill at Katihar, moved to Biratnagar to manage the mill there and was instrumental in establishing Biratnagar's first large rice mill in 1937, a cotton mill in 1942, and a sugar mill in 1946.[18]

Some tarai industry has been established by hill people with their own capital. For example, Nepal's largest rice mill was built in Janakpur in 1938 by the father of Gauri Narayan Giri. Giri's father was born in the eastern hills, and while a government official in a tea-growing foothills district, he began exporting tea to Calcutta. With the capital he acquired, he bought land in the tarai and, in 1926, built a rice mill in the Indian border town of Jaynagar. After Juddha Shamsher constructed a narrow-gauge railroad from Jaynagar to Janakpur to facilitate the logging operations on his extensive forest holdings north of Janakpur, the Giris moved their mill to Janakpur, and Gauri Narayan became its manager.[19] Chamaria and Giri wanted to move their industries from India into the tarai for several reasons. First, the railroads provided cheap and reliable transportation. Second, they wanted to avoid the payment of Indian excise taxes. Third, they wanted to locate closer to the source of primary materials, i.e., jute and rice, in order to obviate dependence on middlemen.

Although some Ranas and Shahs, members of the King's extended family, and other hill people like the Giris have invested capital in the development of tarai industry, much of the capital for the tarai's large-and medium-scale industry appears to have come from Indian businessmen or from plains people who are settled in the tarai and

[18]Interview with Shyam Narayan Singhania, younger brother of Aish Narayan Singhania, in Biratnagar on Jan. 1, 1967. Aish Narayan was manager of the Biratnagar Jute Mills at the time of the interview.
[19]Interviews with Gauri Narayan Giri in Janakpur, Dec. 5 and 7, 1966.

have access to capital through marriage or business associations in India. This cannot be documented by reference to Industry Department records because Indian investors have found it advantageous to associate themselves with hill people, particularly those who have government connections, in order to obtain government licenses for their industries. Therefore, Industry Department records often list hill people as owners and managers of industries in which they have little or no capital investment. Government officials tend to distrust businessmen of plains origin, even those who have lived in the tarai for many years or even generations. This distrust arises from the complex and, from the officials' point of view, often confusing relationships between businessmen living in the tarai and in India. Some officials tend to suspect that Indian economic interests may threaten Nepal's political integrity.

Except for several stainless-steel and synthetic-fabrics factories,[20] one cotton mill (not operating at present) and one steel-rolling mill, nearly all of Nepal's industry, whether large- or small-scale, processes timber and agricultural produce grown in the tarai. Table 7 organizes information about small-scale industry in the five districts of the 1967–68 field survey. The great majority of these enterprises are rice mills, most of them small diesel-driven mills which husk rice and press oil seeds only for the population in surrounding villages. However, a few of the mills in each district are large and process thousands of tons of rice for export to India.[21] Along the Indian border there are many bidi factories[22] that operate in Nepalese territory, again to avoid Indian excise taxes. Until recently, timber was generally exported to India in the form of logs and milled there, but now the milling process is beginning to take place in the tarai. The sugar, brick, and soap industries have been established mainly for local consumption.

COMMUNAL CHARACTERISTICS OF OWNERS OF SMALL-SCALE INDUSTRY

Unlike large- and medium-scale industry in which part-ownership and management may be shared with individuals who have made little or no capital investment, small-scale industry is generally owned

---

[20]These were established during the 1960s, apparently by Indian businessmen to avoid Indian excise taxes.

[21]Much of the tarai's rice is still milled in India.

[22]A bidi is a handmade cigarette and a bidi factory may be no more than a shade tree under which village women and children roll bidis and a one- or two-room brick structure nearby where the factory manager keeps his records and stores the bidis.

TABLE 7
Small-Scale Industry in the Tarai,
by District and Type of Industry [a]

District	Jhapa	Mahottari Dhanusha	Bara	Kapila-bastu	Kailali
Rice mill	85	155	102	87	55
Bidi factory	2	46	20	9	2
Brick factory		7		20	
Saw mill	5		1	1	2
Soap factory		1	3	1	
Sugar mill			4	1	
Miscellaneous	1		4	2	
Total	93	209	134	121	59

[a] The data for this table were collected from the unpublished records of the revenue office in each of the districts. The revenue office is under the supervision of the Anchaladish (zonal commissioner) or Assistant Anchaladish. Small-scale industry means single-owner industries. All public limited and private limited industries, i.e., those with more than one owner, have been excluded from the data in this table.

and managed by the same individual or family. The caste of the owners is therefore easily identified in the district revenue-office records. Table 8 indicates that hill people are better represented among the owners of small-scale industry than among shopkeepers or itinerant traders. In Jhapa district, where the hill people constitute 16 percent of the population, they account for 58 percent of small-scale industrialists. In Kailali, only 10 percent of the population are hill people, yet they represent 73 percent of the small-scale industrialists. A few of the small rice mills in these two districts are owned by plains tribals, indicating the possibility that these people are beginning to adapt to the complex world beyond the fringe of their isolated forest habitat.

Even in the most populous subregions of the tarai, represented by Mahottari-Dhanusha, Bara, and Kapilabastu districts, the percentage of hill people among owners of small-scale industry is higher than the percentage of the hill people in the population of those districts. The best example of this is in Bara, where they own nearly 13 percent of small-scale industry despite the fact that they represent only about 2 percent of the district population.

It is difficult to know why the hill people appear to be more highly

TABLE 8
Owners of Small-Scale Industry in Five Tarai Districts, by Regional and Communal Groupings[a]

Regional and communal groupings	Jhapa	Mahottari-Dhanusha	Bara	Kapila-bastu	Kailali
Hill people	58.1	15.3	12.8	13.2	72.9
Plains Hindus	25.8	76.1	75.2	61.2	3.4
Muslims		6.2	9.0	25.6	
Plains tribals	16.1	2.4	3.0		23.7
Total	100.0	100.0	100.0	100.0	100.0

[a] These data were collected for each district as a whole, not simply for the villages in the field survey. The data were obtained from unpublished records of the revenue office in each district. Generally, the owner's caste could be identified by his name, but in cases where this was difficult, the revenue officer was consulted.

commercialized with regard to light industry than shopkeeping or itinerant-type trade. Although hill people represent a small percentage of the tarai population, a relatively large number of them, because of their contacts with the various Kathmandu governments over the past several generations, have sizable holdings of rice-producing land in the tarai. For an enterprising producer of large rice surpluses, it is a rather natural step to establish a small rice mill, husking the rice in order to enhance its value before it is sold to Indian wholesalers. Also, as already mentioned, it tends to be easier for hill people than plains people to obtain the necessary government licenses for such an enterprise.

There is a concentration of small-scale industry in the subregions of the tarai represented by Mahottari-Dhanusha, Bara, and Kapilabastu. Despite the involvement of the hill people, the Hindus and Muslims together own over 80 percent of all small-scale industry in these districts.

NEPALESE ATTITUDES TOWARD INDIAN ECONOMIC DOMINATION

Nepal's economic dependency on India involves, along with others already mentioned, dependence on India for the supply of skilled labor for Nepal's several large-scale industries and of essential goods such as cloth, salt, kerosene, and sugar. Moreover, Nepal is susceptible to the inflationary trends that grip the Indian economy. Discussion of these must be left to scholars focusing their attention upon the economic relations between Nepal and India.

It is relevant here to mention the earnest desire of the hill people to lessen their economic dependency upon India. The construction of a transportation system which ties together various regions of the country is one way they seek to lessen this dependency and, therefore, they hail the construction of the east-west highway as a move toward greater self-sufficiency. Some kind of an east-west artery to link the isolated subregions of the hills has been considered since the early 1950s, but it was first seriously proposed by King Mahendra only in 1961. Because the cost of constructing such a road through the hill region would have been prohibitive, the highway was planned to run through the tarai, all the way from the Mahakali River in the west to the Mechi River in the east.[23] The American and Russian governments have completed segments of the road, and the British and Indian governments have agreed to build other segments. It is hoped that the entire highway will be completed by the mid-1970s.

The road cuts across the traditional north-south trade routes between India and Nepal; hence the Nepalis hope that it will facilitate the process of national integration. Soon, Nepalis will be able to travel from one part of the country to another without traveling through India. Until recently, the quickest and easiest way for them to travel from one subregion of the hills to another was to walk south to the nearest Indian railhead and take the train to the station south of their destination, then walk north into the hills. In 1972 the Nepalese government contracted an Italian firm to make surveys for eighteen north-south roads to connect the east-west highway and various parts of the hill region.[24] However, until these feeder roads are built—and the actual construction may still be a long way off—the east-west highway will be effective only in unifying the tarai subregions and linking the tarai with the Kathmandu and Pokhara Valleys, which already have feeder roads.

It is doubtful that the highway will make Nepal less dependent upon the Indian economy. As an agricultural society, much of it

[23]At the two points where the Indian border runs along the Siwaliks foothill range, interrupting the Nepalese-controlled tarai region, the east-west highway runs north of the range, through the central and western inner-tarai valleys.
[24]*Navin Khabar,* Jan. 30, 1972.

operates on a subsistence or near-subsistence level. Indeed, Nepal is probably less a part of the larger Indian economic sphere than it would be as an industrialized nation. Industrial nations that border each other tend to develop much greater economic interdependence than do neighboring agricultural nations, because of the greater flow across national boundaries of capital, labor, and goods that is stimulated by industrialization.

India's economic domination of the tarai and of Nepal as a whole is inevitable, given the close proximity of the two countries and their disproportionate sizes. Yet, this is a dependency relationship that is resented by the Nepalis. As one empathetic Indian journalist has put it, "A country of 10 million people, tied by geography and much else to the Indian colossus, is apt at times to feel like someone having to share a bed with an elephant."[25] One Nepalese newspaper editor has warned: "If the Government of India wants to see Indians in Nepal looked upon in the same way as Indians in Ceylon, Burma, and Africa" it has only to continue its present policy of attempting to protect its economic monopoly of Nepal.[26] The government daily, *Gorkhapatra*, in a statement reminiscent of Indian journalistic comment about American economic domination, complained: "India expects developed nations to follow a policy which will encourage its trade and industry. How can Nepal, which is lagging far behind India in industrial and commercial development, undergo such adverse and reactionary treatment at the hands of its intimate friend, India?"[27]

It is not possible to explore in this study whether the Indian government is actively encouraging Nepal's economic dependency or attempting to accommodate Nepal's frustrations. However, the fact that Nepalis tend to perceive the Indian government as playing a "neocolonialist" role has its effects on the question of national integration. These effects will be discussed in the concluding chapter. Let it suffice to say here that the economy of the tarai is so closely linked to that of northern India that some government officials and other members of the Kathmandu elite, almost all of them hill people, have difficulty thinking of the tarai as more than a Nepalese-administered but otherwise alien region.

---

[25] Inder Malhotra, "India-Nepal Relations: Delhi's Diplomacy on Trial," *Statesman* (Calcutta), June 12, 1970, p. 6.
[26] *Samaj*, June 19, 1969.
[27] *Gorkhapatra*, Aug. 14, 1969.

EXTENSION OF THE NEPALESE CURRENCY SYSTEM INTO THE TARAI

The economy of Kathmandu Valley has been monetized for many centuries, perhaps since the third century B.C., when the influence of the great Mauryan Emperor, Ashoka, was felt there. Gradually, over the past several centuries, monetization has occurred in the economy of the tarai and in the hill region outside Kathmandu Valley. Because Nepal is a part of the larger Indian economic sphere, Indian currency has been until recently the major circulating currency in much of the country, almost to the total exclusion of Nepalese currency in the tarai. This situation is responsible for one of the interrelated problems of national integration. The unrestricted entry of Indian currency into Nepal and its use, particularly in the tarai, as the currency of daily commercial transactions, have prevented the Nepalese government from exercising monetary control over much of the national economy.

The demand for Indian currency began growing rapidly during the 18th century. During the latter half of that century, the Nepalis used Indian currency to buy more sophisticated arms than they could produce themselves in order to defend their territory against threatening Indian and British armies. In the second half of the 19th century, Nepalese nobility, particularly the Rana family, developed contact with European culture and acquired a taste for the trappings of upper-class western living, baroque-style palaces with cut-glass chandeliers, motor cars, watches, and so forth. Although some of these goods were purchased directly from Europe, many were acquired in India.

The Nepalis tapped a number of sources to obtain Indian rupees for these purchases. The most productive source was land revenue from the tarai. The 1861 administrative regulations for tarai districts state specifically that "Company Rupees," as British East India Company money was called, would be accepted in payment of taxes.[28] Until the last decade, Indian currency was used almost exclusively in the tarai. Both Nepalese and Indian currency were used in Kathmandu Valley and in the hill districts, Nepalese currency generally for local transactions. Thus there was a dual-currency system, and the extension of the use of Indian currency resulted from what might be called a commercial acculturation process taking place among upper- and more recently middle-class Nepalis who created a demand

[28]Nepal, Department of Land Revenue, *Administrative Regulations for Tarai Districts*, 1861, vol. I, p. 20, and vol. V, p. 14. (Trans. by Regmi Research Project, 1967.)

for goods and services that could be met only by the Indian economy.

Now that nationalism has taken hold, at least among educated Nepalis, the Indian businessman in Nepal and the Indian rupee are often viewed as symbols of Nepal's economic dependence on India. In addition, there are more practical economic reasons for favoring the termination of the dual-currency system. Since the late 1940s, there has been a general deterioration in the value of the Nepalese rupee in relation to the Indian rupee. The fluctuation in value has created many problems for those who must deal with the two different currencies, not only the large-scale businessman and the Nepalese government itself, but also the villagers. Fluctuating currency rates harass both buyers and sellers and discourage creditors and borrowers alike from becoming involved in long-term loans at fixed interest rates. In other words, the fluctuating values of the two currencies inhibited the process of economic growth. The problem existed not only in trade between Nepal and India, but also between the two currency areas of Nepal, that is, between the hills, particularly Kathmandu Valley, and the tarai. The dual-currency system encouraged economic interaction between the tarai and India. It created a barrier to economic interaction between the two regions of Nepal and, therefore, a formidable barrier to national integration.

The government took its first step to abolish the system in 1957, when it passed the Nepalese Currency Circulation Expansion Act.[29] There have been many subsequent efforts to make the Nepalese currency area coincide with the nation's borders, but it has been a difficult task. For example, because customs and currency-exchange facilities along the border are inadequate, the government has no records from which to estimate how much Indian curency is circulating in Nepal. Indian currency continues to be used for major transactions, but the government's effort to discourage its use as the everyday currency for minor transactions has been making considerable headway. Even in the tarai, one seldom sees Indian currency being used in the open market.

It is not the government's intent literally to push Indian rupees out of Nepal, but rather to have them converted into Nepalese currency in Nepalese banks so that they will be available to the government for use in purchasing from India various development goods needed to modernize the economy. Despite the fact that Nepalese currency is now used for daily transactions throughout Nepal, the government

[29] *Nepal Gazette*, vol. VII, No. 15, July 20, 1957.

has difficulty obtaining the Indian rupees it needs from the private sector. A major reason for this is the variety of means by which Indian currency is brought into the country. It can be mailed in, as a Nepalese soldier serving in the Indian Army might do when he wishes to send part of his pay to his family. It can be transferred in through the banking system, as the Indian and American governments do with their economic-aid funds. However, most Indian currency finds its way into Nepal in a less organized fashion. More than 95 percent of Nepal's trade is with India and most of the Indian-currency-earning exports are produced in the tarai. The Nepalese businessman may go to a nearby Indian market to sell his goods and bring Indian currency back into the tarai, or the Indian businessman may bring Indian currency into the tarai and buy goods with it there. The Nepalis may hold their Indian currency to reinvest in their trade, they may invest it in other sectors of the tarai economy or in India, or they may spend it on consumer or development goods in India. In any case, except for the Indian currency they convert into Nepalese currency for living expenses or taxes, the government obtains little of it.

Besides gaining access to the use of Indian-currency surpluses in Nepal, the government wants to prevent the outflow of these surpluses for investment in India. During the Rana period, the Rana prime ministers and family members invested large amounts of capital in India, primarily in urban real estate and industry. Since then, big landowners, businessmen and some government officials have done the same. In the early 1960s, the government enacted laws to prevent this, but there is no government apparatus to enforce them. How can the outflow be stemmed? Because adequate control of the border appears too difficult from the administrative point of view, the government can only hope to create investment opportunities in Nepal as well as an atmosphere of confidence in the Nepalese economy, so that Nepalis who would otherwise invest their money in India will invest it at home instead. In order to persuade the plains people to invest their money in the tarai or in other parts of Nepal, the government will have to draw these people more fully into national politics and policy making, to assure them that they have a stake in national development.

Chapter III

NEPAL-INDIA BORDER PROBLEMS

Throughout this study, Nepal-India relations constitute a secondary theme, interwoven with the primary national-integration theme, but in this chapter, international relations come to the fore, because problems that develop along the border generally affect both nations and often require joint action. The border problems also relate directly to the question of national integration. Until the Nepalese government is able to control the movement of people and goods across its border with India, it can not establish full control over the tarai. The government's success with administration of activities along its border is a measure of its capacity to administer more complex, nontraditional economic- and political-development programs in the tarai, indeed, to ensure progress toward more complete unification of the tarai with the hill region.

Approximately 850 miles of Nepal's international border is shared with India and the Indian protectorate, Sikkim.[1] Most of Nepal's border problems have been along the Indian segment of the border, and this can be attributed to two factors. First, at least 550 of these 850 miles run through flat plains land, either cultivated fields or forest. Except for an occasional stretch of border that follows a river or stream, there are no natural geographical features to distinguish Nepalese from Indian territory, and even the rivers and streams cause problems now and then. During the dry season they twist and turn gently through the rice fields and forests, but during the rainy season they swell and frequently overflow their banks, occasionally cut new beds, and put fields and even entire villages on the opposite side of the border. Second, much of the Nepal-India border is demarcated by stone pillars erected about every quarter mile. The population of the border area is fairly dense, and sometimes disputes occur between people living on opposite sides, drawing the two governments into

[1]Approximately 670 miles of Nepal's international border is also shared with the Tibetan region of China. Over the years, the Nepalis have had a number of border difficulties with the Chinese. However, these are beyond the scope of this study.

conflict. For example, this may happen when local inhabitants destroy or remove the border pillars in order to avoid taxes or to claim land.

There are four types of border-related problems, all of which have been cropping up for at least several hundred years. The first of these concerns border demarcation. The second involves outlaws and political terrorists who operate either in the tarai or in India and use territory on the opposite side of the border as sanctuary. Smuggling from Nepal into India and vice versa constitutes the third problem. These three types of border problems will be the subject of this chapter, and the fourth, the migration of settlers from one country into the other, will be taken up separately in chapter IV.

BORDER-DEMARCATION DISPUTES

The British administrator and historian, Francis Hamilton, related the existence of demarcation disputes between the Nepalese and British Indian governments in the first decade of the 19th century.[2] In 1829, the two governments signed an agreement establishing procedures for reerecting "a minaret, a pillar, or a border stone" when one was destroyed.[3] Usually, since then, when demarcation problems have arisen, local Nepalese and Indian officials have studied maps of the border alignment and have replaced markers in mutually agreed locations.

Occasionally, a demarcation problem flares into a dispute between the two governments, the most notable example being the dispute over the Susta forest in Nawal Parasi district. This forest is situated on a small piece of tarai territory that extends south into Indian territory along the west bank of the Gandak (Narayani) River. The Gandak has been gradually shifting its channel from east to west for the past hundred years or longer, and each time it cuts a new channel, it leaves more of the Nepalese controlled forest on the Indian side. The last major flood and westward shift of the river's course was in 1954, and it left 10,000 acres or more of the forest on the Indian side of the river.[4] For years, local officials have been unable to agree upon a solution to the dispute, which has been aggravated by alleged Indian harassment of Nepalis farming clearings in the forest territory on

[2] *An Account of the Kingdom of Nepal* (Edinburgh, 1819).
[3] "Agreement Made Between Gorkha and British-India for the Conservation of Forests (1829)," in Yogi Narahari Nath, ed., *A Collection of Treaties in the Illumination on History*, vol. II, p. 23. (Trans. by Regmi Research Project, 1967).
[4] *Halkhabar*, Mar. 20, 1960.

the eastern side of the river. The disagreement involves the principles to be applied in settling river boundary-demarcation questions. "Nepal insists upon the boundary delimited in the 1817 treaty between Nepal and British India, while India proposes that the more generally accepted principle under which the boundary follows the river course should be applied in this and similar cases."[5] Even the unusually amicable relations between the two countries in 1972 did not provide a basis for a solution of the dispute.

CONTROL OF CRIME ALONG THE BORDER

The tarai is still a frontier region, government administration is only now in the process of being firmly established, and there is still considerable lawlessness. Bandit gangs from India have been raiding tarai villages for at least several centuries, murdering and looting, and then hurrying back across the border into Indian territory for sanctuary. In the same way, bandit gangs have raided Indian villages and used the tarai as sanctuary. During the early 1950s, when district-level administration in the tarai was particularly disorganized, the Nepalese government was forced to seek law-enforcement assistance from the Indian Army. At the request of the Nepalis, the Indian Army intervened twice in 1951 and once in 1953. Of course, this type of assistance has not been requested since then, but large gangs do continue to operate. An unusually gross example of administrative weakness and gang-style looting and terror occurred in 1971, when four to five hundred bandits rampaged through Rautahat and Bara districts, leaving scores of villages ravaged and 51 persons killed before retreating across the border.[6] Occasionally, in the absence of proper police protection, tarai villagers organize themselves into vigilante groups to defend their villages against such raids.

Once in a while, as one might expect, police cross the border in pursuit of criminals, without consulting their counterparts on the other side, causing ruffled feelings. For example, in April 1969, Indian border police crossed into Parsa district and killed two residents of a village near the border. The Indian police claimed that their victims were members of a bandit gang operating in northern Bihar,[7] but

[5]Leo E. Rose, *Nepal: Strategy for Survival* (Berkeley, 1971), p. 257.
[6]*Gorkhapatra,* Nov. 30, 1971. Hindu-Muslim communalism was a secondary cause of the death and destruction.
[7]*Rising Nepal,* May 8, 1969.

the Nepalis objected to this disregard for their jurisdiction and lodged an official protest.

As a rule, Nepalese and Indian officials cooperate in an effort to maintain law and order along the border, and this cooperation has been facilitated by a series of extradition agreements between the two countries, the first signed in 1834[8] and the latest in 1963.[9] From time to time, law-enforcement officials meet in Indian or Nepalese border towns to discuss their problems. As a result of such meetings in Bhairawa and Janakpur in 1972, a set of simplified border-patrolling and extradition procedures were worked out. Indian police officials agreed to allow Nepalese police to carry arms while traveling through Indian territory and to prevent administrative harassment of these police, and the Nepalis agreed to extend the same privileges to Indian police.[10]

It is not always easy to distinguish between groups that are organized for purely criminal purposes and those that are organized for political purposes, because politically motivated groups occasionally raid and plunder in order to finance organizations with political goals. This was apparently the case with K. I. Singh's "army" in 1951 and with the confrontation between the Communist Party and local-government officials in Rautahat district in 1957. It is possible that some violence labeled purely "criminal" by the government since the royal coup of 1960 has been, in fact, the result of activity organized by the banned political parties. Politically motivated violence naturally adds a complicating dimension to the government's law-and-order problems.

SMUGGLING

Relations between Nepal and India are very close, highly complex, and delicate, given the somewhat different objectives of the two countries. India's major aim in the Himalayas is reinforcement of its defenses against China. Nepal's principal concern is its own national integrity. There have been periods of diplomatic stress when the Indians and Nepalis have felt that their national objectives were particularly at odds. During these periods it has been more difficult for the two governments to resolve problems involving the border,

[8]"A Notice in Connection with the Agreement to Hand Over Criminals, Mutually, on the Southern Borders (1834)," in Nath, *op. cit.*, vol. II, p. 1.
[9]*Nepal Gazette*, vol. XIII, Extraordinary Issue No. 10, Aug. 16, 1963.
[10]*Gorkhapatra*, Jan. 18 and Apr. 12, 1972.

particularly smuggling. Furthermore, the problem of smuggling is linked to that of trade and, therefore, to the larger and more politically sensitive issue of Nepal's economic dependency upon India.

The two governments have had to contend with illegal trade for at least two hundred years. The early Shah kings attempted to prevent the use of many trading routes between the plains and the hills by planting "thorny bushes" on them, hoping that the routes would be overgrown and forgotten, thus facilitating customs administration.[11] However, the problem has persisted because the border is long and there are few customs posts or antismuggling police patrols on either the Nepalese or Indian side. Smuggling has been undertaken with little risk, and it has been practiced by many people living along the border. In fact, as one tarai inhabitant remarked about the people in his village, smuggling has become a habit for them. Any item that is less expensive on one side of the border is likely to turn up for sale on the other side without having followed established customs channels.

There are various smuggling patterns. One that was used frequently in the early 1950s involved Indian "quota" goods. For example, soon after the revolution in 1951, Nepal experienced a critical shortage of cotton goods, and the Indian government began shipping a quota of cotton yarn and cloth to Nepal. These quota goods had no Indian excise tax levied on them and were therefore cheaper in Nepal than in India. Gradually they began to find their way back into Indian markets without alleviating the shortage in Nepal. Finally, the black-market prices for cotton cloth became so high in Kathmandu that the government passed "The Mill Made Cotton Yarns and Cloth Anti-Smuggling and Anti-Black Marketing Act."[12]

Another smuggling pattern developed in the early 1950s, when the governments of the Soviet Union, China, and Eastern Europe began sending aid to Nepal in the form of goods such as cement, sugar, and cloth. These were shipped to Calcutta, and then transported by rail to the Nepalese border. They were usually transferred to trucks at the Raxaul railhead and hauled to Kathmandu, but often found their way back to India. Items such as fountain pens, bicycles, and cosmetics included in aid agreements signed between Nepal and China

---

[11]Mahesh Chandra Regmi, *Land Tenure and Taxation in Nepal*, vol. III (Berkeley, 1965), p. 8.
[12]*Nepal Gazette*, vol. I, No. 49, July 21, 1952.

have been particularly popular among urbanized Indians. Chinese-made fountain pens can be purchased throughout India.[13]

The most complex smuggling pattern developed in the late 1960s. In an effort to shore up its faltering economy after implementation of its poorly conceived revaluation policy in 1966,[14] the Nepalese government encouraged the export of raw jute and burlap to overseas countries by guaranteeing the exporters the right to keep 60 percent of the hard currency derived therefrom.[15] At the same time, the Indian government raised export duties on Indian-grown raw jute to a level which made its export prohibitive. This was done to insure that enough raw jute would be available to supply India's own jute industry. Shortly thereafter, Indian jute began to find its way to overseas countries through Nepal. Indian jute from Bihar and West Bengal was smuggled into the major tarai jute centers of Biratnagar and Bhadrapur, and then shipped as Nepalese-grown jute to overseas countries through Calcutta, Nepal's window on the world.

The 60 percent hard-currency allowance by the Nepalese government was made in late 1966. The following year the government instituted a gift-parcel scheme, under which any Nepali could receive from abroad a gift parcel, no more than one per day, so long as the value of the goods in the parcel did not exceed 1,000 Indian rupees. Until it was terminated in 1971, the gift-parcel scheme was used by Nepalese jute exporters and their Indian business associates to send into Nepal from Hong Kong, Singapore, and other ports such consumer goods as transistor radios, watches, flashlights, cameras, and cigarette lighters. Thus the government received not only 40 percent of the exporters' hard-currency earnings, but also substantial customs revenues. It was estimated that at one point the government was receiving customs revenue from gift parcels at a rate of 200,000 Nepalese rupees a day.[16]

The population of Nepal could absorb only a small percentage of

---

[13]The reverse of this pattern has occurred since the completion of the all-weather road from Kathmandu to Lhasa in 1966. Among the most important quota goods exported by India to Nepal are gasoline and kerosene. Some of these have reportedly reached Tibet. *Statesman Weekly*, Sept. 28, 1968, p. 15.

[14]Goods such as jute burlap that were manufactured in the tarai could no longer compete on the Indian market, because they were priced too high.

[15]Nepal and other developing nations generally require their exporters to convert all or much of their hard-currency earnings into local currency in order to conserve the hard currency for national development needs.

[16]*Nepal Times*, July 30, 1968.

these imported goods, and most of them turned up on the Indian market. Because Nepalese import duties on such goods were considerably lower than Indian ones, these goods, when smuggled into India, were less expensive than those imported through legitimate Indian import channels.

Such consumer goods are smuggled into India in various ways. They are sold in Kathmandu shops to Indian tourists and pilgrims. During important Hindu festival periods such as Shiva Ratri and Dasain, thousands of Indians flock to Kathmandu. It was estimated that Indian visitors bought 10 million Nepalese rupees' worth of imported goods during the 1968 Dasain festival. Most goods apparently cross the border by bullock cart or truck, using well-established routes into India. Small quantities undoubtedly cross in backpacks, over footpaths through the fields. An occasional smuggler is even reported to have floated his goods down the Gandak River![17]

The Indian government has created a fairly effective antismuggling system in its major ports and along its coast, but Indian government officials have viewed the Nepal border as a sieve through which has drained hard currency needed for development purposes. This was particularly the case after Indian devaluation and Nepalese revaluation in June 1966. The Indians began to organize special antismuggling procedures in 1968. Most of the goods were crossing into Bihar State, hence officials of that state created seventeen special mobile-police units along the border. Incidents involving Nepalese traders and Bihar State police occurred, and after the arrest of a trader allegedly inside Nepalese territory, the tactics of the Indian border police came under heavy criticism in the Kathmandu press.[18]

At the end of 1968, India's Excise and Customs Office in the Bihar State capital of Patna released statistics that disclosed the rising rate of smuggling and the increased efforts to prevent it. It reported that during 1966, in Bihar's five districts bordering Nepal, 100,000 Indian rupees' worth of smuggled goods had been seized. In 1967, 400,000 rupees' worth had been seized, and in the first eleven months of 1968, 1,736,000 rupees' worth had been confiscated during 2,133 separate arrests for customs violations. The goods seized in 1968 included synthetic yarn valued at 500,000 rupees, East European sugar valued at 225,000 rupees, and large quantities of watches, fountain pens, and

[17] *Hindustan Times*, Dec. 30, 1968, p. 5; *Gorkhapatra*, May 26, 1969; *Matribhumi Weekly*, May 27, 1969.
[18] *Motherland*, July 11, 1968; *Gorkhapatra*, Aug. 14, 1968.

cigarette lighters. The seizures also included 62,000 rupees' worth of Indian jute bound for Nepal.[19]

The establishment of stainless-steel and synthetic-textile factories in the tarai has resulted in additional problems of illegal trade. In 1966, only one stainless-steel factory and one synthetic-textile factory were in operation. By mid-1969, there were seven stainless-steel factories.[20] Both industries mushroomed as a result of Nepalese-government industrial-licensing policies, excise-tax benefits, and the opportunity to purchase raw material from overseas countries with hard currency earned from the export of jute or tea or black-market hard currency smuggled in from India. By 1968, these factories were exporting products in large quantities to India, and despite Indian import duties, selling these goods at prices below those of similar Indian-made products. As a result, Indian industrialists, particularly members of the Indian Silk and Art Silk Mills Association, began to protest to the Indian government.

During the last several months of 1968, the questions of smuggling and the import of inexpensive goods were raised in the Indian Parliament. In the lower house, in answer to charges that the Indian government was doing too little to prevent the illegal movement of goods across the Nepal-India border, Deputy Prime Minister Morarji Desai spoke of India's need to strike a balance between its concern about these problems and its concern for its friendship with Nepal.[21] Nevertheless, because of this criticism, the Indian government initiated talks with the Nepalese government in late 1968 and obtained a promise from the Nepalis to restrict the production of goods manufactured with raw materials imported from overseas.[22]

Despite Nepalese moves to restrict the export of such goods, by May 1969, Indian customs officials began holding up shipments on the grounds that they exceeded the quotas agreed upon by the two governments in late 1968. These goods then began to find their way into India in large quantities through unauthorized channels and, by mid-July, the Indian government announced that it had confiscated stainless steel and synthetic textiles worth 6,000,000 Nepalese rupees.[23]

Illegal trade and Indian efforts to prevent it were among the major

[19]*Hindustan Times*, Dec. 30, 1968, p. 5; *Statesman Weekly*, Jan. 4, 1969, p. 8.
[20]*Naya Nepal*, Mar. 4, 1969; *Janavarta*, Aug. 26, 1969.
[21]*Hindustan Times*, Nov. 15, 1968, p. 13. See also Dec. 10, 1968, p. 7.
[22]*Ibid.*, Nov. 20, 1968, p. 16.
[23]*Matribhumi Weekly*, July 15, 1969.

stumbling blocks to renegotiation of the 1960 Indo-Nepal Trade and Transit Treaty, which expired in 1970. The negotiations, accompanied by considerable rancor, spun out through 1970 and most of 1971, as the Indian government sought to win Nepalese commitments to trade policies that would discourage smuggling, policies which the Nepalis resisted on the grounds that they would be detrimental to the Nepalese economy. India finally gained some concessions and, in 1972, the Nepalese government began gradually to discourage the import of luxury goods from overseas.[24] The government also decided to convert all but two of the 17 stainless-steel and synthetic-textile factories in the tarai into plants that would manufacture goods made from domestically produced materials.[25]

For several decades, perhaps longer, smuggling on the largest scale has involved agricultural produce, particularly rice. The tarai has been a rice-surplus region and, until recently, the states of northern India have almost always had food-grain deficits. Although the two governments have sought to control the rice trade across the border in order to gain customs revenue from it, large quantities of tarai rice reach India annually without passing through the customs posts on either side of the border. Neither government has complained unduly about the rice smuggling because India has needed the surplus and the Nepalis have gained large quantities of Indian rupees, much needed for the purchase of other goods from India. However, occasionally, when the hill region of Nepal, a chronically deficit area, has a severe food shortage, as in 1972, the Nepalese government will seek the cooperation of the Indian government to prevent smuggling of rice into India so that the surplus can be diverted instead to the hill region.[26]

As in this case, when the smuggling pattern is detrimental to Nepal, it is the Nepalese government that threatens to take action. In late 1966, when Nepal revalued its currency, goods on the Indian side of the border suddenly became less expensive. They were smuggled into Nepal on a large scale, and in the process Nepal's important Indian-currency reserves were drained. By the end of the year, Nepal's Prime Minister, Surya Bahadur Thapa, threatened to seal the entire border to prevent further economic deterioration.[27] Thus, illegal

[24] *Gorkhapatra*, July 9, 1972.
[25] *Ibid.*, Feb. 18, 1972.
[26] *Ibid.*, Aug. 3, 1972.
[27] *Ibid.*, Dec. 8, 1966.

trade has been damaging to both nations from time to time and has been a frequent source of irritation between them.

ILLEGAL ECONOMIC ACTIVITY AND CULTURAL STEREOTYPES

The illegal economic activity reviewed in the preceding section has been engaged in by Indian citizens as well as Nepalese. Nepalese and Indian sources generally agree that Indian commercial interests overseas and Indian capital were primarily responsible for much of the initiative taken. It has not been uncommon to read in the Nepalese press that Indian businessmen have "infiltrated" into Nepal with their "black" hard currency to import consumer goods from overseas and, with the "connivance" of Nepalese government officials, smuggle them into India.[28] Although the Indian press has generally been more diplomatic about profit-making government officials, both Nepalese and Indian, it has been equally critical of the Indian businessmen. According to one journalist:

> Nepal's economic needs should be treated with the maximum understanding and generosity even if India has to suffer minor losses here and there, and provided no grave damage is done to the Indian economy. Some such damage has been caused in the past because of a diversion of Indian exports, smuggling into India of foreign luxury goods originally brought to Nepal under a dubious gift-parcels scheme, and the hothouse establishment in Nepal of stainless-steel and synthetic-fibre industries. Most Nepalese realize that these have done no good to Nepal or India. But this has yet to be impressed on a particularly unsavoury group of Indian businessmen in Nepal who have been the main promoters as well as beneficiaries of the various rackets. If allowed unchecked, the activities of these ugly Indians may do incalculable damage to India-Nepal relations.[29]

In the past, some Nepalis have branded such Indian businessmen as instruments of an Indian-government policy designed to make Nepal more dependent upon India. Ironically, during the gift-parcel-scheme period, some Indian businessmen appeared to be instruments of Nepal's "independent" economic policy, and it was the Indian government that condemned them.

[28]*Samiksha Weekly*, Oct. 9, 1969.
[29]Inder Malhotra, "India-Nepal Relations: Delhi's Diplomacy on Trial," *Statesman* (Calcutta), June 12, 1970, p. 6.

An unfortunate side effect of the gift-parcel scheme has been increased resentment expressed by some hill people toward the plains people. Particularly the business-caste groups among the plains people suffer from a grossly overgeneralized reputation for crafty and unscrupulous business dealings. By permitting unscrupulous Indian businessmen to operate in Nepal on a particularly large scale during the gift-parcel-scheme period, Nepalese government officials unwittingly reinforced the stereotype. Many hill people have difficulty distinguishing between plains people who are Nepalese citizens and those who are Indian. And, imperceptibly, this stereotype makes it more difficult for plains people to interact with hill people in the course of their daily lives. The problem is most pronounced in the relations between members of the Kathmandu elite and members of the business castes in the tarai towns. When such stereotypes create suspicion and inhibit cooperation across communal lines, they hinder the growth of national unity.

THE BLURRED BORDER

A distinction needs to be made between a closed border and a controlled border. A closed border is one across which there is no movement of people or goods. Neither the Nepalis nor the Indians want to close the border. Such a move would seriously dislocate, if not destroy, Nepal's economy, encourage political instability and undermine India's defenses, limited as they are, in the central Himalayas. Both nations seek to establish a controlled border, across which people and goods move in an orderly fashion.

Before Nepal can hope to establish such control, it must solve some formidable problems. Bijaya Bahadur Pradhan, a Nepalese economist, has attempted to work out the logistics for effective border administration. He assumes that the border that needs careful administration is 800 miles long, and that a customs post is needed every four miles along its length, that is, 200 posts. There are approximately 90 posts at present. He also estimates that an antismuggling check post manned by border police would be needed every quarter mile between customs posts. There would be a total of approximately 3,000 of these check posts. Implementation of the plan would be extremely expensive but, as Pradhan points out, the substantial increase in revenue collected would finance the system. Without such border administration, he suggests that commercial, fiscal, and foreign-exchange policies will be impossible to carry out effectively, and that it will also be impossible to collect the type of statistics about Nepal's trade and international payments upon which national-development planning must be based.[30]

Even if Pradhan's plan could be modified without losing its effectiveness, it is doubtful that the Nepalese government would be able to implement such a plan in the near future. Border control is not only expensive but also administratively complex. Therefore, the nation will be forced to live with the realities of an uncontrolled border. This reality includes the existence of a blurred line of separation between the tarai region of Nepal and India, at least as perceived by many tarai villagers. The blurred border makes it difficult for them to understand clearly the distinctions of sovereignty that also separate Nepal and India. The border therefore remains an unsolved problem for Nepal as it moves to integrate the tarai into its national framework.

---

[30] "A Scheme for Currency Unification in Nepal" (Kathmandu, n.d.).

Chapter IV

MIGRATION INTO THE TARAI

The problem of national integration vis-à-vis the tarai has arisen because people from one cultural background have migrated into a region over which people of another cultural background have established political control. Migration is an important topic in this study, because the movement of people, still in large numbers today, determines to a large extent the cultural composition of the tarai.

MIGRATION FROM NORTHERN INDIA INTO THE TARAI

The early history of the tarai is a record of the ebb and flow of people. Kingdoms successively arose and disintegrated. People have been migrating into the tarai since the first Aryan tribesmen pushed eastward from the confluence of the Ganges and Jumna Rivers around 900 B.C. During the period 900 to 500 B.C., the Aryans penetrated into what is now northern Uttar Pradesh and Bihar, and the powerful kingdom of Videha was established in northern Bihar and the eastern tarai. The capital of Videha was called Mithila, and it may have been located at the site of modern Janakpur in Mahottari-Dhanusha district of the eastern tarai. Janakpur, the centre of extensive ruins, is named after King Janaka of Videha, who married his daughter Sita to the great king-god Ram of the Hindu epic, the Ramayana.

A line of less powerful rulers, the kings of Sakya, had their capital at Kapilabastu in the mid-western tarai. The Buddha was born in about 563 B.C. to a Sakya king at Lumbini, near Kapilabastu. Ruins of the capital have been excavated by a team of Nepalese and Japanese archeologists. Yet another important kingdom of the ancient period established its capital at Simraun Garh in the southeast corner of Bara district. As was likely in the kingdoms of Videha and Kapilabastu, the first ruler of Simraun Garh was probably the leader of a marauding Aryan band who pushed into the tarai forest from the south and west. Archeologists may discover, when excavations are undertaken at Simraun Garh, that the first kings were chieftains in the Vrijjian confederacy, a loose association of Aryan tribes that settled in this region around 600 to 700 B.C. In the tarai exist many other ruins which, when identified, will shed more light on the long and complex history of the region.

It appears that nearly all the settlers in early tarai history were of Aryan or pre-Aryan indigenous stock. The ancient and medieval history of the region is a cyclical one in which men and forest have dominated in turns. From time to time, people from more settled parts of the Gangetic plain pushed back the forest, cleared the land, and established settlements that grew into kingdoms. When the kingdoms withered away because of natural calamities or war, the forest reclaimed the land.

Information about settlement in modern times comes from three sources—records of British East India Company officials, records of Nepalese government officials, and oral histories of the tarai villagers themselves. The British records, particularly the reports of Colonel William Kirkpatrick and Francis Hamilton, provide the earliest information. Kirkpatrick crossed the tarai at the head of an expedition to Kathmandu in 1793 and described the settlement pattern in what is now Bara and Parsa districts. He observed that the land was cleared and settled from the border north for about four miles and then partly cleared for another four or five miles. From there, dense and uninterrupted forest extended north to the Siwaliks.[1] Hamilton found that a majority of the inhabitants of the eastern tarai were plains tribals, Tharus throughout and Rajbanshis, Mechis, and Gangais in the far-eastern tarai.[2] He reported that they practiced slash-and-burn cultivation, shifting their location every three or four years when the land lost its fertility. Although the land fell into disuse, it was not reclaimed by the forest because of continual grazing by herds of cows and buffalos driven north from India during the dry season by Ahirs and other caste Hindus.

The Nepali-speaking Sen kings of Palpa and Makwanpur gained control of the mid-western tarai in the fifteenth or sixteenth century and extended their control to the eastern tarai around the mid-seventeenth century. They looked upon the dense, malarial tarai forests

[1] William Kirkpatrick, *An Account of the Kingdom of Nepaul* (London, 1811), pp. 12–16.
[2] Francis Hamilton, *An Account of the Kingdom of Nepal* (Edinburgh, 1819), pp. 156, 164, 169. Hamilton was an administrative officer of the East India Company in the early 1800s. His account is much more detailed than Kirkpatrick's and furnishes a considerable amount of valuable information about the tarai's economic and cultural history.

as a defense against invasion from India and, therefore, did not encourage settlement. Instead, they drew tarai revenue from logging, the trapping and selling of elephants, and taxing the seasonal pasturing of cattle. The Shah kings wrested the eastern tarai from the Sen kings in the 1770s and permitted some settlement.[3]

Still, it was not until the 1860s that those who controlled the tarai[4] felt that the region had lost its utility as a defense perimeter and that diplomacy was a more effective defense against increased British intervention. For its military assistance to the British during the Indian Mutiny, 1857–58, Nepal received title to the far-western tarai, territory the British had taken away from Nepal during the Anglo-Nepali War of 1814–16. Jung Bahadur Rana, the founder of the line of hereditary Rana prime ministers, immediately began to encourage settlement in the far-western tarai and in other parts of the tarai as well. For example, he promised to grant the status of free men to all Nepali slaves who would settle there.[5] Details of the new government policy are included in government documents of the period.[6]

The policy of settling the tarai was not solely the result of more stable and friendly relations between the Nepalis and British following the Mutiny. It was also due to population pressure and the expansion of the economy throughout the subcontinent, accompanied by rising prices and a need for increased revenue to finance the government and to purchase goods in India for the nobility. Revenue could be increased most readily by expanding logging operations and agricultural activity in the tarai. Since logging and clearing land for farming went hand in hand, settlers moved in large numbers to forested areas, encouraged by promises of land ownership and low tax rates.

The oral history of tarai inhabitants sheds further light on tarai settlement patterns in modern times. Oral history in this case refers to the stories told by village elders of their fathers' and forefathers' journeys through the wilderness to seek new opportunities. Despite the problems with oral history caused by the limitations of memory and the distortions of time, some valuable generalizations can be drawn from that source. Much material of this type was gathered in

[3]*Ibid.*, pp. 64, 131–132.
[4]By this time, the Rana prime ministers of Kathmandu; the Shah kings still reigned, but the Ranas had gained control over them and exercised their power.
[5]Chittaranjan Nepali, "Nepal ma Kariya Mochan ko Itihas," *Nepali*, XX (July-September 1964), 10–11.
[6]See Nepal, Department of Land Revenue, *Administrative Regulations for Tarai Districts*, 1861. 5 vols. (Trans. by Regmi Research Project, 1967.)

villages and towns of the tarai during the period 1966–68, but very little of it can be included here.

Generally speaking, the oldest continually inhabited villages in the tarai are those established near a religious site such as Sita's birthplace at Janakpur or near a fort of some long-forgotten king. Still other villages grew up around customs posts, police stations, or rest stations along trade routes between the plains and the hills. Early settlements were also cut out of the forest along riverbeds which, during the dry season, furnished broad, flat roads for travel through the dense jungle.

Some of the earliest settlements were those of Tharus, deep in the forest, isolated from nontribal people. None of the headmen in Tharu villages could even hazard a guess as to how many generations ago their ancestors settled in those villages. Of the eleven villages in Bara district for which oral histories were collected, seven had been settled by Tharus, but all the Tharus had moved away from the four closest to the border, thus evidencing their retreat further into the forest in the face of competition for land with more sophisticated caste people. Plains Hindus and Muslims appear to have moved into Mahottari-Dhanusha and Bara and the districts contiguous to them earlier than into other parts of the tarai. Villages in the southern part of both districts were mostly settled seven to ten generations ago, although one village in each of the two districts was reportedly established fifteen generations ago. Farther north in the district, villages were settled four to five generations ago, and the northernmost villages were begun by hill people in the 1930s. In Kapilabastu and its two neighboring mid-western tarai districts, the villages were all settled within the last eight to ten generations, and even the Tharus could recall how many generations ago their villages were established. Jhapa district is experiencing in a three-generation span the transition that Mahottari-Dhanusha and Bara districts underwent in two or three hundred years, from a dense forest region hiding a few tribal villages to an uninterrupted, cultivated plain dotted with many villages. Kailali district, representative of the far-western tarai, is about at the stage of settlement in which Kirkpatrick found Bara district in 1793, or the stage in which the first Newar businessman found Jhapa district when he moved to Bhadrapur in 1917 and built the first tile-roofed house there.

The first plains caste people to settle in the tarai often were Ahirs, cowherds by occupation, who grazed cattle in the tarai during the dry season and gradually turned seasonal huts into permanent dwellings. Other early arrivals were yeoman-farmer groups such as the Kurmis and similar quasi-caste groups among the Muslims. Lower-caste agricultural people also arrived early, followed by occupational- and business-caste people after the agricultural economy had developed beyond the rudimentary stage.

The pattern of extending agricultural settlements gradually north from the border was followed by trading settlements. As the Indian railroads were extended to the border in the late nineteenth century, frontier trading communities grew up around the railheads. People living in the tarai and the hills would bring their produce to these places to sell or barter for such items as salt, sugar, cloth, and metal utensils. Gradually, businessmen from these railhead communities moved across the border into the tarai to out-maneuver their competition by making it unnecessary for villagers to transport their produce so far south. The first commercial centers in the tarai were just across the border from the railheads, and many of these centers have developed into important towns. Finally, the businessmen began to establish their trading locations at the foot of the Siwaliks in order to make themselves available to the hill people as they reached the plains. Today, such a trading community is located at the foot of every major trail leading out of the hills.

Between the 1860s and 1951, the Nepalese government encouraged economic development in the tarai and made an effort to settle hill people in the region. However, the hill people responded only in small numbers, because the tarai seemed unfamiliar and unpleasant to them, being hot, flat, and malarious. Therefore, the government had to content itself with letting migrants from India develop the economy of the tarai. Until the last several decades, tarai history has been dominated primarily by events farther south on the plains, by Pax Britannia, by population growth and the spill-over of people into the tarai, by economic expansion represented by the railroads, by new trading communities and adventuresome businessmen. This has been a progression of events which the Nepalese government could not be expected to control to any significant degree.

MIGRATION FROM THE HILLS INTO THE TARAI

Many of the demographic and economic problems that plague the Gangetic plain also plague the hill region, forcing people to leave their ancestral villages to look for land that will support them. Although the Himalayas have always attracted adventurers and mystics, they have offered little more than subsistence-level living conditions for most hill people.

This is apparently not a recent phenomenon, and may have begun as long as 3,000 years ago. Some of the Aryan tribes may have separated from those moving east onto the Gangetic plain and instead moved eastward along the Himalayan foothills. The balance between population and available resources must have narrowed quickly for the settlers in the dry and inhospitable western Himalayas, pushing them eastward into less densely populated and less dry hill regions. This process—migration, settlement, gradual overpopulation, agricultural deterioration, famine, migration—produced a kind of Malthusian peristalsis, pushing people farther and farther east along the hill ranges. The eastward migration of people speaking a Sanskrit-based language, an early form of Nepali by the time they reached the central Himalayas around the twelfth century,[7] began to sweep the hill tribals along with it.

This west-to-east migration can be documented in Nepalese and Indian censuses. For example, many Magars and Gurungs have left their ancestral villages in the western hills of Nepal and have migrated into the eastern hills. The 1961 census of Nepal enumerates 67,327 Magars and 6,938 Gurungs living in the eastern hills.[8] The Indian census data are even more illustrative of this west-to-east movement of people. Already in 1901, the Indian census enumerates nearly 200,000 speakers of Nepali and hill-tribal languages settled in India,[9] most of them in Darjeeling and Jalpaiguri districts of West Bengal, in Sikkim and Assam. By 1961, slightly more than one million speakers of these languages were enumerated in India.[10]

Demographic and economic problems have also been responsible for the much more recent migration from the hills into the tarai. Many writers have explored these problems as they exist on the Gangetic plain, but few have studied or written about them as they affect the hill people. In 1954, a United Nations forestry specialist was one of the first to issue the warning that "erosion is slowly but surely robbing the Mahabharat of habitable land," because its drainage basins are

---

[7]T. W. Clark, *Introduction to Nepali* (Cambridge, England, 1963), p. vii.
[8]*Census of Nepal*, 1961, vol. II, pp. 18–19, 22–23. These figures include the eastern inner tarai as well as the eastern hills.
[9]See relevant volumes of the *Census of India*, 1901.
[10]*Census of India*, 1961, vol. I, part II-C (ii), pp. 97, 141–183.

being deforested. He went on to observe that the deforestation and erosion were causing a decline in soil productivity and water supply and were even changing climatic conditions.[11] Decline in agricultural productivity is itself one of the spurs to deforestation. When exhausted soil and a drier climate reduce the crop yield, farmers attempt to bring more land under cultivation to make up the difference. New land brought under cultivation is generally forest land of marginal value, high on the mountain slopes. It must be terraced, and the terraces often wash away during the rainy season, precipitating the erosion problem. It becomes a vicious cycle: decline in productivity, more land brought under cultivation, more erosion and less water, still greater decline in productivity. The American anthropologist, John Hitchcock, and his wife Patricia have produced a film, "The Himalayan Farmer," which is a poignant story of a Magar farmer caught in this vicious cycle. Two Nepalese scholars, Pashupati Shamshere and Mohammad Mohsin, have completed an interesting study of leadership in the villages of the eastern hills, in which 59 percent of the 243 village leaders they interviewed stated that the productivity of their land was declining.[12]

Charles McDougal, another American anthropologist, has undertaken the most detailed study of these economic problems to date. He studied 640 families in six villages of the far-western hills and documented the growing imbalance between living expenses and locally producible income, a factor which has forced a large number of people from these villages to seek employment in India or the tarai.[13] He describes three types of migration from the hills into the tarai and India. The first is permanent migration. Of the 640 families that lived in five of the six villages in 1965, 39 had moved away during 1965–67 (6 percent of the sample), a large loss of population for a two-year period.[14] Thus, McDougal's study begins to measure the

[11]Earnest Robbe, *Report to the Government of Nepal on Forestry* (Rome, 1954), F.A.O. Report No. 209, pp. 14, 45.

[12]*A Study Report on the Pattern of Emerging Leadership in Panchayats* (Kathmandu, 1967), p. 14.

[13]McDougal produced two preliminary reports of his survey, both mimeographed. The first, issued in June 1967, is entitled *Economic Survey of Doti District: Preliminary Report*, and the second, issued in September 1967, is entitled *Village Economy in Far Western Nepal*. His final report, which includes the results of his surveys in Doti, Sallyan, Kailali, and Dang-Deukhuri districts, was subsequently published as *Village and Household Economy in Far Western Nepal* (Kathmandu, 1968). He uses the term "household" for family.

[14]*Village Economy in Far Western Nepal*, p. 15.

magnitude of the problem that has resulted in the permanent settlement of more than a million Nepalis in India.

The second type of migration is semipermanent, that is, migration for periods of six months to ten years or even longer. Whereas permanent migration involves women and children and is often migration to rural areas, the semipermanent migration consists almost exclusively of men going to urban centres, leaving their wives behind to manage family affairs in the village. Of the 640 families in McDougal's sample, 234 (36 percent) had one or more members working in India or the tarai for more than six months. The average stay away from the village was three years.[15] Semipermanent migrants work chiefly as gatekeepers and night watchmen for businesses and wealthy families in India's cities. Nepalis are given preference for these jobs because of their reputation for fearlessness, physical ruggedness, honesty, and loyalty.

> This type of employment is in many ways comparable with army service, long a source of livelihood for the hillmen of many parts of Nepal. Men often remain employed with the same company for several years, returning to their homes for 2–3 months on leave at intervals of 2 years or so, when they bring back savings, cloth, and other consumer goods to their families.[16]

The third type of migration is seasonal and usually occurs for a period of three to four months during the winter season. It is cold in the hills at that time of year, particularly at the higher altitudes. The harvest season is over, and little agricultural work is to be found. In the tarai the harvest season does not end until February or March, and hill people are often able to find work harvesting and threshing rice and mustard. Both the seasonal and semipermanent migrations serve important economic needs for the hill people. The migrants earn their subsistence, which is difficult for them to do in the hills, and they save a little money for essential goods needed by the families they left behind in the hill villages. As might be expected, those who are most frequently forced to seek employment in the tarai or India are members of families with little or no land. Most of the land is owned by upper castes, Brahmins and Chetris and, in the case of McDougal's villages, Magars as well. Therefore, it is the lower-caste people such

[15]*Ibid.*, p. 17.
[16]*Ibid.*, p. 15.

as the Kamis, Sarkis, and Damais who leave their villages in the greatest numbers.[17]

Although McDougal's study emphasizes the greater vulnerability of low-caste people to economic hardship,[18] it should be pointed out that a large number of upper-caste people have also been forced to migrate out of the western hills. For example, during a severe drought in 1966–67, large numbers of people moved from the far-western hills into Kailali district in the far-western tarai. Although approximately 200 families belonged to the lower castes, 250 to 300 families were Brahmins and 400 to 500 were Chetris, all as destitute as their lower-caste brethren.[19]

THE TARAI AS A POPULATION VACUUM

Economic deterioration in the hills and in parts of the Gangetic plain has necessitated out-migration, and positive factors in the form of economic opportunities have encouraged migration into the tarai. Most important has been the opportunity for the land-hungry to obtain land, either free or at relatively little cost. As agriculture has developed, the tarai has presented businessmen with new opportunities as well. The tarai can be called a population vacuum, as a comparison of population densities in the tarai and surrounding areas indicates. The most important point illustrated by map 5 is the greater population density to the north and south of the tarai than in the region itself. The density in the eastern Indian border districts is two or three times greater than in the eastern tarai districts, and the density is three to four times greater in the western Indian border districts than in the western tarai districts. If one keeps in mind the fact that there is much less cultivable land available in the hills, the density of population on cultivable land is much higher in the hill districts than in the tarai, and perhaps even higher than in the Indian border districts. The greatest disparity is in the far west where, for example, the tarai district of Kanchanpur had a density of 31 people per square mile in 1961 and the neighboring hill district, Dandeldhura, had a density of 146, nearly five times greater.

[17]*Ibid.*, pp. 14, 16–17.
[18]The same vulnerability among low-caste people in the hill region of Uttar Pradesh is documented by Gerald Berreman in "Caste and Economy in the Himalayas," *Economic Development and Cultural Change*, X (July 1962), 390–394.
[19]Interviews with leaders of these settlers, several miles north of Malakheti bazaar, Jan. 3, 1968.

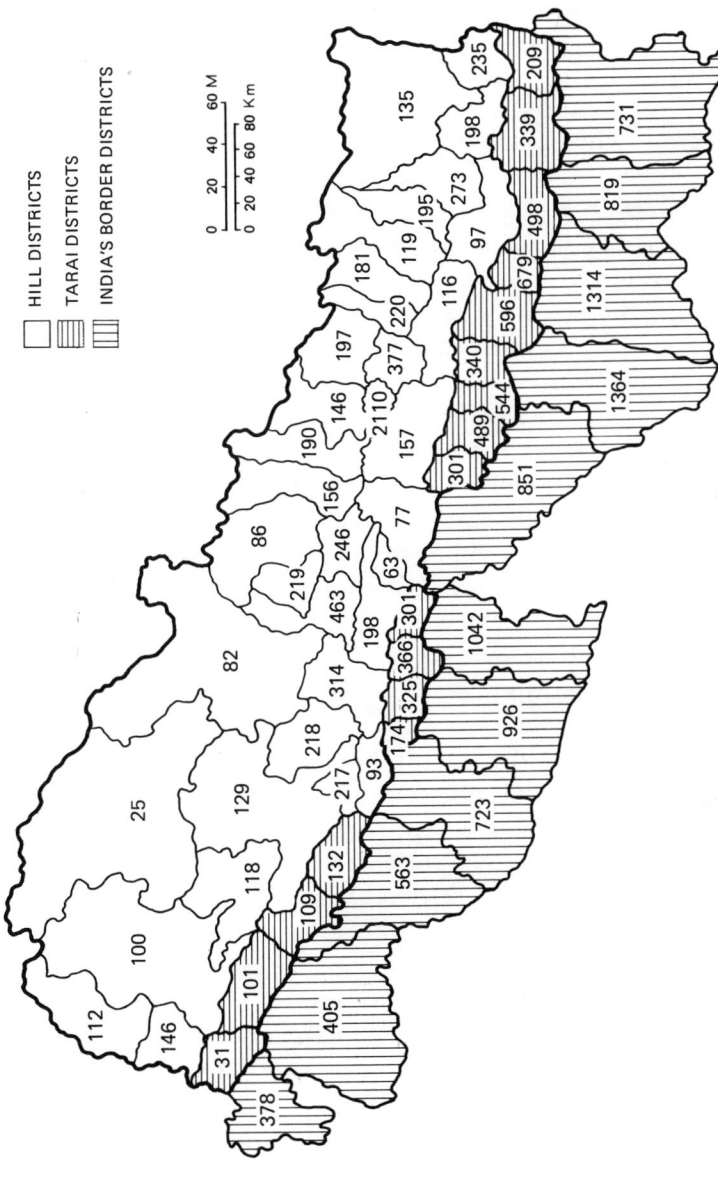

Map 5. Population density in districts of Nepal and India's border districts, 1961. Sources: *Census of Nepal*, 1961, vol. II, pp. 1–4; 1961 *Census of India*, vol. I, part II-A(i), pp. 74–75, 86–88. Base map: Survey of India, 1:2,534,400, 3d edition, 1959.

Population pressure in the hills and on the Gangetic plain has persisted for many decades. This has been evidenced by the large-scale migration of hill people into northeastern India, Sikkim, and Bhutan over the past sixty or seventy years. One is likely to ask why the tarai did not begin to draw large numbers of hill people earlier. A partial answer is to be found in their preference for resettling in other hill regions when possible, because the surroundings were more familiar. However, malaria is largely responsible, and references to the malaria scourge punctuate historical records about the tarai. That disease was one of the defenses of the hill kings against military threats from India. It was as responsible for decimating Captain Kinloch's expeditionary force in 1767 as were the long, curved kukris (knives) of the hill warriors. A saying current among hill people until recently illustrates the prevalent fear of malaria. "In Morang (eastern tarai) one rupee's worth of rice is enough to last a man until his funeral."

In view of the high death rate caused by malaria before the Nepalese government, in cooperation with the World Health Organization and U.S./A.I.D., began its eradication campaign in the 1950s, it is amazing that settlers were willing to clear and cultivate land there throughout the modern period. Long-term inhabitants of the tarai recount tragic stories of their families being decimated by the disease; asked why they chose to remain, they often reply that simply nowhere else could they find land to make a living. During the past few years, the malaria-eradication campaign has been highly effective, and the fear that once discouraged so many potential settlers is no longer a factor. More than anything else, eradication of malaria has turned the tarai into an in-migration region.

In order to assess the extent to which the tarai has potential for absorbing a rapid increase in settlers, one must find out how much cultivable forest land is still vulnerable to the settlers' girdling knives and axes. As map 6 indicates, the most heavily forested tarai districts are in the far-eastern and far-western tarai, although some other districts still retain heavily forested areas. The clearing has been taking place from south to north, although now some hill people are beginning to clear areas at the foot of the Siwaliks. Forty percent of the entire tarai was forested in 1967. Kanchanpur district had the highest percentage of forested area, 71 percent. Saptari and Siraha districts had the least, a little less than 6 percent.

Of the 3,662 square miles of forested land recorded in 1967, 1,227 square miles lie on the steep, stony, and uninhabitable southern slopes

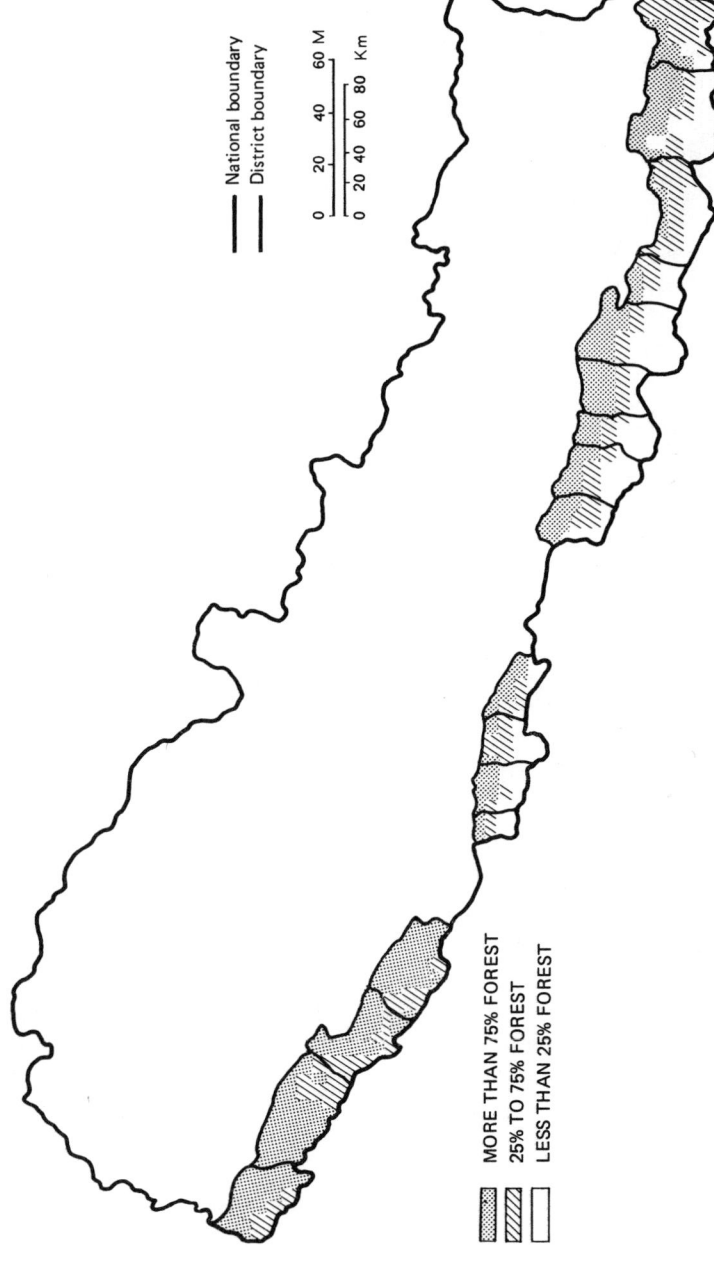

Map 6. Forested and cultivated areas of the tarai. Source: 1-inch-to-30-mile foldout map, Government of Nepal, Dept. of Forests, Forest Resources Survey, *Forest Statistics for the Tarai and Adjoining Regions*, 1967, p. 2.

of the Siwaliks. If the remaining 2,435 square miles were cleared and were settled at a density of 311 people per square mile, the light average density of the entire tarai in 1961,[20] the forest area would provide a habitat for 757,285 people. In the not-too-distant future, the population density of the tarai is likely to reach that of Indian border districts. When that unfortunate time arrives, the tarai may support at a subsistence level a population of 800 people per square mile,[21] a total of about 6,626,000 people, 3,741,000 more than lived in the tarai in 1961. If this is allowed to occur, the population vacuum will be, in the minds of Nepal's leaders, no more than a wistful recollection of lost opportunities for systematic regional planning.

THE SCALE OF MIGRATION

Let us turn now to a discussion of current migration into the tarai, especially to the four following characteristics: scale of migration (the number of people migrating), the caste and communal characteristics of migrants, the location of their previous residence, and their economic status. This study of migration patterns in Nepal is the first of its kind because the necessary data have not been available. The data for the study were collected as part of the 1967–68 field survey.[22]

From the data in table 9 it is immediately apparent that there is little migration into the sample villages of Mahottari-Dhanusha, Bara, and Kapilabastu districts. In Kailali district, the number of newly arrived settlers is more significant, but only in Jhapa district is the scale of migration great enough to effect rapid population growth. One should bear in mind that statements made about these five selected districts are meant to be applied, albeit with caution, to the subregions of the tarai in which they are located.

The table breaks down migration for Mahottari-Dhanusha, Bara, and Kapilabastu into two subcategories, the plains cultivated area in the southern part of each district, where most of the population is concentrated, and the forest and fringe-of-forest area in the northern part, where land clearing is in process. More settlement is taking

[20] *Census of Nepal,* 1961, vol. I, pp. 1–4.

[21] In 1961 the average population density of the eleven Indian districts bordering the tarai was 831 per square mile.

[22] All data on migrants for the 1967–68 field survey were collected in terms of family units, not individuals.

TABLE 9

Migrant[a] Families as a Percentage of All Families in Sample and Nonsample Villages, by District and Subregion of District

District and subregion of district	No. of sample villages surveyed	No. of families in village	No. of migrant families	Migrant families as a percentage of families	No. of nonsample villages surveyed	No. of families in village, 1958	No. of migrant families, 1958–67	Migrant families as a percentage of families
Jhapa (total)	10	509[d]	167[f]	32.8	6	133	238	179.0
Mahottari-Dhanusha:								
Subtotal, P.C.A.[b]	16	3,487[e]	33[g]	1.0				
Subtotal, F.F.F.A.[c]	8	874	83	9.5				
Total	24	4,361	116	2.7	2	124	49	39.5
Bara:								
Subtotal, P.C.A.	16	3,409[d]	50[f]	1.5				
Subtotal, F.F.F.A.	4	333	46	13.8				
Total	20	3,742	96	2.6		No data collected		
Kapilabastu:								
Subtotal, P.C.A.	15	1,348[d]	29[f]	2.1				
Subtotal, F.F.F.A.	4	168	63	37.5				
Total	19	1,511	92	6.1	2	118	61	51.7

TABLE 9

District and subregion of district	No. of sample villages surveyed	No. of families in village	No. of migrant families	Migrant families as a percentage of families	No. of nonsample villages surveyed	No. of families in village, 1958	No. of migrant families, 1958–67	Migrant families as a percentage of families
Kailali: Total	8	290[d]	45[g]		No data collected			
Five-district-survey total	81	10,413	516	15.5	10	375[d]	348[f]	

[a] "Migrant" is a general term used here to include immigrant, one who has moved across the Nepal-India border to settle in the tarai, and in-migrant, one who has simply moved from some other part of Nepal. Out-migration has not been taken into account, however, there is so little out-migration that it is unlikely to affect significantly the total migration picture in the villages surveyed. All data were collected during field survey, 1967–68.
[b] P.C.A. = Plains cultivated area.
[c] F.F.F.A. = Forest and fringe-of-forest area.
[d] Number of families in villages in 1958.
[e] Number of families in villages in 1962.
[f] Number of migrant families, 1959–67.
[g] Number of migrant families, 1963–67.

place in the fringe of forest areas than in the plains cultivated areas. The only villages into which strikingly large numbers of settlers are moving are the most recently settled villages of each district, represented by the nonsample villages in the table.[23]

CASTE AND COMMUNAL CHARACTERISTICS OF MIGRANTS

Many Nepalese government officials tend to assume that migration into the tarai is primarily from the hills and that these migrants, as their numbers grow, will gradually change the hill-plains cultural equation, bringing about a Nepalization of the region. This assumption results from the fact that hill settlers are more conspicuous than settlers of plains origin. The plains people tend to settle in relatively large, established villages where visiting officials have more difficulty in identifying them. On the other hand, many of the hill settlers are cutting down the forest, bringing themselves to the attention of forest rangers. They also present malaria-eradication teams with a special problem: their newly established forest dwellings must be found so that their huts can be sprayed and the people treated if they are carriers of malaria. Furthermore, touring government officials tend to notice settlements that did not exist on their previous visits to the area. However, if we assume that the five districts of the survey represent the entire tarai with fair accuracy, the majority of migrants are, in fact, of plains origin: 59 percent of plains origin, 35 percent of hill origin, and the remaining 6 percent tribals indigenous to the tarai.

To be more meaningful, this generalization must be analyzed more closely because migration patterns vary greatly from one subregion to another. In Kailali, 71 percent of the migrants are caste Hindus and tribals from the hills. In two other districts, Jhapa and Kapilabastu, the numbers of migrants are distributed evenly between the castes and tribes of hill origin on the one hand and those of plains origin on the other. In Bara and Mahottari-Dhanusha, the majority of migrants are of plains origin, 71 percent and 94 percent respectively. It must be emphasized, however, that a larger percentage of plains migrants than hill migrants are shifting from one location to another within the same district, and thus not altering the cultural equation of the district.

[23]Some fringe-of-forest villages that were not part of the sample were surveyed, despite the fact that they were not representative of the districts as a whole, because of the interesting socioeconomic developments taking place in them.

The majority of migrants from the hills are high-caste people, whereas the majority of plains migrants are of low caste. Bara district had the lowest percentage of high-caste hill migrants, 57 percent of all hill migrants. Kapilabastu had the highest, 89 percent. On the other hand, the low-caste plains migrants represented the majority of plains migrants in four of the districts, if we add together the low-caste plains Hindus, the plains tribals, and the Muslims.[24] They represented 75 percent of the plains migrants settling in Jhapa, 70 percent in Mahottari-Dhanusha, 78 percent in Bara, and 77 percent in Kapilabastu.

In terms of a changing cultural equation, the fact that the majority of hill migrants are from the upper castes and the majority of plains migrants from the lower castes serves to counterbalance the fact that the majority of all migrants are of plains origin. The caste ranking of migrants is an important determinant in the role they play in changing the economic, political, and cultural matrix of the tarai. The hill Brahmins and Chetris are relatively well educated, compared to the lower castes. They also have more land and more capital with which to acquire land. They tend to be more aggressive in economic, social, and political matters, and this enables them to gain control of the available resources and assert a leadership role much more easily. In addition to these advantages, the high-caste hill migrants tend to have the sympathy and at least passive support of local government officials, arising from their common cultural backgrounds. Some of the high-caste hill settlers may even have family connections among these local officials or with more important officials in Kathmandu.

It is clear, therefore, that numbers of migrants alone do not determine the acculturation process. A minority of high-caste hill migrants can achieve leadership dominance wherever they settle. In districts such as Jhapa and Kapilabastu, where there are large minorities of migrants from the hills, Nepalization is making rather rapid inroads on the still-dominant plains culture.

Another factor that determines the extent to which Nepalization may take place is the caste composition of the population already settled in the area. If the upper-caste hill people settle in an area where large numbers of upper- and business-caste plains people are

[24]There are high-caste as well as low-caste people among the Muslims; however, in the 1967–68 field survey, no attempt was made to differentiate Muslims according to caste. The Muslims have been put into the low-caste plains-Hindu and tribal category because their economic conditions are generally more similar to those of that category than to the high-caste groups.

already installed, the hill people will find it difficult to gain control of economic resources and political power. If, on the other hand, the hill migrants settle among the relatively unsophisticated plains-tribal people, the hill people are able to acquire local leadership rather quickly. Plains tribals such as the Tharus tend to have little sophistication about economic affairs. They are prone to borrow money without understanding the interest terms or the consequences of indebtedness, and thus fall prey to the false dealings of money-lenders and lose control of their land.

The village of Kushmaha in northern Kapilabastu district provides a fairly typical example of the land-alienation process which the Tharus experience. The village was settled by Tharus but, sometime after the turn of the century, the Nepalese government granted it as part of a zamindari to a businessman of plains origin. During the 1930s, the price of rice fell sharply on the Indian market and the businessman could not raise the revenue needed to pay the government tax on the zamindari. In 1936, the zamindari was turned over to a Chetri with family connections in Kathmandu. Gradually, because of relatively high land taxes and the Tharus' mismanagement of their finances, many of them became indebted to the Chetri, who eventually foreclosed on them, gaining title to their land but retaining them on the land as tenants. In 1963, when the Chetri heard that the government was planning to pass land-reform laws for the Ukhada land-tenure region of the mid-western tarai which would force him to return land titles to tenants on holdings that exceeded a 40-acre ceiling, he decided to sell the land before he was forced to forfeit it. Although loopholes in the law have made it possible for individuals to control much larger acreage than the established 40-acre ceiling, the Chetri had considerable land elsewhere and, because his Tharu tenants could not afford to buy the land, he sold it to thirty-one Brahmin families from the western hills. In late 1963, when the Brahmin families arrived in Kushmaha, the sixteen Tharu families that were tenants or day laborers of the Chetri were evicted and forced to move away. They left behind nine Tharu families that had managed to hold title to their land.

Until recently, the plains people were primarily responsible for encroaching on the Tharus and other plains-tribal groups. Nevertheless, today the hill people more than the plains people are moving into the fringe of forest areas where the plains tribals live and, therefore, are currently putting more pressure on plains-tribal lands.

In a few limited areas of the tarai, hill-tribal people such as Magars, Gurungs, Rais, Limbus, and Tamangs have been settled for a number of decades. These people share with the plains tribals a propensity for indebtedness and vulnerability to eviction. They migrated to the tarai in the first place because they lost control of their land in the hills, mostly to upper-caste hill people. Now they are again losing control of their land in the tarai, often to upper-caste hill people, sometimes to plains people.

When the hill tribals and low-caste hill people such as the Sarkis, Kamis, and Damais migrate into tarai areas already under the control of plains people, they find themselves at a disadvantage. This has occurred in northern Mahottari-Dhanusha district, and the acculturaration process is one in which the plains culture is gaining a continually stronger position. Upper- and business-caste plains people are gradually acquiring control of land settled by hill tribals.

The village of Bimban in northern Mahottari-Dhanusha is a good example of this process. Where Bimban is now located, two sons of the Rana Prime Minister, Bir Shamsher, had been granted a birta, or tax-free land. During the early 1950s, these brothers persuaded Tamangs and Magars to fell timber in return for tenancy rights on the cleared land. After the Birta Abolition Act in 1959, the tenants acquired title to the land they had settled. However, since then, most of them have fallen in debt to Teli and Sudi moneylenders and have lost their land titles. Although the moneylenders preferred that the hill tribals stay on as tenants because they work hard and are undemanding, most wandered off. The moneylenders then brought members of their own castes and other low-caste plains people to Bimban as tenants—eight families, four of which are Telis and two Sudis.

It is not possible, therefore, to conclude that all fringe-of-forest areas are becoming Nepalized. Nepalization is taking place throughout the far-western tarai and in forested areas of Jhapa and Morang districts in the far-eastern tarai. It is also occurring in or near the forest in the mid-western tarai. However, in the northern part of the tarai between Mahottari and Saptari districts and perhaps to a lesser extent also in northern Parsa, Bara, and Rautahat districts, the plains people are consolidating and extending their control.

PREVIOUS RESIDENCE OF MIGRANTS

The place-of-previous-residence data in table 10 reconfirm the movement of hill people into the tarai, particularly into the heavily

TABLE 10

Percentage of Migrant Families Settling Permanently in Sample Districts, by Region in Which Migrant Families Resided Previously[a]

District	Total number of migrant families	Other parts of same district	Other tarai districts	Hill districts (including Kathmandu)	Northeastern[b] India (A)	India except northeastern region (B)	All India (total, columns A and B)	Burma	Location unknown
Jhapa, 1959–67	167	21.0	5.4	33.5	3.0	35.3	38.3		1.8
Mahottari-Dhanusha, 1963–67	116	51.7	16.4	4.3		27.6	27.6		
Bara,[c] 1959–67				Data not available					
Kapilabastu, 1959–67	92	21.7	2.2	46.7		28.3	28.3	1.1	
Kailali, 1963–67	45	15.6	13.3	64.4					6.7

[a] Data collected during field survey of eighty-one villages, 1967–68.
[b] Northeastern India includes the two hill districts of West Bengal, Darjeeling and Jalpaiguri districts. It also includes Sikkim, Assam, and Manipur. The migrants from those areas are predominantly people of Nepalese hill origin.
[c] Place-of-previous-residence data were not systematically gathered for the migrants of Bara District.

forested districts of the far-eastern and far-western tarai. The data also confirm the migration of similar numbers of people from India into all parts of the tarai except the far-western districts. These data disclose two additional patterns of migration. The first is the significant intradistrict migration in the most populous districts, such as Mahottari-Dhanusha, where people are moving from the more crowded southern villages to the more recently established villages farther north. This is part of the process that is strengthening the plains culture in these populous districts. The second migration pattern[25] is from east to west in the tarai, exactly the opposite direction of the general west-to-east migration in the hills. For example, there is a movement of people from the relatively densely settled districts of Saptari, Siraha, and Mahottari-Dhanusha into the less densely settled neighboring districts of Sarlahi and Rautahat to the west. There is also a western movement of people from Banke district in the far-western tarai and Dang district in the western inner-tarai valley into the two most far-western tarai districts of Kailali and Kanchanpur. This is mainly a migration of Tharus who have lost title to their land and are looking for land to settle in the dense far-western tarai forest.

ECONOMIC STATUS OF MIGRANTS

As important to the question of hill or plains cultural dominance in the tarai as the factor of caste ranking is the factor of economic status. The two are usually related, that is, low-caste migrants usually have low economic status. Complete economic data exist for only three of the five districts surveyed: Jhapa, Kapilabastu and Kailali. A comparison of the economic status of migrants into the three districts is given in table 11.

The economic categories are landowner, tenant farmer, farm laborer, caste-occupation worker, and shopkeeper. A tenant farmer is defined as one who rents land from a resident or absentee landowner, and a farm laborer is one who works on a daily or hourly basis for other farmers who are either landowners or tenants. One who earns his living by following his traditional caste occupation may be, for example, a Sonar who makes jewelry, a Halwai who makes sweets, or a Chamar who cleans latrines and skins dead animals. Of these five economic groups, the tenant farmer, farm laborer, and caste-

[25] The data that identify this pattern are not included in the highly condensed data presented in the table.

TABLE 11

Migrant Families Settling Permanently, 1959–67, as a Percentage of Total Population in 1967, by District and Economic Status[a]

District	Total migrant families	Migrant families that have purchased land	Migrant families that are tenant farmers	Migrant families that are farm laborers	Migrant families doing caste occupation	Migrant families that are shopkeepers
Jhapa	167	22.8	34.1	18.0	9.0	16.2
Kapilabastu	92	47.8	10.9	23.9	4.4	12.0
Kailali[b]	45	64.4	6.7	17.8	11.1	

[a] Data for Jhapa, Kapilabastu, and Kailali collected during field survey, 1967–68. No data collected for Bara and Mahottari-Dhanusha districts.
[b] For Kailali, migrant families enumerated only for 1963–67.

occupation worker are usually poor, low-caste people, who have little capacity to exert influence in local community affairs. Such affairs are, as a rule, the domain of the largest of the landowners and occasionally shopkeepers of importance.

The data indicate that a considerably larger percentage of migrants into Kailali and Kapilabastu districts are landowners than is the case for Jhapa district. Although a caste breakdown is not included in the table, caste data indicate that there are no tenant farmers and few farm laborers among the caste and tribal people from the hills who are settling in Kapilabastu and Kailali districts. On the other hand, 43 percent of the hill caste people and 79 percent of the hill tribals settling in Jhapa district are either tenant farmers or farm laborers. The probable explanation for the considerable difference in the economic status of the hill people in Jhapa district and the other two districts is the fact that the hill migrants arriving in Jhapa find much of the land under the control of two tribal groups, the Rajbanshis and the Tajpurias, which have managed to protect their interests much more effectively than have the Tharus in the other two districts.

Data in the table indicate that a significant number of migrants into Jhapa and Kapilabastu districts are shopkeepers. Most of these businessmen establish small village shops. Few bring enough capital with them to become large-scale businessmen. In none of the survey villages of Kailali were there any recently settled shopkeepers, because there is still little commercialization in the district.

Although a few shopkeepers may be economically and politically important in their villages, most of the migrants who assert leadership roles are landowners, particularly the largest landowners. In the Jhapa district sample, twenty-six of the thirty-eight migrants who acquired land are hill Brahmins and Chetris, and six others are of the two plains tribal groups, Tajpurias and Rajbanshis. Only two hill-tribal migrants and three caste Hindus from the plains were able to acquire land. No Muslims or plains tribals in the sample were able to do so.

Evidently, the hill Brahmins and Chetris made the largest inroads in terms of land ownership in Jhapa, and it is interesting to note from whom they acquired their land. Of the twenty-six Brahmin and Chetri migrants who acquired land, four obtained it from the government's Land Reform Office, ten from other hill Brahmins and Chetris, seven from Tajpurias and Rajbanshis, three from hill tribals, and two from other plains caste people. The transfer of land from one high-caste hill family to another does not alter the economic standing of the high-caste people relative to other caste groups. The high-caste hill people made their gains primarily at the expense of hill and plains tribal people.

In the Kapilabastu-district sample, thirty-seven of the forty-four migrants who acquired land are hill Brahmins and Chetris, the other seven are hill tribals, plains Hindus, and Muslims. The hill Brahmins and Chetris obtained their land from nineteen other Chetris, sixteen plains Brahmins, one hill tribal, and one Tharu. Although these data seem to indicate that the transfer is mainly from high-caste plains people to high-caste hill people, this is due to the distortion caused by the small sample. Evidence obtained from oral histories of sample villages indicates that the pattern of land transfer in the district has been from Tharus both to high-caste hill people and to plains people of business and yeoman-farmer castes such as the Kurmis and Ahirs. Because there is a considerably lower rate of migration into Kapilabastu from the hill region than is the case in other districts surveyed, it is unlikely that a shift in land control will occur rapidly enough to make a substantial difference in the cultural equation for a long time to come.

In the Kailali-district sample, twenty of the twenty-nine migrant families acquiring land were hill Brahmins and Chetris, one was Newar and eight were low-caste hill families. Of the twenty high-caste hill-migrant families, eighteen acquired their land from Tharus and from the Land Reform Office. The Newar and eight low-caste hill families also obtained their land from the Land Reform Office. All this was land confiscated from Tharus who owned more than the legal limit. Although the Kailali sample is small, it appears to be fairly representative of the shift in land control from the Tharus to the high-caste hill people in the district and throughout the far-western tarai.

In all three districts for which these economic data were collected, therefore, the hill Brahmins and Chetris represented by far the largest percentage of migrants who acquired land: 50 percent of all migrants acquiring land in Jhapa, 75 percent in Kapilabastu, and 48 percent in Kailali. Given the large-scale migration into Jhapa and Kailali, this will eventually put much of the land in these two heavily forested districts into the hands of hill Brahmins and Chetris. The government is reinforcing this trend by putting most, if not all, of the land confiscated through the land-reform program into the hands of settlers from the hills.

The government finds itself caught in a particularly difficult bind with regard to the large-scale unplanned settlement of hill people in the forest areas of the tarai. On the one hand, there is a growing awareness of the important economic resource represented by the stands of commercial timber in tarai forests, the sale of which is a major source of revenue for the government. As settlers move into the forest, they destroy it. On the other hand, the government views this pattern of settlement as an answer to its problem of Nepalizing the tarai. Both protection of forests and Nepalization of the region are important to the government, and this results in policies which sometimes appear contradictory. For example, in years like 1972, when heavy rains made the growing season in the hill region unusually short and the food scarcity more acute than usual, destitute hill people migrated in very large numbers to the tarai forests to clear land and reestablish themselves. Therefore, the confrontations between them and forest rangers, often backed by local police, were numerous, with shootings reported in a number of tarai districts. The most serious incident occurred at Ramailo-Jhora in northern Morang district, where more than 4,000 landless hill people resisted police attempts to burn their huts and force them out of the forest. The government admitted that one settler was killed when the police fired into the angry crowd, but press estimates of those killed ran as high as seventy-five.[26] Yet in 1972, the government moved ahead more vigorously with the granting of ownership certificates to those who had recently cleared forest land, in effect bestowing its blessing upon a process which it does not yet have the administrative apparatus to control. Despite the occasional efforts to force hill settlers out of the forest, the government is not likely to object as strenuously to this settlement pattern as it would if the forest areas were being settled by plains people, whom government officials suspect of being migrants from India.

GOVERNMENT-SPONSORED RESETTLEMENT PROJECTS

Not all settlement is unplanned, nor do government officials make public statements about their interest in Nepalization of the tarai through resettlement of hill people there. Such statements would confirm the government's discomfort about the predominance of plains people in the region, would invite the Indian government to express similar attitudes toward the large number of Nepalis living

[26]*Gorkhapatra,* Mar. 1, 1972; *Nepal Times,* Apr. 12, 1972.

in India, and would add another serious irritant to the always sensitive relations between the two countries. The only publicly stated evidence that some people in Kathmandu endorse resettlement for political purposes appears occasionally in Kathmandu newspaper columns suggesting that Gurkha soldiers retired from the British, Indian and Nepalese armies be settled along the border as a paramilitary force to prevent smuggling detrimental to Nepal and to prevent raids by bandit gangs from India.[27] The Gurkhas, being hill people, are assumed to be more loyal to the government than others who might settle along the border. One Nepalese newspaper, noted for its public support of plains people, has charged that the main object of the government's policy to settle ex-servicemen and other hill people in the tarai during the past ten years has been to change the cultural composition of the population so that the plains people will find themselves in a minority. The paper warned that this would encourage "communal tension" and suggested that the government avoid this by providing landless plains people of the tarai with an opportunity to resettle on forest land.[28]

There are a few small-scale resettlement projects, and the government plans to undertake others in the future. Despite the political implications of these projects, the government is careful to justify them in strictly economic terms: relief of population pressure in the severely overcrowded hill region, and increased food production on the land brought under cultivation by the settlers.[29] The stated economic problems are certainly real and are compelling reasons for government action in this sphere. Moreover, government officials naturally want to make the nation's resources available to people already living within its borders rather than to people from outside.

The government's second economic plan, 1962–65, allocated funds for the resettlement of 6,000 families on 50,000 acres of land.[30] In 1963, the Israeli government agreed to undertake the resettlement of approximately 800 families in the central inner tarai and, three years later, in Banke district of the far-western tarai.[31] In 1967, the Nepalis reached an agreement with the Israeli and Australian governments to

[27]*Gorkhapatra*, Apr. 26, 28, 1968.
[28]*Dainik Nepal*, Mar. 3, July 5, 1972.
[29]Nepal, Department of Agriculture, *Resettlement Project, Nawalpur* 1963, pp. 1, 9.
[30]Nepal, National Planning Council, *The Three Year Plan*, 1962–65, p. 228.
[31]Israel [Nepal Aid Mission], "Summary of Nepal-Israel Cooperation" (Kathmandu, n.d.), pp. 1–2.

resettle ex-soldiers on nearly 3,000 acres of land in Jhapa district.[32]

Resettlement projects such as these affect the lives of few migrants because, as already mentioned, the government has as yet been unable to direct or control the large number of hill people moving into the tarai forest. The government has been unable to play a more active role because resettlement projects require the availability of unused but cultivable land, capacity to finance the settlers' development of the land, and resettlement administrators with the skills needed to undertake this highly complex economic and social operation.[33] Although the first of these three prerequisites, cultivable land, is available to the government, the other two are not. The minimum cost of resettling a five- or six-member family was estimated at 1,390 Nepalese rupees in 1965. Most families are without capital funds, and they need this amount in the form of a long-term loan, if not an outright grant, to invest in material to build a house and dig a well and to buy farm tools, seed, and fertilizer. This figure does not include funds the government must spend on access roads, schools, and hospitals.[34] The government is unable at present to allocate adequate funds. They must be provided by foreign governments, but most aiding nations do not appear to be interested in settlement projects.

The unavailability of Nepalese personnel trained to manage resettlement projects is another handicap. Indeed, aside from Israel and Malaysia, few nations have personnel trained for this task. The success of the Israeli-sponsored projects can be largely attributed to the loan of Israeli resettlement administrators to the Nepalese government. Without such personnel, resettlement funds tend to be invested unwisely. These funds and the land itself tend to fall into the hands of local vested interests.

Let us conclude by turning briefly from the question of planned resettlement to the general migration phenomenon. Some Nepalese leaders have mourned the existence of this phenomenon. However, the focus of their attention has not been on the large-scale migration of Nepalis into the rural and urban areas of India but on the comparatively small migration of men out of Nepal to join the British and Indian armies.[35] Because Nepalese mercenaries are stationed by the British in Hong Kong and by the Indians along the Tibetan border,

[32]*Naya Sandesh,* Jan. 13, 1967.
[33]J. B. Melford, "Planning and Implementation of Land Settlement Schemes (Five Year Plan 1965–1970)," (Kathmandu, 1965).
[34]*Ibid.,* p. 4.
[35]Rishikesh Shaha, *Nepal and the World* (Kathmandu, 1955), p. 18.

they constitute an irritant to the otherwise cool but correct Nepal-China relations.

If migration creates one problem for the Nepalese government, it alleviates several others. Migration into the tarai and into India represents a kind of pressure-release valve for the hill people, preventing discontent that might otherwise be translated into organized opposition. The migration also provides the government with an instrument for national integration through Nepalization of the tarai. Because the government's administrative capability for implementation of various national integration-oriented programs is still limited, migration becomes a central factor in the integration process. It requires no direction from the government, no investment of funds, and little administrative effort.

Perhaps somewhat unexpectedly, malaria eradication has become the most effective of all government programs that encourage Nepalization, apparently without conscious design on the part of its initiators. The eradication of malaria has been a far more important stimulus to settlement of hill people in the tarai than the resettlement projects. For generations, a few landless hill people were willing to clear and settle forested areas because the odds of dying from starvation in the hills were greater than the odds of dying from malaria in the tarai. The malaria-eradication program now has eliminated the fear that previously impelled a great many migrating hill people to settle in India instead.

To what extent is the tarai being Nepalized through the migration process? In another generation or two, when most of the remaining forest has been cut down, one will be able to draw a line east and west across a map of the tarai, separating fairly clearly the settlement areas of the hill people and the plains people. The line will follow closely the southern fringe of the forest as it stood at the time of the 1951 revolution. Most of the four far-western tarai districts, half or more of Sunsari and Morang districts, and most of Jhapa in the far-eastern tarai, the northern third of Parsa, Bara, Rautahat, Sarlahi, and the three mid-western tarai districts will be settled predominantly by hill people. The rest of the tarai will remain settled mostly by plains people. Of course, there will be a mixing of hill and plains people in the towns of the region. Hill Brahmins, Chetris and Newars will probably continue to become more influential in district-level politics. Members of these three castes, along with the more aggressive upper- and business-caste plains people, will penetrate each other's settlement areas, gaining control of land and forming commercial ties. Migration is therefore an essential factor in the economic and political integration of the hill and plains regions of Nepal, a prerequisite for the more complete cultural integration that is likely to take place in the more distant future.

Chapter V

THE POLITICS OF CITIZENSHIP

Citizenship bestows the right to participate in the governing process. It grants access to power. It is a symbol of legitimacy for people living within their national boundaries. Citizenship is a bond between the individuals and the government of a nation and, therefore, important in the process of national integration. The definition of citizenship eligibility is a complex and often vexing dilemma for leaders of developing nations faced with the need to create stable national polities out of populations composed of competing, occasionally hostile groups from different geographical, ethnic, and linguistic backgrounds.

This has been a dilemma in Nepal. People of the nationally dominant hill culture and people of the regionally important plains culture have lived separate existences until the last several decades, often with suspicion of each other. Citizenship legislation framed by representatives of the nationally dominant hill culture during the 1960s reflects this suspicion, for it makes the acquisition of citizenship more difficult for people of plains origin living in the tarai. For this reason, the political dynamics surrounding Nepal's citizenship policy, the motives behind it, and responses to it in the tarai provide insights into the national-integration process.

STATUS OF TARAI SUBJECTS BEFORE 1951

Changing citizenship regulations reflect changes in the attitudes of Kathmandu's decision makers toward the plains people of the tarai. Let us first take a brief look at attitudes that prevailed in Kathmandu before 1951, before citizenship was defined in modern, constitutional terms. In 1769, Prithvi Narayan Shah, king of the western hill principality, Gorkha, conquered Kathmandu Valley. During the next four years, he extended his sway over the eastern hills and the eastern tarai, creating the geopolitical entity which has become Nepal. With the conquest of the tarai came the need to define the responsibilities and rights of the people who lived there. Government documents of the mid-19th century tell us that zamindaris and minor government posts in the tarai were given to tarai inhabitants in three preferentially ordered categories. First preference was given to "hill folks," and second preference to "those who are settled in our territory with their family members, those who are rich, ...faithful and of respectable ancestry. ..." Only if such individuals could not be found, could "an Indian" be appointed, an Indian being defined by inference as a plains person living in the tarai without his family, i.e., living there temporarily.[1] It is likely that this distinction was made soon after Prithvi Narayan Shah conquered the tarai, because it was necessary to establish criteria for recruiting people into local administrative service. Hill people were given preference over plains people settled in the tarai, so that the plains people were relegated to a second-class status. This is understandable when one remembers that the tarai was viewed before 1951 more as a colony than an integrated part of a modern nation-state.

Culturally different from the hill people and geographically isolated from Kathmandu, plains people living in the tarai were considered to be at least quasi-foreigners. No administrative procedure was established in the tarai to determine an individual's status as a Nepalese or Indian subject. Therefore, except during the Shiva Ratri festival, when Indians were allowed to make pilgrimages to Pashupatinath Temple in Kathmandu, tarai residents as well as Indians were required to stop at the border town of Birganj to obtain a passport before proceeding to Kathmandu; passports were then checked at Chisapani Garhi on the route to Kathmandu. This procedure was not modified until the early 1950s and not abandoned entirely until 1958. Before 1951 one's nationality appears to have been determined primarily on a linguistic basis. Nepalese subjects were the "hill folk" who spoke Nepali or hill languages such as Newari, Magar, or Gurung. For this reason, passports were not required for people traveling into Kathmandu Valley from the eastern or western hills.

Indeed, it has always been difficult for the average hill person to draw a distinction between plains people living in the tarai and Indians. Whether the hill person was a village agriculturalist or a merchant, before the advent of the malaria-eradication program, his trips across the tarai to sell produce and buy supplies in the Indian border towns were always hurried. His attitude toward the unhealthy tarai and its

[1]Nepal, Department of Land Revenue, *Administrative Regulations for Tarai Districts*, 1861, vol. I. p. 16. (Trans. by Regmi Research Project, 1967.)

different-looking people was generally a negative one, as illustrated by the following saying common among hill people until recently: "Don't perform the funeral rites for one who goes to Hitaura (actually in the central inner-tarai valley) during the spring (March-April) or for one who goes to Tibet during the winter (October-November)." The implication was that a person unwise enough to go to those places during those seasons did not deserve to have funeral rites performed for him.

CITIZENSHIP LAWS IN THE 1950s

After the negotiated settlement that ended the period of political turmoil in 1950–51, the need was voiced for drawing up a voters' list and holding an election. Since there was no formal definition of citizenship, the Public Representation Act of 1951 affirmed the right to vote for any inhabitant who had resided in any constituency for at least sixty days.[2] This act, with its liberal, straightforward voting requirements, set the tone for the Citizenship Act of the following year. Like most citizenship laws, it declared a citizen anyone who was born in Nepal, anyone permanently settled in Nepal who had at least one parent born in Nepal, or any woman married to a citizen. It also stated that anyone who had lived in Nepal for at least five years could acquire citizenship.[3] The five-year-residency requirement for naturalization is part of citizenship laws in the neighboring countries of India and Pakistan and, indeed, most other nations. If discrimination against minority groups occurs in citizenship legislation, it is usually found in the naturalization requirements. This is the case in citizenship laws passed by Nepal's South Asian neighbors, Burma and Ceylon. Those countries, like Nepal, have experienced substantial immigration, which the laws are designed to limit.

What caused the pre-1951 discrimination against the tarai population to be absent from the legal documents written immediately after the end of the Rana period? The influence of the Indian government in Kathmandu in the early 1950s was one factor, although it is difficult to document. While Nepalese leaders were adjusting to the changes brought about by the 1951 revolution and were, so to speak, finding their political feet, the Indian government, which engineered the

[2] *Nepal Gazette,* vol. I, No. 27, Feb. 10, 1952.
[3] United Nations, Legal Department, *Laws Concerning Nationality* (New York, 1954), pp. 320–321.

settlement of 1951 among the Ranas, the Nepali Congress, and King Tribhuvan, exercised considerable influence in Kathmandu through the appointment of Ambassador C. P. N. Singh, Govinda Narayan, personal advisor to the King, and other Indian officials. As might be expected, Nepalese legislation of the early 1950s was similar in content to corresponding Indian legislation. The 1951 Interim Government of Nepal Act was "a hastily prepared adaptation of the 1950 Indian Constitution."[4]

Indian citizenship legislation, from its first enactment in 1852, has been nondiscriminatory with regard to naturalization eligibility. The Nepalis who found themselves in positions of political prominence immediately after the revolution had no experience at drawing up their own laws and, although there is no evidence that Indian advisors wrote laws such as the Public Representation Act and the Citizenship Act, it is likely that they influenced the spirit of such legislation.

The second and most important reason for the nondiscriminatory citizenship legislation of the early 1950s was the close association of the hill people and plains people in the politics of that period. Young men from Kathmandu Valley and from the tarai obtained their education in the same colleges and universities of northern India; many of them were swept up in the Indian national movement, and occasionally spent time in the same British jails. After Indian independence in 1947, these young men turned their attention toward their own country, viewing the Ranas with much the same antipathy that they viewed the British. The Nepali Congress Party, founded in 1946, was the anti-Rana political organization into which most of them were drawn. Unfortunately, during the tumultuous history of the party, there have been occasions when its headquarters and the homes of its leaders were raided and its records destroyed, making it difficult to document the close association of many plains people with the party.

The results of the general election in 1959 and the composition of the Nepali Congress government that followed the election give some indication of this association during the preceding decade. Of those who won seats in Parliament on the Nepali Congress ticket from tarai constituencies, twelve were plains people and eleven were hill people. Although it is surprising that so many were hill people, given the very small percentage of hill people in the region, the hill people

[4]Bhuwan Lal Joshi and Leo E. Rose, *Democratic Innovations in Nepal* (Berkeley, 1966), p. 488.

included a number of party leaders such as B. P. Koirala, S. P. Koirala, Rudra Prasad Giri, and Subarna Shamsher, men who had close personal ties with the region. Two of the seven ministers in the Nepali Congress cabinet were plains people—Ram Narayan Mishra, a Maithili Brahmin from Janakpur, and Parashu Narayan Chaudhari, a Tharu from Dang in the western inner-tarai valley. One of the eleven deputy ministers was of plains origin, Suryanath Das Yadav, an Ahir from Saptari.[5]

These data are not as illustrative of the association between hill people and plains people in the party as are stories told by plains people of their fathers' and brothers' involvement in the party during the dangerous days of the late 1940s, when party leaders and weapons were hidden from Rana officials, jails were attacked, and political prisoners were released, despite superior Rana forces. The elders of many tarai villages tell such stories. The heroic content has perhaps swelled with the passage of years, but the message is clear. There was a time when men of the hills and plains worked, fought, and occasionally died together and, when the struggle was over, they governed together.

CITIZENSHIP LAWS IN THE 1960s

Citizenship legislation of the 1960s was formulated in a much different atmosphere. The royal coup had taken place. Both hill people and plains people associated with Nepali Congress leadership were in jail or in exile along with the leaders of the several other political parties that had included representatives of the tarai population. Few people in Kathmandu could command attention when speaking for the interests of the plains people. In addition, during the first several years of the decade, when citizenship requirements were being reformulated, there was underground Nepali Congress activity in the tarai and border areas of India. As this posed a threat to the royal government, it tended to undermine whatever willingness to accommodate tarai interests might have existed in the Palace.

Citizenship received detailed attention in articles 7 and 8 of the 1962 Constitution. Article 7 of the 1962 Constitution is a repetition of article 2 of the 1952 Citizenship Act; it gives qualifications for those who can be classified as citizens automatically, that is, by birth and marriage. The major difference between the two documents

[5] Nepal, Election Commission [Results of the First General Election, 1959].

lay in the requirements for naturalization. Article 8, section 2, of the 1962 Constitution states:

> 2. While making law in pursuance of clause (i) it shall be, *inter alia*, stipulated that a foreigner may qualify for the acquisition of citizenship if—
> (a) he can speak and write the national language of Nepal;
> (b) he, engaged in an occupation, resides in Nepal;
> (c) he has taken steps to renounce the citizenship of the country of which he is a citizen; and
> (d) he has resided in Nepal for not less than a period of two years in case of a person of Nepalese origin, and for not less than a period of twelve years in case of a person other than of Nepalese origin.[6]

Clause (a) of article 8, section 2, requiring knowledge of the national language, Nepali, was not included in the 1952 Citizenship Act because the linguistic ramifications of nationalism had not yet been debated by Nepalese leaders in the early 1950s. Although it is not unreasonable to require applicants for citizenship to speak Nepali, given the very low literacy rate of Nepal's population (4 percent in the early 1950s and not much higher a decade later), it does seem unreasonable to require applicants to write it as well. Most developing nations insert a language-speaking but not a reading or writing requirement in their naturalization legislation. In the case of such multilanguage nations as India and Pakistan, where language has been more a disruptive than a unifying factor, the language requirement tends to be liberal, allowing applicants to speak one of a number of languages commonly spoken within the country.

What does this clause mean for people migrating into the tarai from India? For businessmen it is likely to mean little, because they learn Nepali relatively quickly from government officials and other Nepali speakers with whom they have contact. For tenant farmers and farm laborers who settle in areas of the tarai where there are few if any Nepali speakers, it is very difficult to learn to speak Nepali, to say nothing of learning to write the language. The 1968 Citizenship Rules[7] made no provision for a language test, and there is no evidence that this requirement is enforced. If the rules should be changed, the requirement would represent a major stumbling block for many applicants.

[6]Nepal, Ministry of Law and Justice, *The Constitution of Nepal* (Kathmandu, 1963); see pp. 3–5 for articles 7 and 8.
[7]See Rules, schedule 6, *Nepal Gazette*, vol. XVIII, No. 8, June 3, 1968.

Clause (b) places an unusual requirement upon citizenship applicants. In many countries, immigrants must provide proof of their financial solvency at the time they immigrate. Since there is no control of immigration in Nepal, this requirement would be impossible to enforce. However, at the time one applies for citizenship, he must prove that he earns a living in Nepal. No such requirement is included among the naturalization requirements of other South Asian nations. Clause (b) is worded in a way that implies there are people who reside in Nepal without any occupation, presumably Indian businessmen who are attempting to evade Indian taxes. If they are the object of this restriction, this reflects yet another way in which the Indian business world is intertwined with Nepalese affairs and also reflects Nepalese resentment of Indian businessmen.

Clause (c) is another requirement for naturalization not included in the 1952 Citizenship Act. Most citizenship laws forbid dual citizenship, and it is likely that the inclusion of this proviso is the result of the not-infrequent public debate which has swirled around prominent Nepalis allegedly holding both Indian and Nepalese passports.

Clause (d) is the most restrictive of the four naturalization clauses. It extends by seven years the length of residence required for some people who seek citizenship, and it shortens the period for others. This is not uncommon. Burma has extended the period to eight years and Sikkim to fifteen years. By so doing, these countries hope to discourage immigration, or at least limit the influence of immigrants. It is doubtful that the extended residency requirement is having this effect in Nepal. It may give a few large-scale businessmen second thoughts. However, most of the migrants are villagers who cross the open border in search of land and employment, unaware of citizenship laws.

It is in this clause (d) that discrimination against people of plains origin is evident, more in the vagueness of wording than in the stated fact. "Nepalese origin," or as it is occasionally translated, "Nepali origin," is not defined in the 1962 Constitution or in the Citizenship Act of 1964;[8] interpretation is left to officials granting citizenship certificates. There are two possible definitions. One, that the applicant's parents, grandparents, or even great-grandparents were born within the political borders of Nepal, which, of course, include the tarai. Two, that the applicant is of hill origin, that he, his parents, or even his more distant ancestors were born in the geocultural region called

[8] *Nepal Gazette,* vol. XIII, Extraordinary Issue No. 28, Feb. 28, 1964.

the hills. There is a linguistic dimension to this definition, that the person of Nepalese origin speaks Nepali either as a mother tongue or, if a hill-tribal person, as a second language. This is essentially a cultural definition rather than one limited by political geography. The cultural definition excludes the tarai plains people but includes many hill people living in Sikkim, Bhutan, and parts of northeastern India. The failure of the authors of the Constitution to make the same clear distinction regarding "Nepalese origin" that was made by the authors of the 1952 Act, i.e., "A person one of whose parents was born in Nepal," may have been unintentional. However, it would not have been difficult to write a straightforward statement for clause (d).

It is understandable that lawmakers of a small nation might feel threatened by migration from a large neighbor nation and that they might wish to discourage this migration by legal means. But such means are not effective, and the citizenship laws of the 1960s are an affront to the plains people, many of whom have lived in the tarai for generations.

CITIZENSHIP REQUIREMENTS FOR VARIOUS TYPES OF ECONOMIC ACTIVITY

To protect its citizens from the competition of other nationals, the Nepalese government required citizenship for continually more forms of economic activity during the 1960s. For example, importers and owners of small-scale firms must now be citizens. On the basis of citizenship status, the government has instituted a policy of preferential hiring for laboring jobs in Nepal's largest industries. The management of these industries has been directed to seek permission from the Industries Department before hiring Indian citizens or firing Nepalese citizens. Teaching is yet another activity for which citizenship is now required. The requirement was first made in 1957 and included in the Education Code of 1961 as follows: "First priority shall be given to Nepali citizens, and then to emigrant Nepalis. If persons of neither category are available, or lack the essential qualifications, foreigners may be appointed on a temporary basis."[9]

Citizenship is also now required for land acquisition, and this has been the most controversial application of the requirement. The 1952 edition of the *Muluki Ain* (Legal Code) allows foreigners to settle on land, pay taxes on it, and become landowners; in continuance

[9]"Education Code, 1961," art. 12, sec. 27. (Trans. by Regmi Research Project.)

of this policy, noncitizens can retain title to their land under the Lands Act of 1964.[10] However, one must now be a citizen to acquire land. This requirement has been incorporated into land-reform measures enacted since 1964, and it has caused difficulty for some people of plains origin living in the tarai, particularly tenants. Most of the agriculturalists in the tarai are tenants, a much higher percentage than in the hills,[11] and they must prove that they are citizens before they can buy land, or before the title to land they work can be registered in their names.

Neither the 1964 Lands Act nor the 1964 Lands Rules state specifically that a tenant must produce a citizenship certificate before purchasing land. However, schedule 1A of the Rules[12] is a form for recording in considerable detail information about tenants' citizenship, as required in article 3, section 3 of the Rules. Thus, in practice, tenants are being required to prove their citizenship. The reason the Nepalese government has not made the citizenship requirement for land ownership more explicit in the land-reform laws may be its concern that the Indian government would retaliate. This would cause serious trouble for many Nepalese families migrating from the hill region into the agricultural regions of West Bengal and Assam. According to the 1950 Indo-Nepal Friendship Treaty, article 7, nationals of either country are guaranteed the right to own property in the other country.

The citizenship requirement has caused tenants of plains origin the most difficulty in the Ukhada land-tenure subregion of the tarai, the three mid-western tarai districts of Nawal Parasi, Rupandehi, and Kapilabastu. The Ranas encouraged the settling of the mid-western tarai between the 1890s and 1930s. Under the Ukhada system, zamindars, most of them Indians, were given title to large land holdings which they parceled out to tenants, also mostly Indians, for clearing and farming at rental rates low enough to attract the tenants. Most of the tenants did not acquire citizenship certificates between 1952, when it was first possible to do so, and 1964, when the land-reform program was inaugurated. The 1964 Ukhada Land Tenure Act states that title to Ukhada lands in excess of land-holding ceilings shall be transferred from the zamindars to their tenant cultivators,

[10] *Nepal Gazette*, vol. XIV, Extraordinary Issue No. 18, Nov. 16, 1964.
[11] Nepal, Central Bureau of Statistics, *National Agricultural Census*, 1962. A comparison of table 7 in the volumes for various tarai and hill districts will verify this.
[12] *Nepal Gazette*, vol. XIV, Extraordinary Issue No. 21, Nov. 23, 1964.

unless the tenants are proven to be aliens.[13] The Ukhada Land Tenure Rules enacted shortly thereafter provide: "In case a controversy arises with regard to the citizenship of Nepal, the peasant shall submit a Nepali citizenship certificate within a time limit not exceeding seven days as prescribed by the Ukhada authority. In case such certificate is not produced, the land shall not be registered in the name of the peasant."[14] The Rules add: "Land of the following categories shall be retained by and registered in the name of the landowner in the following circumstances: (a) Ukhada land cultivated by any peasant who is proved to be an alien in accordance with the particulars submitted by the landowner under Rule 3, or, (b) land registered under these rules in the name of any peasant who is proved to be an alien."[15] By giving the zamindars license to accuse their tenants of being aliens, the government provided the zamindars with an opportunity to retain control of the land. These large landowners could then sell the land, if it exceeded the land ceiling in size, or transfer the title to relatives or other associates, making informal arrangements to retain de facto control. Thus, the law and accompanying rules perpetuated the economic and social status quo by encouraging a kind of class struggle in which the government legitimized the landowners' interests.

These provisions of the Ukhada land reforms yield an insight into the traditionalist nature of the "reforms." The reforms reflect the attitudes of decision makers in the government about landlord-peasant relationships and about fundamental social and economic change. In respect to these attitudes, the land reforms are discussed at greater length in chapter IX. Here the focus must remain on the question of citizenship, and the attitudes of decision makers about distinctions between people of hill and those of plains origin. Particularly with regard to the Ukhada reforms, there is some conflict of attitudes. Although the citizenship laws discriminate against all plains people, the land reforms have been of benefit to many landowners who are plains people. It must be remembered that hill people represent a considerably higher percentage of large landowners in the tarai than of the general tarai population. Many of the largest landowners in the tarai are hill people with considerable influence in Kathmandu, and it is likely that they helped to shape the provisions of

[13]Act, article 3, section 1, *Nepal Gazette*, vol. XIV, Extraordinary Issue No. 15, Oct. 2, 1964.
[14]Rules, section 7, *Nepal Gazette*, vol. XIV, No. 41, Jan. 25, 1965.
[15]*Ibid.*, section 11.

the reforms. The benefits to them accrued also to the landowners of plains origin who, being considerably more sophisticated and influential than their tenants, were usually able to acquire the citizenship certificates they needed. But, because the process of obtaining certificates often involves months of bureaucratic delay and sometimes considerable financial outlay, when landowners filed claims in local land-reform offices alleging that their tenants were not Nepalese citizens, large numbers of tenants, most of whom had lived in the tarai for longer than twelve years, were helpless.

Growing popular discontent in the mid-western tarai was the result. Perhaps the government grew uneasy about the situation, because it drew up the Ukhada Land Tenure First Amendment Act in 1965, designed to alleviate the landowner-tenant conflict. The Act declared: "In case such peasant is, or is subsequently proved to be, an alien, the Ukhada lands cultivated by him shall be registered in the name of His Majesty's Government, which may sell or distribute such lands to landless Nepalese peasants on any condition."[16] This made it useless for landowners to take action against their tenants. However, it placed the tenants in an even more precarious position. Under the 1964 Rules, being unable to prove their citizenship, they would have remained tenants of their landlords. In reality, they would have lost nothing but the prospect of owning the land they worked. According to the 1965 law, however, the tenants were threatened with dispossession. It was now to the landowner's advantage to evict his tenants and cultivate as much of the land as possible himself, with the help of daily paid farm labor, as a means of retaining control. It became the government's responsibility to prove that tenants were not citizens. When this happened, the government, after making financial compensation to the landowner, could confiscate the land, evict the tenants and resettle "Nepalese peasants." Because of the hill-culture-oriented definition of citizenship, the Nepalese tenants would tend to be people of hill origin.

If the government had carried out the provisions of the Ukhada land-reform program, there would have been widespread uprooting of the population in the mid-western tarai districts and the relocation there of many hill people. This has not occurred, although eviction of tenants has been common and the population has become more restive than anywhere else in Nepal. Rioting in Nawal Parasi district

[16] Act, replaces article 3, section 1, of the 1964 Act, *Nepal Gazette*, vol. XV, Extraordinary Issue No. 11, July 14, 1965.

in 1966 and in the other two mid-western tarai districts in 1969 was at least partly the result of alienation caused by the government's citizenship and land-reform policies. These disturbances are discussed in chapter IX.

In 1972, the government announced that it was formulating legislation to prevent "foreigners" from working as agricultural laborers in Nepal and to make the appointment of all new tenant farmers the responsibility of government officials,[17] which probably also means that the selection of new tenants would be based on their citizenship qualifications. If such legislation is enacted, it will use citizenship as an instrument to discourage migration from India into the tarai. Because it is often difficult for government officials to distinguish between landless laborers of plains origin who meet citizenship qualifications and those who do not, if the legislation can be effectively implemented—a doubtful prospect—it is likely to result in yet more hardships for many disadvantaged plains people in the region. According to one observer:

> Kathmandu's failure to consult with New Delhi before enacting legislation discriminating against Indian nationals may ... constitute a violation of the 1950 [Indo-Nepal Peace and Friendship] treaty. The Indian government presented Nepal with an aide memoire on the subject in June 1966, and Mrs. Gandhi also discussed it with King Mahendra during her visit to Kathmandu in October of that year. The Indian government's policy has been to wait and see how thoroughly Kathmandu implements the discriminatory legislation.[18]

If the Nepalese government continues to add citizenship restrictions to more and more forms of economic activity and the disadvantages experienced by the plains people of the tarai, whether eligible for Nepalese citizenship or not, become discernibly more acute, the Indian government might retaliate with reciprocal restrictions against the large community of people of Nepalese hill origin living in India. This is a possibility of which the Nepalis are aware, and it undoubtedly inhibits the enactment of legislation applying citizenship restrictions to an even wider range of activities.

The current citizenship legislation gives formal recognition to the cultural divisions within Nepal. By including provisions for granting hill people citizenship after two years' residency and plains people

[17]*Gorkhapatra*, Mar. 23, 1972.
[18]Leo E. Rose, *Nepal: Strategy for Survival* (Berkeley, 1971), pp. 260–261.

citizenship after twelve years' residency, the legislation creates discrimination reminiscent of an earlier period. If the growth of hill-oriented nationalism results in the Kathmandu leadership reverting to pre-1951 attitudes toward the large and economically important tarai minority, the process of national integration will suffer a serious setback.

CITIZENSHIP-APPLICATION PROCEDURES

The citizenship-application procedures are difficult because they involve considerable contact with government officials, considerable filling out of forms and, occasionally, some politics. Whether applicants apply for citizenship by birth or by naturalization, they must obtain the written endorsement of a gazetted officer, a town panchayat chairman or a district panchayat chairman.[19] Prominent merchants are likely to have easy access to at least one of these officials, whereas such access is a greater problem for most villagers.

If the application is for citizenship by birth, the applicant must provide evidence of birth in Nepal. Inasmuch as there are no birth-registration procedures in Nepal, outside the several hospitals in Kathmandu Valley, this can become a problem. Officials are generally ready to accept the fact that an applicant of hill origin was born in the country, but an applicant of plains origin often needs to find one or two prominent people from his village to verify that he was born there. If the applicant is following naturalization procedures, he must furnish evidence of having relinquished Indian citizenship or of having started the procedures toward that end. One familiar with Indian bureaucracy will understand that even a wealthy merchant's resourcefulness could be tested by the task of acquiring the necessary evidence.

If an applicant has powerful political enemies, he may have additional difficulties. If he is involved in factional politics in one of the urban centers of the tarai, and members of the opposing faction have influence with government officials, they may attempt to persuade officials to investigate and reject his application on technical grounds. There are reports that charges of alien status have been leveled against candidates for panchayat office in several tarai towns

---

[19]"Nepal Citizenship Rules, 1968," *Nepal Gazette*, vol. XVIII, No. 8, June 3, 1968. Most tarai districts have ten to twenty gazetted officers posted in them at any one time.

as a maneuver designed to disqualify them. It is likely that wealthy and powerful individuals not eligible for citizenship have used their influence upon occasion to obtain citizenship certificates in order to buy land or participate in politics.

Citizenship-application procedures present problems chiefly for tarai villagers with little or no education or influence. As in the old days, they must take advantage of paternalistic patterns, seeking advice and support from locally important men who have connections with government officials. In return for guiding villagers' applications through the proper channels, these "benefactors" sometimes expect financial remuneration. If a villager can not find a locally influential person willing to assist him or if he can not afford the expense involved, a citizenship certificate may be beyond his reach.

CONTROVERSY OVER CITIZENSHIP

Considerable public controversy has been generated by the citizenship issue. The issue first arose in 1951, when there was public demand for national elections. Virtually everyone in the tarai was eligible to vote after the Public Representation Act of 1951, which gave voting rights to everyone who had resided in a constituency for six months or more. After the 1952 Citizenship Law was passed, defining a citizen as a resident of five years or more, the voting lists were drawn up again, but local administration was inadequate for the task during that chaotic period, and there were many charges that Indians were included in the lists. The charges were renewed with greater intensity after the general-election date was set for early 1959.

The most extreme claims were made by the Citizenship Amendment Committee and the Nepal Prajatantrik Mahasabha. The Citizenship Amendment Committee was formed in September 1958. Its president, Jagadish Nepali, declared: "The voters' list prepared by the Election Commission is defective in many respects. Several foreigners have got their names registered, especially in the tarai districts. It was with a view of having the elections held fairly and impartially that this committee was formed."[20]

In August 1958, Ranganath Sharma, president of an ultranationalistic party, the Nepal Prajatantrik Mahasabha, demanded that in the elections only those who had lived in Nepal for at least eighteen

[20]*Citizenship Amendment Committee Bulletin*, Sept. 23, 1958.

years have the right to vote.[21] The daily newspaper *Halkhabar*, sympathetic to the Mahasabha, agreed with Sharma that no Indian or Pakistani who had migrated into Nepal since 1942 should be granted citizenship. The newspaper accused many businessmen and cultivators who had moved into the tarai since 1942 of remaining loyal to India. "We fear that these elements can have great influence on the elections in the tarai. And these elements may even be able to enter Parliament to work as fifth columnists."[22] Members of the Mahasabha claimed that Indian businessmen flocked to the tarai to avoid Indian income taxes, that these Indians purchased a few acres of land in the tarai, but carried on business in Banaras and Calcutta. *Halkhabar* continued during the months before the election to articulate the concerns of those hill people whose nationalism was at least in part an expression of hostility toward Indians and toward the plains people of the tarai.

More moderate spokesmen advocated that the government take steps to insure that only those qualified for citizenship be allowed to vote. As the election date approached, it became obvious that the crescendo of voices raising the citizenship question was not motivated entirely by the purest patriotic sentiments. Only those who were members of Kathmandu-based political parties, which had depended on Palace favor rather than popular support, could raise the citizenship issue. For these parties, alienation of the tarai population could do little harm, and the issue might block the election which would otherwise lay bare their claims of popular support. The tarai region, with a third of the parliamentary seats, had to be taken seriously by any party contending for the national-leadership role.

The two parties with the broadest national organizations, the Nepali Congress and the Communist Party of Nepal, played down the issue. The editorials of the Nepali Congress newspaper, *Kalpana*, urged the King and the Election Commission to proceed with the election and to ignore demands for amendment of the Citizenship Act because, these editorials observed, the controversy had been motivated by various political factions wanting to sabotage the election.[23] There were also reports that some election officials sympathetic to these factions were demanding that tarai villagers produce citizenship

[21]*Halkhabar*, Aug. 7, 1958. This party was formed in November 1957, advocated a limited form of democracy under the King's guidance, and was rumored to be financially supported by the Palace. See Joshi and Rose, *op. cit.*, pp. 206–207.
[22]*Halkhabar*, June 9, 1958.
[23]*Kalpana*, Sept. 19, 1958.

certificates before their names could be included on the voters' list. Because it was impossible for most villagers to produce certificates, large numbers of them were being disenfranchised.[24] Even the United Democratic Party and the Gorkha Parishad, parties with more limited support in the tarai, were determined that the issue not be allowed to delay the long-awaited first national election. This determination appears to have been a deciding factor with wavering officials in Kathmandu. The election was held in 1959, and the advocates of a more restrictive citizenship policy had to wait another several years until the political parties had been banned and leaders of the major parties could not oppose them.

The question of citizenship was also raised during the 1950s and 1960s with regard to students selected by the government to study abroad. Scholarships for study abroad are highly coveted in Nepal, because the nation's educational institutions have yet to develop graduate programs in many fields. Furthermore, some scholarships offer the opportunity to travel widely and to earn prestigious degrees from overseas institutions. A number of cases have been reported of Indian students and Indian teachers from colleges in the tarai claiming to be Nepalese citizens in order to apply for these scholarships. With a more highly developed educational system in India, there is even greater competition for the few scholarships available in India and, no doubt, some Indians have taken advantage of the "blurred border" discussed in chapter III to apply for Nepalese scholarships.

A fairly typical case in point is that of K. N. Jha, reported by *Bachhita* in 1958:

> It is reliably learnt that K. N. Jha, an Indian citizen, was sent by the Government of Nepal to study electrical engineering at the Bihar Institute of Technology as a Nepali student. K. N. Jha had, however, applied for a seat in the same institution as a citizen of the village of Masahia in Darbhanga district (India), prior to the award of the scholarship to him by the Government of Nepal under the Colombo Plan Technical Cooperation scheme. He claimed himself a resident of Madhwa Birta, Mahottari district of Nepal at the time of the grant. No inquiry was made due to the gross negligence of the Education Department, and hence he was sent on the scholarship. . . . It is reported that an Education Department employee is his relative and has been trying his best to suppress the matter. The students of Kathmandu are reported to be terribly dissatisfied.[25]

[24]*Nepal Times*, Sept. 9, 1958; *Halkhabar*, Sept. 4, 1958.
[25]*Bachhita*, Jan. 8, 1958.

Jha is a Maithili Brahmin name. The Maithili Brahmins are perhaps the most aggressive of all the castes in the tarai in pursuing modern as well as traditional forms of education. Only 31 of Madhwa's 100 families are Maithili Brahmins, but Madhwa, the village in question, is a Maithili Brahmin village in every other sense of the word. All 4 of the village's representatives to the local panchayat are Maithili Brahmins; one of them is chairman of the panchayat. All of the large landowners in the village are Maithili Brahmins. All 5 students from Madhwa working toward B.A. degrees, a large number for a village of this size, are Maithili Brahmins, as are all but 2 of the 25 students attending nearby high schools.[26]

Madhwa is a five-minute walk from the Indian border, and the Brahmins of the village have marriage ties in villages across the border. The children receive their high school and college education across the border simply because those are the high schools and colleges nearest to Madhwa. Whether K. N. Jha or his father was born in Madhwa is unknown. However, he most certainly has a number of close relatives who live there, one of whom, according to *Bachhita*, worked in the Education Department at the time. Madhwa is an extremely atypical tarai village because twenty-seven of its inhabitants are Government of Nepal employees, all of them Maithili Brahmins, five of them in Kathmandu.[27]

If we accept the *Bachhita* account as true for the purposes of discussion, we can assume that K. N. Jha had acquired two citizenship certificates. Perhaps he was actually born in Madhwa and applied for an Indian citizenship certificate by stating that he was born in his cousin's village across the border in Darbhanga district. Or he may have been born in India and have applied illegally for Nepalese citizenship, as *Bachhita* suggests. The main point, however, is that people who live along the long, open Nepal-India border, particularly people of the higher castes, use their family connections on both sides to their best advantage. When reports similar to the one in *Bachhita* appear in the Kathmandu press, they serve to reinforce suspicions that indeed, the tarai plains people feel little loyalty to Nepal. This, in turn, makes it increasingly difficult for persons from the tarai to gain entry

---

[26] By coincidence, Madhwa was one of the 12 villages that were included in the field survey of Mahottari district in February 1968.

[27] It is a rare tarai village from which a person of plains origin is working for the government in Kathmandu. The Maithili Brahmins and the Kayasthas represent the majority of tarai people of plains origin in government service in Kathmandu.

into government service, and for students and teachers from the tarai to obtain scholarships to study abroad.

DUAL CITIZENSHIP

Both the Indian and Nepalese governments prohibit dual citizenship, and during the 1950s there were acrimonious debates about individuals who allegedly possessed this status. Accusations were occasionally made against students or teachers, but more often against businessmen and political leaders. A well-publicized example occurred in 1951, in Birganj, an important tarai town. Birganj is the grain depot for the rich rice-growing districts, Bara, Parsa, and Rautahat. In the chaotic days of 1951, when local administration was almost nonexistent, rice disappeared almost completely from the Birganj market and the local people, angered by the hoarding of local merchants, rioted. A crowd estimated at 10,000 looted the stores and threatened merchants' lives. The army had to be called in to stop the looting. In the meantime, some of the merchants who had previously claimed that they were Nepalese citizens hurried to Delhi. On the plea that they were really Indian citizens, they requested the Indian government to intervene.[28]

Similar stories are told of merchants in Kathmandu. The majority of the large-scale merchants on New Road and Juddha Sarak, Kathmandu's business center, were of plains origin during the early 1950s. Of the twenty-five largest cloth merchants, thirteen were Marwaris and two were Rauniyars, another caste of merchants of plains origin. Only six were definitely of hill origin, three Newars and three hill Brahmins.[29] The fact that a high percentage of Kathmandu's large-scale merchants have been in the past and still are of plains origin has been a source of irritation to the people of the Valley, particularly the Newars, the traditional merchant class of the Valley and hills. The resentment was heightened in the early 1950s when Marwari merchants, who had earlier sought acceptability from the local population by claiming Nepalese citizenship, presented themselves to the

---

[28] *Samaj*, Mar. 3, 1958.
[29] This is based on a list of twenty-five cloth merchants permitted by the government to import cloth from India in 1952. See *Nepal Gazette*, vol. I, No. 29, Feb. 24, 1952. The assumption here is that the cloth merchants were among the largest merchants in Kathmandu at that time. Four names could not be identified by caste.

Indian Embassy for assistance in several disputes with the Nepalese government.[30]

From time to time during the 1950s, some Nepalese leaders were accused by their political rivals of holding dual citizenship. For example, after the election of 1959, members of parties in opposition to the Nepali Congress government claimed that Tulsi Giri and Nageshwar Prasad Singh held Indian as well as Nepalese citizenship. Both were prominent members of the Nepali Congress, and Giri was a deputy minister. Giri is of hill origin and Singh of plains origin, but both were born in the tarai. They were accused of having attempted to join an Indian delegation to a medical conference in the United States in 1954. Whether or not this particular accusation had any legitimacy, an occasional Nepali has used dual citizenship to his advantage in India. Dual citizenship was most frequently a problem during the early 1950s, before the administrative machinery in either Nepal or India was functioning well enough to prevent it. Along with other aspects of the citizenship problem, dual citizenship was debated most frequently during the intense political campaigning of the 1958–59 period. Since then, fewer plains people have been influential in Kathmandu. They have felt more constrained about supporting the interests of other plains people and have been more sensitive to the need to document their own citizenship carefully.

THE SPECTER OF MIGRATION

The demand for restrictive citizenship regulations has generally arisen during periods of large-scale migration, and the specter of significant, if not massive, migration of Indians into Nepal is undoubtedly one of the factors that contributed to the restrictive citizenship regulations incorporated in the 1962 Constitution of Nepal. Large-scale migration from eastern and southern Europe into the United States during the early twentieth century led to restrictive U.S. immigration legislation in 1924. Similar demands have recently received attention in Great Britain because of migration from South Asia and the West Indies. The flow of Tamils from South India has

[30]Resentment against Indian merchants in Kathmandu is of long standing. Jung Bahadur Rana had tried to force the Indian merchants out of the Valley just a hundred years earlier, and the merchants were successful in seeking intervention from the British Mission in Kathmandu. Letter from G. Ramsay to G. F. Edmonstone, Secretary to the Government of India, Foreign Dept., Dec. 26, 1856, Secret Correspondence No. 47–48, pp. 2066–78.

resulted in Ceylonese citizenship legislation which discriminates against the Tamils. Nepal's neighbors, Sikkim and Bhutan, have reacted similarly, ironically enough to the large-scale migration of hill people from Nepal.

Reports of large-scale migration from the Indian border states of Uttar Pradesh, Bihar, and West Bengal periodically find their way into the Kathmandu press, most of them reports of Muslims escaping the wrath of their Hindu neighbors. Only the vaguest estimates of the numbers of migrants accompany these reports. During the 1950s, there were occasional reports of large migrations of Muslims from Bengal into Jhapa district, but the 1961 census of Nepal indicates that little more than 3 percent of the district's population was Muslim. In 1972 the press reported that large numbers of "Bihari" Muslims were moving into Jhapa from Bangladesh because of persecution at the hands of Bengali Muslims following the establishment of an independent government there.[31] Although it is doubtful that significant migration of Muslims is occurring as a result of the Bangladesh crisis, data presented in chapter IV document the fact that there is substantial migration from India into some parts of the tarai. Because Nepalis have not yet attempted to study this migration systematically, there remains only a vague awareness of it in Kathmandu, but one which is disturbing to those most anxious to extend the dominance of the national hill culture into the tarai.

ANTI-INDIAN SENTIMENT AND CITIZENSHIP RESTRICTIONS

Anti-Indian feeling was certainly an important factor contributing to the citizenship restrictions included in the Constitution. As the liberal Citizenship Act of 1952 was partly the result of a very close relationship between India and Nepal at the time, so the citizenship articles in the 1962 Constitution were partly a response to antagonism between the two nations during the early 1960s. The 1950s and early 1960s encompass a period of traumatic father-son-type relations between India and Nepal—the paternalism of India and the dependency of Nepal during the early 1950s, followed in the late 1950s and early 1960s by a striving for independence, even defiance upon occasion, on Nepal's part. The period culminated in late 1962 with India's adjustment to the fact of Nepal's political maturity. The volumes that analyze this love-hate relationship are well known

[31] *Jana Jagriti Weekly*, Aug. 11, 1972.

to students of Himalayan affairs.[32] There is no need to retell the drama here. Indian leaders, including Jawaharlal Nehru, went on record disapproving King Mahendra's termination of Nepal's parliamentary system and, during the period 1961–62, the Indian government did little to discourage Nepali Congress rebels from attacking Nepalese government officials and installations from Indian territory. When the 1962 Constitution was being written, reinforcing the King's position at the apex of Nepal's political system, anti-Indian feeling was at its height in Kathmandu. The citizenship restrictions are to some extent at least an expression of a kind of nationalism fostered by anti-Indian feeling, a reaction among Kathmandu's governing elite to Indian influence. And, in this respect, the plains people living in the tarai could not escape their association with India.

[32]See Girilal Jain, *India Meets China in Nepal* (Bombay, 1959), Anirudha Gupta, *Politics in Nepal* (Bombay, 1964), Joshi and Rose, *Democratic Innovations in Nepal*, and Rose, *Nepal*.

Chapter VI

THE POLITICS OF LANGUAGE

The Nepali language has been developing for at least 700 years, perhaps longer, and now it is a major component of Nepalese nationalism. The language was carried along the footpaths which have served as trade routes through the hill region and, more recently, it has spread into all parts of the country through the educational system. As nationalism became a force in the 1950s and national leaders began to encourage the teaching of Nepali in the schools, representatives of other language groups resisted, and the language question became a hotly debated political issue. As in many other developing nations, language became a stumbling block along the road to national unification.

The end of Rana rule in 1951 brought with it a whole series of changes, perhaps none more pronounced than those in the field of education. A new generation of young Nepalese leaders came into prominence in 1951. Although most of them had studied English in India during the 1940s and knew it well, they were nationalists, anxious to establish for Nepal its own national image. For most of them, those with Nepali as their mother tongue, this included the implementation of Nepali-language instruction in the schools and colleges that began to mushroom during the immediate post-Rana period. The first effort to organize a national educational system began in 1954 with the appointment of a National Education Planning Commission. In 1956 the Commission published its report, *Education in Nepal*. Much of the report was subsequently ignored, but the following recommendations formed the basis for the government's language policy:

> Nepali should be the medium of instruction, exclusively from the third grade on, and as much as possible in the first two grades.
> No other languages should be taught, even optionally, in the primary school because: few children will have need for them, they would hinder the teaching of Nepali. ....[1]

[1]Nepal, National Education Planning Commission, *Education in Nepal* (Kathmandu, 1956), p. 104.

Although a few of the fifty Commission members objected to the use of Nepali as the sole medium of instruction, the majority listed the justifications for their recommendation as follows:

> 1. If the national language is made the medium of instruction, [this would avoid] preparing textbooks in many languages. ...
> 2. It will be imperative to adopt a general policy to give status to a language which is spoken by the majority of the people.
> 3. The national language will be easier to learn than Hindi. No truly Hindi-speaking people inhabit any part of the country.
> 4. As an official language for a long time, Nepali has been current everywhere and therefore is not difficult for the local people to understand.
> 5. ... The different communities of Nepal, easily understand the language. ...
> 6. Nepali bears a closer affinity with Hindi than any other local language.
> 7. ... To solve the problems of multiplicity of language, stress and importance will have to be laid on one language, if the integrity and sovereignty of Nepal is to be maintained.[2]

Justifications 1 and 6 are certainly valid. Nepali may be an easier language to learn than Hindi, as stated in point 3, primarily because Nepali does not have the more complex gender system of Hindi, but, as will be documented later in this chapter, Hindi is already spoken by a significant portion of the tarai population. The most important points are 2 and 7, because they base the language recommendations upon nationalistic considerations.

GOVERNMENT LANGUAGE POLICY AND THE LANGUAGE CONTROVERSY, 1956–58

Although the first jarring notes of the language controversy were not heard until 1956, sentiment against imposition of Nepali on the plains people of the tarai began to be voiced as early as 1951. In that year, the Nepal Tarai Congress was organized under the leadership of Vedananda Jha. The party objectives were stated to be: (a) establishment of an autonomous tarai state; (b) recognition of Hindi as a state language; and (c) adequate employment of tarai people in the Nepal civil service.[3]

[2]*Ibid.*, pp. 62–63.
[3]*Statesman*, May 4, 1953, p. 7.

The genesis of the Tarai Congress is to be found in the tarai's status as a quasi-colony during the Shah and Rana periods. A state of near-anarchy resulting from the collapse of local administration at the time of the revolution gave Tarai Congress leaders the courage to advocate regional autonomy within the Nepalese national structure. Because the government was paralyzed by factional strife, party leaders did not have to fear that their radical demands would be suppressed. Not until 1953 was the government in Kathmandu stable enough to begin reconstructing local administration. The Kathmandu leadership quite naturally viewed with alarm these embryonic separatist sentiments. Once the government had reestablished local control, the Tarai Congress demand for an autonomous state became muted and was dropped from the party's list of demands.

Although Hindi had been advocated as a second national language since 1951, not until 1956 was Nepalese nationalism articulated clearly enough to challenge the role of Hindi and other plains languages in the tarai. Since establishment of schools in the tarai was not permitted during the Rana period, the termination of Rana rule released a burst of school-building activity in the region. A few of these schools were constructed for the Nepali-speaking children of government officials in district administrative centers of the tarai, and these were staffed by Nepali-speaking teachers. Few Nepali-speaking teachers settled in the tarai because it was as unattractive to them as to the agriculturalists from the hills. As a result, most of the schools were established by plains people for their own children. Because there were few qualified teachers among the plains people of the tarai, the founders of these schools were forced to recruit many of their teachers from India. This was not difficult, because of the large number of educated but unemployed young men in the towns and cities of northern Bihar and Uttar Pradesh. In addition, the tarai was climatically and culturally more familiar to the Indian teachers than to their Nepalese counterparts from the hills.

It is difficult to assess the extent to which the National Education Planning Commission report was responsible for provoking the language controversy. Even before the report was officially released, its contents became public knowledge. Pro-Hindi meetings to protest the language recommendations were held in a number of tarai towns during the spring of 1956,[4] but it was not until the summer of 1957 that the language controversy took on serious proportions. In the

[4] *Nepal Samachar,* June 30, 1956.

area around Biratnagar, an ultranationalistic group of hill people called the Nepali Pracharini Sabha (Nepali Publicity Organization) began distributing pamphlets, displaying posters and collecting signatures as part of a campaign to pressure government authorities into using Nepali for local administrative business. Tarai Congress leaders warned government officials that the Nepali Pracharini Sabha was creating conflict between the majority of plains people and the Nepali-speaking minority in the Biratnagar area. The Nepali Pracharini Sabha responded by sending a delegation to Kathmandu to acquaint the government with the intransigence of both local officials and the Hindi advocates. In early September, there were reports of "incidents" resulting from the controversy in the eastern tarai towns of Biratnagar, Rangeli, and Dharan.[5]

In July, the King had appointed K. I. Singh Prime Minister and, in October, the K. I. Singh ministry issued a directive, inspired at least in part by the Commission's report. It ordered all schools to use Nepali as the medium of instruction, unless they received Education Ministry permission to use another language. In addition, it ordered all teachers to demonstrate within two years their ability to use Nepali for instructional purposes, and also ordered all teachers to provide evidence of Nepali citizenship within six months.[6]

The directive was fuel for the fire. An immediate outcry was heard from political leaders in the tarai and public meetings were organized in towns throughout the region. At these meetings, several themes ran through the protest speeches. First, the directive was seen as a government effort to force the hill culture upon the plains people. Second, the rights of the plains people were being undermined because they were being prevented from using the language most familiar to them. Third, the decision was undemocratic, since representatives of the tarai population had no voice in the policy-making process. And fourth, the directive would destroy the unity of the nation by creating dissension between the plains people and the hill people. The Tarai Congress announced its decision to organize a "Save Hindi" campaign, and Save Hindi committees were formed in a number of tarai towns. Although it appears that the Tarai Congress leadership initiated the campaign, the issue cut across party lines, and leaders of the Nepali Congress, the Communist Party of Nepal, the United Democratic Party, and the Praja Parishad quickly joined the campaign.

[5]See *Commoner*, Aug. 13, 1957, p. 1; Sept. 3, 1957, p. 3; Sept. 5, 1957, p. 1.
[6]*Samaj*, Oct. 12, 1957.

The K. I. Singh government was forced to issue a press communique explaining that the introduction of Nepali into the schools of non-Nepali-speaking parts of the country was motivated by the need to develop a national language understood by all citizens and, through this common language, to unify the nation. The government attempted to soften the impact of the directive by insisting that Nepali be introduced immediately only into secondary schools and colleges and not until a later date into the primary schools. However, this did not mollify opponents of the directive. At the end of October, the government issued a ban on all forms of protest against the directive but, despite the ban, protests increased. The Birganj Save Hindi Committee issued an ultimatum to the government, threatening to begin "a struggle" against the directive on November 11 if it were not withdrawn by that time.[7] Committees in other tarai towns supported the Birganj Committee ultimatum and, when the ultimatum deadline expired, there was considerable turmoil throughout the region.

On November 14, King Mahendra dismissed the K. I. Singh government and assumed personal responsibility for Nepal's administration. It appeared to some tarai leaders that the King had been influenced by their agitation; others were not so sure. Their campaign had gained momentum that they did not wish to hinder simply because one of a succession of royally appointed prime ministers had been hustled from the scene. Meetings, protest marches and strikes in Biratnagar, Gaur, Rajbiraj, and Janakpur continued during the days immediately following the dismissal of the short-lived K. I. Singh government. The most serious incident occured in Biratnagar on November 19. The local Save Hindi Committee organized a procession of several thousand people, and the Nepali Pracharini Sabha staged a counter-demonstration. Two hostile crowds soon faced each other. The street fighting and looting that ensued was ended by police action. At least twenty-five were injured, a few seriously.[8]

After the Biratnagar incident, the language controversy began to lose the position it had held for a few months at the center of national political attention, even at the center of political activity in the tarai. The intensity of the feelings aroused in Biratnagar and the violence that resulted caused both pro-Hindi and pro-Nepali leaders to be more cautious in handling the issue. More important, the language controversy was gradually absorbed into the broader United Demo-

[7]*Commoner*, Nov. 1, 1957, p. 2.
[8]*Hindustan Times*, Nov. 23, 1957, p. 1.

cratic Front agitation of late November, December, and January. The language issue became one of a number of grievances important to this loose organization of political parties—the Nepali Congress, the Nepali National Congress, and the Praja Parishad. The major goal of the Front was to obtain from King Mahendra a pledge that national elections would be held. Pro-Hindi advocates were strong supporters of the Front, because they believed a popularly elected government would be much more responsive to their demands than the Palace-oriented governments that had come and gone during the preceding years.[9]

On December 15, the King reached a partial accommodation with the Front and issued a Royal Proclamation setting the national election date for February 1959. Agitation continued until February 1, 1958, over the question of whether the election would be to a parliamentary body or to a constitutional assembly. The pro-Hindi forces, along with other interest groups represented by the Front, felt that a constitution drawn up by a constitutional assembly would give them more power than one drawn up by King Mahendra and his advisors. On February 1, the King issued another Royal Proclamation ruling that the election would be for seats in Parliament. Although the Front reluctantly agreed to accept this, Hindi supporters, at least those who sought for Hindi the status of a second national language, were ultimately proven correct in their assumption that a constitution drawn up in the Palace would not satisfy their demand.

In January 1958, the Ministry of Education, now under the King's direct control, issued a second directive concerning language.[10] It made some concessions to the pro-Hindi forces, but none of the concessions were fundamental, and leadership in the tarai was not mollified. On one point the January 1958 Directive reversed its predecessor. It dropped the citizenship requirement for teachers, a requirement that could not have been enforced without closing down many tarai schools dependent on Indian teachers.[11]

The October 1957 Directive had stated that all schools would be required to adopt Nepali as the medium of instruction. The January 1958 Directive gave up attempts to carry out this requirement at the

[9]*Commoner*, Sept. 4, 1957, p. 1; Oct. 16, 1957, p. 1.
[10]Department of Education, "Notice," *Nepal Gazette*, vol. VII, No. 43, Feb. 10, 1958.
[11]See chapter VII for a breakdown of high-school and college teachers by place of birth. Although many of these teachers have managed to obtain citizenship certificates since 1958, few held such certificates at that time.

primary-school level, conceding the obvious fact that it would be impossible to find Nepali-speaking teachers for the hundreds of primary schools in the villages of the tarai. In 1967–68, 75 percent of primary-schools teachers were of plains origin, 47 percent of these plains Brahmins and Kayasthas.[12] Undoubtedly, the percentage of primary-school teachers of plains origin was even higher in the 1950s, before the substantial migration of hill people into the tarai. Most of these teachers have had little education themselves and little or no contact with the Nepali-speaking world.

It appeared that the January 1958 Directive made yet another concession, worded as follows: "In such schools [Middle and High Schools] about which the Board of Directors, formed according to the foresaid Section 2, decides that it is not feasible to make Nepali Language as the medium of instruction ... instruction shall be imparted through the medium of such language as decided by the Board of Directors for the time being and till another arrangement is made."[13] Although Nepali advocates applauded this as the compromise sufficient to make the language policy workable, Hindi advocates claimed it was no real concession, because another section of the directive put local school boards under the control of district-level government officials.[14] Inasmuch as the large majority of government officials posted in the tarai are Nepali-speakers,[15] the directive, in effect, changed not only the power structure of the boards but also in many cases their cultural composition, thus making them more amenable to the government's policy. An All-Nepal Save Hindi Committee delegation met the King in mid-February, requesting him to withdraw the January 1958 Directive. The delegation was assured by the King of his "proper consideration,"[16] but no action was taken to revoke or modify the directive.

[12]Data collected during field survey, 1967–68.

[13]*Nepal Gazettee*, vol. VII, No. 43, Feb. 10, 1958. Although this notice was published in February, public reaction to it began in mid-January, indicating that it was released to the public before it appeared in the *Nepal Gazette*. It will therefore be referred to as the January 1958 Directive.

[14]Section 2 of the January 1958 Directive stipulated that the Bada Hakim (District Commissioner), District Magistrate, or a nongovernment person appointed to represent them must serve as chairman of each school board. If the chairman appointed by the district officials was not in government service, a government official must also sit on the board. In addition, the Department of Education was given the right to appoint a member. Thus, two or three board members, including the chairman, would henceforth be associated directly or indirectly with the government.

[15]See documentation in section on politics at the district level in ch. VIII.

[16]*Commoner*, Feb. 13–16, 1958.

During 1958, the language controversy received less and less attention in the press and in public meetings, as pro-Hindi and pro-Nepali forces aligned themselves with political parties preparing for the national election on more generalized platforms aimed at attracting support from a broad cross-section of Nepal's population.

IS HINDI THE PREDOMINANT LANGUAGE OF THE TARAI?

This question was debated throughout the period just discussed and needs to be answered before proceeding further. The Hindi advocates answered the question with an emphatic yes and the Nepali advocates with an equally emphatic no. Some Nepali-speaking people maintained that Hindi was spoken nowhere in the tarai. On the other hand, Tarai Congress leader Vedananda Jha claimed that Hindi was the language of four million tarai inhabitants.[17] However, until the 1952/54 census of Nepal was released to the public, all judgments about the number of Hindi- and Nepali-speakers, and for that matter, all judgments about numbers of people living in the tarai, were based on personal estimates of claimants in the controversy.

Although the census was not ready for public distribution until late 1958, the language figures found their way into the press in January 1958, while the lingering echo of the language controversy could still be heard. The figure supported the contention of the Nepali advocates that few Hindi-speakers lived in the tarai. According to the 1952/54 census, 29 percent of the tarai population spoke as "mother tongues" plains languages such as Maithili, Bhojpuri, or Bengali, or plains-tribal languages such as Tharu, Rajbanshi, or Satar. By far the largest number of tarai inhabitants, 63 percent, were assigned to no recognized language classifications but appeared instead under headings such as "eastern tarai dialects," "mid-western tarai dialects," or "Morang Pradesh dialects." Another 5 percent were listed as speakers of Nepali or various hill-tribal languages such as Magar, Gurung, or Tamang. Most important for our consideration here is the fact that the census claimed that only 3 percent of the tarai population spoke Hindi as their mother tongue.[18]

[17]*Ibid.*, Nov. 22, 1957, p. 2.
[18]Nepal, Department of Statistics, *Census of Population, Nepal, 1952/54 A.D.* (Kathmandu, 1958), pp. 44–45. The population of the tarai, that is, of the seventeen outer-tarai census districts, was 2,386,813. Nepal's first census was taken in two stages, the first in eastern Nepal in 1952 and the second in western Nepal in 1954.

Since these figures undercut the position of Hindi advocates, their rejection of the validity of the statistics was predictable. Jha accused the Department of Statistics of manipulating its data for political purposes. Perhaps because of this criticism, the Department of Statistics discarded the vague dialect categories while preparing the 1961 census. Speakers of Maithili Pradesh and Morang Pradesh dialects were included in the Maithili category, those of eastern-tarai dialects in the Bhojpuri category, and those of mid-western and far-western-tarai dialects in a category called Awadhi. If Hindi advocates had hoped that more clearly defined categories would force the census enumerators to admit the existence of large numbers of Hindi speakers, they were disappointed. The number of Hindi-speakers in the entire country was reduced from 80,181 in the 1952/54 census to 2,867 in the 1961 census.[19]

In defending the 1961 language categories, administrators of the Department of Statistics, subsequently renamed the Central Bureau of Statistics, used a line of argument followed by South Indian academics who want to buttress their position against Hindi as the national language for India. According to them, Hindi is the language spoken by the people of Delhi, Lucknow, and Allahabad. The people living elsewhere in northwest India speak somewhat differently, therefore they do not speak Hindi but languages such as Rajasthani, Bihari or, as the Central Bureau of Statistics administrators claim, Awadhi. In this way, the opponents of Hindi reduce the language to its dialects and call the dialects languages.

In the past, pro-Hindi census administrators in New Delhi have included under the broad Hindi rubric both Maithili and Bhojpuri, which they claimed are dialects of Hindi. This was done for the same underlying political reasons that lead anti-Hindi South Indians and Nepalis to insist that Hindi dialects are separate languages. Because it is difficult to make purely linguistic distinctions between dialects and languages, nonlinguistic considerations are used, and this has fanned the language controversy in both countries. Now that the controversy is abating in India, census administrators there are changing their policy. It was reported that in the 1971 census they were taking Maithili and Bhojpuri out of the Hindi dialect category.

Pro-Nepali census administrators in Kathmandu have used a broad

---

[19]Nepal, Central Bureau of Statistics, *Census of Nepal,* 1961 (Kathmandu, 1967), vol. II, pp. 18–21. The categories Maithili and Bhojpuri were used in the 1952–54 census, but relatively small numbers of people were included in them.

definition for Nepali, including in the Nepali category speakers of various dialects and perhaps also some other languages, thus inflating the figures so that Nepali could be claimed as the mother tongue of a majority of the population. For example, in Baitadi and Dandeldhura, districts in the far-western hills bordering on the Kumaon region of India, the inhabitants are enumerated as Nepali-speakers, despite the fact that Nepali-speaking district administrators deputed from Kathmandu understand little of the local language. It appears that the people of Baitadi and Dandeldhura speak Kumauni, the language of 96 percent of the people in the contiguous Indian hill district of Almora.[20]

The 1961 census of Nepal reported 447,090 Awadhi-speakers living in the mid-western and far-western tarai.[21] According to a grouping of dialects in the 1961 census of India, Awadhi is one of six dialects comprised in the "Eastern Hindi" category.[22] The 1961 census of India lists only two districts of Uttar Pradesh in which Awadhi-speakers represent a significant percentage of the population— 24 percent in Lakhimpur Kheri district and 14 percent in Sitapur district.[23] Only one of these two districts, Lakhimpur Kheri, borders on Nepal, but it is contiguous to the far-western tarai districts where almost no Awadhi-speakers were recorded by the 1961 census of Nepal. In the mid-western tarai census districts of Palhi, Majkhanda, Khajahani, and Shivaraj, the census of Nepal reports that 87 percent or more of the people speak Awadhi. In contiguous border districts of Uttar Pradesh, the census of India reports that 85 percent or more of the people speak nondialect Hindi. Thus, those classified by the Nepalese census as Awadhi-speakers are obviously speaking the language classified by the Indian census as Hindi.

Members of Kathmandu's governing elite tend to view Hindi as the symbol of the plains people's resistance to the hill culture. This attitude has prevailed in the absence of an effective political-party system, during the periods when both the 1952/54 census and the 1961 census were produced. It is not improbable, therefore, that Nepalese census administrators in Kathmandu have found it difficult to avoid pressure to deemphasize the importance of Hindi in the

[20]*Census of India*, 1961, vol. XV (Uttar Pradesh), part II-C (ii), p. 271.
[21]*Census of Nepal*, 1961, vol. II, p. 18.
[22]*Census of India*, 1961, vol. I, part II-C (ii), p. clxix. The other five dialects are Bagheli, Chhattisgarhi, Kosali/Baiswari, Baghelkhandi/Riwai, and Laria/Khaltahi.
[23]Vol. XV, part II-C (ii), pp. 256–355.

tarai by putting Hindi-speakers into a "mid-western tarai dialects" category in 1952/54 and then into an "Awadhi" category in 1961.

Although Hindi advocates were justified in questioning the government's language data, they were not justified in claiming the vast numbers of Hindi speakers they did. The Central Bureau of Statistics figures for speakers of Awadhi, Hindi, and Urdu[24] combined represent only 17 percent of the tarai population. Even if this were an underestimate of 10 to 15 percent, the fact remains that people who speak Hindi as a mother tongue would still be a minority of the tarai population. The tarai has larger numbers of both Maithili and Bhojpuri speakers.

Hindi is important in the tarai because of its use as a second language by plains people who need to communicate across regional language barriers. It is the language in which business activity is carried on throughout most of the Gangetic plain, and it is used in the tarai wherever itinerant traders or craftsmen meet the local people. One hears Hindi spoken in the village markets and in the streets of the towns. It is the language used by tarai villagers when they travel to India, a relatively frequent experience for many who visit relatives or attend religious festivals.

Many people in the tarai and, incidentally, also in Kathmandu, learn Hindi by attending the Indian films that are shown in the local cinema halls. Although attendance at these Hindi films is the major pastime of only a small, affluent segment of the urban population in either the tarai or Kathmandu Valley, the Hindi films, with their singing, dancing, and melodramatic plots, represent an occasional enthralling escape from the mundane existence of all but the poorest villagers. Nepalis also learn Hindi by listening to All India Radio and reading Indian newspapers printed in Hindi.

The 1952/54 census of Nepal reported only 68,932 people in Nepal who could speak Hindi as a second language. Of this number only half, that is, less than 2 percent of the tarai population, were listed as people whose mother tongues were other plains languages.[25] This

---

[24]It is more difficult to define Urdu than to define Hindi. The Urdu of educated and urbanized Muslims contains many more words of Arabic and Persian derivation than does Hindi. However, Muslims and Hindus at the village level use about the same vocabulary for speaking. The difference is primarily in the script; literate Muslim villagers employ the Arabic script and literate Hindus the Devanagri.

[25]*Census of Population, Nepal*, 1952/54 *A.D.*, p. 47. At the time this study was completed, no 1961 census data were available on the use of various languages as second languages. It should be noted that questions about the use of second languages are

is a gross underenumeration. We can safely assume that at least half of all speakers of Maithili, Bhojpuri, Bengali, and the plains-tribal languages speak Hindi as a second language. Among the speakers of non-Hindi plains languages, almost all males and those females who have contact with the world beyond their villages speak Hindi as a second language. On the basis of these assumptions, it can be concluded that in 1961 at least 46 percent of the tarai population spoke Hindi as a second language. If one adds to the 46 percent the 17 percent who speak Hindi or dialects of Hindi as mother tongues, at least 63 percent of the tarai population spoke Hindi as either a first or second language in 1961. It is doubtful that this percentage has declined since 1961, given the growing commercial contacts between the tarai and India. Although the point was never made clear by either the pro-Hindi or anti-Hindi forces in the language controversy, the use of Hindi as a *lingua franca* of the tarai population rather than its use as a mother tongue made it a symbol around which regionally conscious political activity could be organized.

TO WHAT EXTENT IS NEPALI SPOKEN IN THE TARAI?

At the same time that a few Hindi advocates were claiming that nearly half the population of Nepal spoke Hindi, Nepali advocates were claiming that Nepali had become a generally understood second language in the tarai. The Nepalese historian, Dilli Raman Regmi, went so far as to say: "In the whole Nepal tarai, with the exception of some Indians who have recently migrated there, all the people, even along the Indian border, cannot only speak but also plead in Nepali in the courts."[26] As a result, debate about the use of Nepali among the tarai people became as much a part of the language controversy as the question about Hindi.

According to the 1952/54 census, only 4 percent of the tarai population spoke Nepali as a mother tongue. Another 1 percent spoke other hill languages as mother tongues, and it can be assumed that they spoke Nepali as a second language, because Nepali is the *lingua franca*

---

generally asked only of heads of households, and census enumerators tend to assume that women in these households have the same language facility. However, this is often not true, because women have less education and less contact with the world beyond the household and village in which the mother tongue is spoken. The data are therefore unreliable.

[26] Nepali National Congress, *Ghoshanapatra* (Kathmandu, n.d.).

of the hill region, except in the far-western hill districts bordering on India.[27] According to the 1961 census, 6 percent of the tarai population spoke Nepali as a mother tongue and another 2 percent spoke other hill languages.[28] Perhaps because of inadequate enumeration procedures, the 1952/54 census data on plains people who can speak Nepali seem to suffer from the same underenumeration as the data on those who speak Hindi as a second language. We can be sure that 5 percent of the tarai population, that is, the hill segment of the tarai population, spoke Nepali as a first or second language in 1952/54 and 8 percent in 1961. To this must be added the plains people who speak Nepali as a second language. Many plains people living in the towns and district centers have learned Nepali through contact with government administrators and the few Nepali-speaking businessmen. Villagers of plains origin who live in close contact with hill people settled along the fringe of the tarai forest, particularly in the far-eastern and far-western tarai districts, undoubtedly acquire a rudimentary knowledge of Nepali. Students attending high schools and colleges in the tarai are also learning Nepali. But, because there is only a small urbanized population in the tarai and because the far-eastern and far-western tarai districts are sparsely settled, it would be reasonable to estimate that no more than 20 percent of the plains people have learned the language. If the people of hill origin living in the tarai are included, perhaps 25 to 30 percent of the tarai population speak Nepali as a first or second language, certainly a much lower percentage than the 60 to 65 percent who speak Hindi as a first or second language.

When government administrators, scholars, and journalists in Kathmandu assert that Nepali is now understood by most of the people in the tarai, they mean that it is understood by most of the people they have contact with in the tarai: businessmen, students, teachers, office clerks, messengers, and those relatively wealthy and sophisticated villagers who serve as "brokers"[29] or communication links between other villagers and government officials in the district centers.

---

[27]*Census of Population, Nepal,* 1952/54 *A.D.*, pp. 44–47.
[28]*Census of Nepal,* 1961, vol. II, pp. 18–21.
[29]As F. G. Bailey calls them in *Politics and Social Change: Orissa in* 1959 (Berkeley, 1963), pp. 60–66.

THE LANGUAGE ISSUE DURING THE PERIOD OF THE NATIONAL ELECTION CAMPAIGN AND THE NEPALI CONGRESS GOVERNMENT, 1958–60

In preparation for the 1959 election, all political parties drew up platforms that contained statements on the language issue. These language planks closely resembled each other and, in some cases, were almost identical in wording. Although this appears surprising at first, a closer examination reveals few fundamental differences among the aims of most parties. The Nepali Congress language plank was typical of most others. It recognized Nepali as the national language, but encouraged the development of local languages at the same time.[30] K. I. Singh's United Democratic Party, which a year earlier had forbidden the use of regional languages even in primary education, now followed the line of other parties.[31] Even the ultra-nationalistic, hill-oriented Nepal Prajatantrik Mahasabha unbent on the language issue, conceding that "Our national language is Nepali and will remain Nepali, but proper regard will be given for the growth and presentation of the regional languages."[32] With minor variations, this was the approach of other parties except the Communist Party and the Tarai Congress.

The Communist Party produced a language plank that placed a greater emphasis than those of other parties on the importance of regional languages. The party agreed that Nepali should be the language of government business, but did not specify Nepali as the national language. It supported the use of Hindi as the medium of instruction in tarai schools, but stated that it would be "the correct national attitude to encourage all the languages of the country equally."[33]

The Tarai Congress advocated that both Hindi and Nepali be adopted as national languages. The party's election manifesto played down the importance of Nepali, referring to it as Gorkhali,[34] and suggested that Gorkhali had become important because it was "the court language" in Kathmandu. On the other hand, the manifesto

---

[30] Nepali Congress, *Chunao Ghoshanapatra* (Kathmandu, 1958).
[31] United Democratic Party, *Chunao Ghoshanapatra* (Kathmandu, 1958).
[32] *Nepal Prajatantrik Mahasabha ko Abashyakata ra Uddeshya* (Kathmandu, 1958).
[33] Nepal Communist Party, "Chunao Ghoshanapatra," *Navayug,* Nov. 26, 1958.
[34] Although Nepali was the court language of many minor hill kings in the past, it was commonly called Gorkhali after the kings of Gorkha conquered Nepal and this is still a commonly used term in the hill villages.

continued, Hindi is the only language understood by people throughout the tarai.[35]

Factionalism within the United Democratic Party illustrates how divided a party could become as a result of the language controversy. K. I. Singh, a Chetri and the mainspring of the party, while serving his brief tenure as prime minister, had been responsible for issuing the October 1957 Directive that brought the language controversy to a head and, in effect, put him at the forefront of the pro-Nepali forces. The party's general secretary, Kashi Prasad Shrivastava, a Kayastha from the mid-western tarai was, like Singh, a strong personality. After the United Democratic government issued its controversial directive, Shrivastava embarrassed his party by advocating Hindi as a second official language for Nepal. The language controversy caused considerable strain within the party at the time, but it was Shrivastava's view that prevailed a year later when the party prepared its election platform. The about-face of the United Democratic Party aptly illustrates how easily the professed goals of a party could be altered with a shift of its power base from the Palace to the popular electorate, and how much the tarai population served to gain from this shift.

Just a week before the voting, King Mahendra proclaimed a new Constitution. It was publicized as the product of a consensus among leaders of the major parties but, according to Joshi and Rose, it was the best accommodation that these leaders could make with the King. "The establishment of the Crown as the source of all legislative, executive, and judicial authority, an essential feature of the 1954 proclamation, was retained in the new Constitution."[36] One of the last and shortest articles of the 1959 Constitution affirmed that "The national language of Nepal shall be Nepali in the Devanagri script."[37] In effect, this resolved the issue before the election took place. It not only undercut the Tarai Congress effort to promote Hindi as a second national language but also deemphasized the importance of regional languages by neglecting to mention them.

Although the Constitution failed to mention Hindi, the question of its status arose as soon as Parliament was first convened in July 1959. A member of Parliament from the tarai presented a speech in Hindi, and another member objected. The Nepali Congress leadership sup-

[35] *Nepal Tarai Congress ko Ghoshanapatra* (Raxaul, 1957).
[36] Bhuwan Lal Joshi and Leo E. Rose, *Democratic Innovations in Nepal* (Berkeley, 1966), p. 285.
[37] *The Constitution of the Kingdom of Nepal* (Kathmandu, 1959), art. 70.

ported the use of Hindi and the debate lasted only briefly. Hindi as a language of communication in Parliament was thereafter accepted, if somewhat grudgingly in some quarters, throughout the eighteen months of the Nepali Congress government.

Except for Pashupati Nath Ghosh of the Praja Parishad and Kashi Prasad Shrivastava of the United Democratic Party, the leaders of the Save Hindi committees appear to have been drawn primarily from the Tarai Congress and Nepali Congress parties. Vedananda Jha and his Tarai Congress associates were the first to capitalize upon the issue, but Nepali Congress leaders gradually came to dominate many of the local committees and finally, in the person of Mahendra Narayan Nidhi, chairmanship of the All-Nepal Committee. This can be explained by the fact that a large number of the tarai's most active and experienced political leaders were drawn into the Nepali Congress ranks and by the fact that the party had superior organizational ability.

The Tarai Congress had attempted to capitalize upon the resentment felt by educated plains people toward Kathmandu officials and toward the encroachment of the hill culture upon their lives. However, after the party cast off its demand for a semiautonomous state, it became, in effect, a one-issue party. Other parties anxious to gain support in the tarai were forced to include in their platforms at least a few sympathetic words about the regional languages. In so doing, they defused the language controversy and undercut the *raison d'être* of the Tarai Congress. Throughout the period of campaigning, Jha claimed that the Tarai Congress had the support of the tarai population. However, the election proved a disaster for his party. All twenty-one candidates who ran on the party's ticket lost. Even more humiliating, they all lost their deposits of 250 rupees because they received less than 20 percent of the votes cast in their constituencies. Jha contested the election in his home district of Saptari and lost his deposit there.[38]

Most of the tarai people were illiterate and probably little concerned with the government's language policy because it did not affect the village primary schools. The directives of October 1957 and January 1958 had direct bearing only on the high schools and a few small colleges in tarai towns and, therefore, affected only the children of the urbanized business and landowning elites of the region. This segment of the tarai population was important, because from it were drawn most of those who became politically active. They were concerned about the language issue and felt that Hindi was a symbol of

[38]Nepal, Election Commission [Results of the First General Election, 1959].

the need for greater recognition of tarai interests. However, the results of the election proved that they were not attracted by the regional orientation of the Tarai Congress. They were willing to compromise some of their regional interests by joining nationally focused political parties in the hopes that thereby they would be able to obtain a share of the political power and, through their participation in the government, safeguard their more fundamental economic and political interests.

THE GOVERNMENT'S LANGUAGE POLICY SINCE 1960

In early 1961, King Mahendra appointed a nine-member National Education Commission to study the existing educational system and to submit suggestions for the adoption of "a national system of education." The Commission produced its report in the same year and recommended that Nepali be the medium of instruction for all grades.[39] The report was followed by the Education Code later in the year and the Education Act in 1962. Article 5 of the code put into law the Commission's recommendation regarding the medium of instruction.

In February 1962, the King elaborated on the government's policy, explaining that Nepali would be the medium of instruction in the high schools, and that this policy would be implemented only in stages.[40] Although the King's statement seemed to indicate that regional languages could be used as the medium of instruction in primary schools, the Education Act of 1962 confused the issue with the following declaration: "The medium of education in every school shall be the Nepali language. But the teaching and examination of any subject prescribed in the curriculum may be held in languages other than Nepali, in the prescribed manner."[41] Considering that the medium of education is the language of teaching and examination, the statement is contradictory and probably intentionally vague in order to permit exceptions to be made to what would otherwise be a strong stand.

The 1962 Constitution included a requirement that applicants for naturalization write as well as speak Nepali and, in 1964, the

[39]National Education Commission, *Report of the National Education Commission* (Kathmandu, 1961). (Trans. by Regmi Research Project.)

[40]A. S. Bhasin, *Documents on Nepal's Relations with India and China, 1949–66* (Bombay, 1970), p. 61.

[41]Act, *Nepal Gazette*, vol. XII, Extraordinary Issue No. 12, July 25, 1962.

Nepal Company Act required all companies, small as well as large, to maintain their records in either Nepali or English.[42] The majority of Nepal's registered companies are located in the tarai, primarily managed by people of plains origin, hence it is likely that many have records that are kept in Hindi or some other plains language. Inasmuch as most Nepalese government officials speak and understand Hindi,[43] the government's refusal to recognize Hindi for the use of company records is a pointed assertion of national consciousness.

One minor reaction to the government's language policy occurred in 1965, and it was not the Hindi but the Newari advocates who were heard publicly. In April of that year, Radio Nepal terminated its daily ten-minute news broadcasts in Newari and Hindi. A number of Newari organizations reacted indignantly, but not a note of protest was heard from the tarai.[44]

Thus, soon after the ouster of the Nepali Congress government, King Mahendra's government took an unequivocal stand on the language issue, confirming the January 1958 Directive that had been issued by a preelection government under his control. The type of Nepalese nationalism represented by the requirement that Nepali be used outside the Nepali-speaking region of Nepal has received its most forceful support from the King. In an atmosphere that has discouraged criticism of government policy since December 1960, no public protest has been raised in the tarai. Dissatisfaction has remained a muted, privately expressed sentiment.

---

[42]"Nepal Company Act 1964," *Nepal Gazette*, vol. XIV, Extraordinary Issue No. 18A, Nov. 16, 1964.

[43]Many of them have studied in Indian colleges and universities.

[44]*Matribhumi Weekly*, Apr. 22, 1965. Some tension has long existed between advocates of Nepali and Newari, dating back to 1769, when the Newari-speaking people of the Valley were conquered by Nepali-speaking people from the western hills. During the Rana period, Newari, then called Nepal Bhasha, or language of Nepal, was vigorously suppressed. Since the 1951 revolution, some revival of Newari has occurred in Kathmandu, Bhaktapur, and Patan, the urban centers of the Valley where Newars are concentrated. The Nepali-Hindi controversy spurred Newari advocates to increased activity in support of their language. At the time of the Biratnagar incident, for example, the Patan District Committee of the Nepal National Students' Federation demanded that Newari be used in the schools of Patan. See *Sahi Sandesh*, Nov. 19, 1957.

Chapter VII

LANGUAGE, COMMUNICATION, AND NATIONAL INTEGRATION

An essential aspect of the national-integration or nation-building process is the definition and articulation of economic, social, and political ideals and goals for the new nation. In Nepal, this process has been going on during the past several decades among the educated Nepalis living in Kathmandu and a few other urban centers. These goals must now be communicated to the rest of the nation's inhabitants, which is a difficult task because most Nepalis live in relatively isolated villages. In regions of the country where people do not speak Nepali, there is an added dimension to the problem. The government can communicate with Nepali-speaking villagers through various channels: radio, newspapers, local-government officials' personal contact with villagers, and the educational system. But the government must also be willing to communicate in languages other than Nepali if it hopes to do so effectively with most tarai villagers.

THE PRESS AND THE RADIO

Low literacy rates make it difficult, but not impossible, for the government to communicate with villagers through the printed word. According to the 1952/54 census, only 4 percent of the population of school age or older could read or write a letter. Although the rate has undoubtedly increased significantly since then, Nepal still has one of the lowest literacy rates in the world. Rates in various subregions of the tarai vary considerably, depending upon the extent of urbanization. In Mahottari-Dhanusha, perhaps the most-urbanized tarai district, the literacy rate was 9 percent. In Kailali, where there is no urbanization and the few inhabitants are predominantly tribal people living in settlements isolated from the rest of the world by dense forest, it was 2 percent.[1] What still makes some communication possible is

[1] Nepal, Department of Statistics, *Census of Population, Nepal,* 1952/54 A.D. (Kathmandu, 1958), pp. 39–41. The 1961 census data on literacy were not available at the time this study was completed.

the tradition of reading by literate villagers to illiterate neighbors.

Although it is easier to deliver mail in the tarai than in the hill region, mail service in the tarai does not yet appear to have been established effectively, even during the dry season. Literate villagers throughout the region complain that they receive only an occasional issue of newspapers and magazines to which they subscribe. This limits the government's ability to communicate by printed word beyond the limits of the tarai's urban centers, where literacy is higher and the mail-delivery system is better established. Whatever the reasons, circulation of newspapers in tarai villages is quite limited, as verified by the following statistics. In the eighty-one villages of the 1967–68 field survey, individuals in only ten villages were receiving newspapers. Five English-language papers published in India were received in four villages, seven Hindi language papers published in India were received in six villages, the government's Nepali-language daily, *Gorkhapatra*, published in Kathmandu, went to five villages, and nongovernment Nepali publications[2] to three villages.

These statistics are instructive. Only ten villages (12 percent of the sample) received any publications, and in only half of these villages did any individual subscribe to the government-published paper. Of the twenty newspapers received in the ten villages, thirteen were published in India; these papers naturally focus on Indian rather than Nepalese events. Of course, these papers also tend to present the Indian point of view in matters of mutual concern to the two governments. Of the twenty papers, eight were Nepali-language publications, seven were in Hindi, and five were in English. Although the government publishes newspapers and magazines in Nepali and English, it does not publish in Hindi or in other tarai languages. It is difficult for the government newspapers to compete with many of those published in India because the latter, particularly the English-language papers, tend to be much more comprehensive in their coverage of international news. This is particularly the case in urban centers of the tarai, where many members of economic elite groups speak English and have an interest in international affairs. However, the government could compete more effectively with the Indian press in the tarai villages if it modified its language policy, published also in Hindi, Maithili, and Bhojpuri, and concentrated on events

---

[2] *Nepal Sandesh* (Patna, India), *Dhanuka* (Janakpur, Nepal), and *Ruprekha* (Kathmandu).

of local interest. Of course, improved mail delivery would also be imperative.

The radio provides the government with at least a partial solution to the problem of illiteracy and the logistical difficulties of mail delivery. By radio, the government can communicate with villagers who can not read, and communication can take place even during the monsoon season, when bullock-cart tracks are flooded and bridges are in disrepair. Transistorized radios have become available in the shops of Kathmandu and major Indian cities, and they are now prestige symbols in the homes of wealthy villagers. These radios provide semi-public channels of communication between villagers and the outside world. It is not uncommon for villagers to gather, particularly at the end of the day, in the courtyard of a large landowner to listen to Indian (Hindi) film music and farm reports.

As part of the 1967–68 field survey, village headmen were asked whether there were any radios in their villages. Headmen in fifty-six of the eighty-one villages surveyed, 69 percent of the sample, answered affirmatively. However, some underenumeration is likely. Radios are subject to an annual tax, which villagers seldom pay, and headmen were therefore occasionally hesitant to answer this question. In Kapilabastu district, where the Ukhada land reforms had been causing considerable tension between villagers and government officials at the time of the survey, there was particular reluctance to answer questions related in any way to land ownership or taxation. In only 35 percent of the sample villages in the district were radios reported, a suspiciously low figure as compared with other districts surveyed. Even in the relatively poor district of Kailali, there were radios in 63 percent of the sample villages. In the more prosperous districts, Mahottari-Dhanusha and Bara, the respective percentages were 79 and 80. Ninety percent of Jhapa's sample villages had radios. No attempt was made to ascertain the number of radios in each village, because of the sensitivity of the question. Nevertheless, if the discordant sounds of competing Hindi film songs heard above the rooftops in the larger and more prosperous villages is any measure, some of these villages had a number of radios.

Headmen were asked which radio stations villagers listened to. In the 56 villages with radios, various stations were mentioned, some many times, for a total of 130 responses.[3] Of these responses, 76 were

[3] In some villages, headmen listed only one or two stations, in other villages three or four. No attempt was made to rank these responses in terms of villagers' listening preference or listening frequency.

All India Radio or its regional stations at Patna, Lucknow, Calcutta, or Kurseong in Darjeeling district. Radio Nepal was mentioned 42 times, Radio Ceylon 8 times, and each of the following once: Radio Sikkim, Moscow, B.B.C., and Voice of America. Thus, of the 130 responses, 59 percent were All India Radio, 32 percent Radio Nepal, and the other 9 percent stations in other countries.

Most popular with the villagers seemed to be programs of Indian film music. Villagers mentioned listening most to news on Radio Nepal. It is not clear why Radio Nepal music programs did not seem to be very popular, even among the villagers of hill origin. Possibly Indian film music is not broadcast as much by Radio Nepal as by All India Radio. Villagers talked at greatest length and with the most enthusiasm about All India Radio evening programs in the regional languages. These programs are broadcast from Delhi and Lucknow in Hindi, from Patna in Maithili and Bhojpuri, from Calcutta in Bengali, and from Kurseong in Nepali, and they focus upon farming problems, local customs, festivals, and other information of interest to people in the various linguistic regions.[4]

Despite the fact that the Nepalese government appears to reach a considerably larger segment of the tarai population by radio than through its publications, it is communicating less effectively than the Indian government through its All India Radio programs, especially since the Nepalese government terminated its ten-minute news broadcasts in Hindi and Newari. The Nepalese government may be unaware of the popularity of All India Radio regional-language broadcasts, but as a result of its failure to broadcast similar programs, it is losing an opportunity to establish a more significant channel of communication. If regional-language programs could be produced attractively enough to win an audience in the tarai, they could be used to inform large numbers of people about government policies and development programs and could begin to build a sense of national identity among many who heretofore have had little contact with Nepalese national concepts. The government can not persuade Hindi, Maithili, and Bhojpuri speakers to learn Nepali by broadcasting programs in Nepali only. As long as people have the option to tune in these regional-language programs broadcast by All India Radio, the government only succeeds in cutting itself off from these people, thereby eliminating

[4]There may have been some overreporting of Radio Nepal because village headmen usually thought that my assistant and I were associated with the Nepalese government and some appeared anxious to please us by mentioning Radio Nepal.

perhaps the most effective form of communication presently available.

GOVERNMENT OFFICIALS' CONTACT WITH VILLAGERS

Although radio may be the government's best channel of communication with villagers at present, direct personal contact between local-government officials and villagers has the potential of even more impact. Although district-level administration has improved greatly since the Rana period, it is still severely hampered by a rudimentary transportation system. Motorized travel is still difficult and sometimes impossible, even during the dry season. Bullock-cart tracks, which serve as the only roads in most parts of the tarai, are intersected by irrigation ditches and occasionally disappear into streams and rivers. Tracks to villages in the forest narrow to footpaths. During the monsoon season, the tarai becomes a sea of mud, and villages are cut off to all forms of transportation except by elephant and arduous foot travel.

As the transportation system is improved, there will be continually more contact between government officials and the villagers. Of course, tax collectors and law-enforcement officers have been familiar to generations of villagers, but now other types of government officials are beginning to make their appearance. During the 1967–68 field survey, the headmen of seventeen villages in Bara district were asked how frequently various types of government officials visited their villages. Since the data were based solely on memory, reliability is limited, but they do provide some indication of the frequency of contact between government officials and villagers.[5] In 1967–68, the zonal commissioner was the most important official in a group of districts called a zone. The most important official in each district was the chief development officer. The chief development officer of Bara district had visited five of the seventeen villages. Because there are hundreds of villages in a district, the chief development officer can get to only a few of them in any given year.

More important in terms of direct contact with villagers are the middle-level officials, who are the land-reform and cooperative-program officers. Land-reform officers had visited ten of the seventeen villages, once or twice a month in some cases. Cooperative inspectors

[5]Because the village headmen in the sample villages of Bara found it difficult to recall the frequency of visits by government officials, no attempt was made to collect corresponding data in the other four districts surveyed.

had visited eight of the seventeen villages, also rather frequently in some cases. These officials are attempting to implement government programs, hence they must be informative and effective in persuading villagers to cooperate.[6]

Potentially the most effective communicators of government policy are the lower-level government workers called junior technical assistants, who are individuals assigned as agricultural advisors to groups of villages. They live in the villages they serve and are responsible for creating a link between demands for agricultural improvement in their villages and district-level supply centers for seed, fertilizer, and farm implements. Junior technical assistants lived in nine of the seventeen villages and regularly visited five others. Only three of the seventeen villages received none of their attention. The majority of junior technical assistants in the tarai are semiurbanized young men of plains origin. Because of their at least superficial urbanization and their extremely low salaries, they tend to be unenthusiastic about their jobs. Also, because they are on the lower rungs of the government-employee ladder, they are not in close contact with the pulse of government activity and usually are not able to articulate government policy to villagers as clearly as some of the middle-level officials. On the other hand, they have visited Kathmandu, can speak Nepali, and understand the workings of the panchayat system. Therefore, along with the various other officials who visit villages less frequently, they are beginning to create a significant channel of communication to the villagers.

Language is probably not as great a barrier to personal communication between government officials (most of whom are Nepali-speaking hill Brahmins, Chetris, and Newars) and tarai villagers as might be expected. Many of the officials have studied in India or travelled extensively there and have learned Hindi as a second language. However, officials tend to post in Nepali announcements of government policies or programs. More often than not, these announcements, in highly Sanskritized Nepali, can not be deciphered by villagers. Even though printed announcements have limited value among largely illiterate populations, the refusal of the government to

[6]There have been numerous administrative changes since the field survey. The chief development officer has now received some of the law-enforcement powers of the zonal commissioner. The land-reform program will eventually be completed and the land-reform officers withdrawn. The cooperative program has not proved to be successful, and the cooperative inspectors may be less in evidence than they were in 1967–68.

print such announcements in the regional languages limits further its ability to communicate with the village population of the tarai.

THE INTEGRATIVE FUNCTION OF THE EDUCATIONAL SYSTEM

A nation in which all citizens speak the same language is one that naturally avoids a whole set of language-oriented administrative problems and the disruptive conflicts of language factionalism. Nevertheless, there are nations which have welded diverse cultural groups into a stable polity despite the absence of a language that is shared by all or even the majority of the population. Nepal has an advantage over many other nations in this respect. A majority of Nepal's inhabitants speak Nepali either as a mother tongue or a second language. Even if there were no policy to encourage the learning of Nepali, gradually more people in both the hill region and the tarai would learn the language through the slow process of acculturation. Government policy seems to be based at present upon the assumption that ability to speak Nepali is associated with first-class citizenship. Although Nepali is a primary symbol of Nepalese nationalism, the two need not be viewed as inseparable. As demonstrated in other multilanguage nations, loyalty to the nation need not be tied to the ability to speak the designated national language. Whatever the assumptions that underlie the government's language policy, the government is pushing ahead with efforts to introduce Nepali into the tarai schools, and it is useful to assess the outcome of this effort.

Before the government could expect Nepali to be taught in tarai schools, it had to ensure that teachers could use the language and that Nepali-language teaching materials would be available to teachers and students. The October 1957 Directive stipulated that schools should start using Nepali-language textbooks immediately. However, few Nepali textbooks were being used at that time, even in Kathmandu Valley, and no system had been developed for their distribution outside the Valley. Most of the textbooks were written in Hindi or English and published in India. The National Education Commission in its 1961 report recommended that textbooks be written by Nepalese citizens and published by Nepalese publishers, and that a committee of Nepalese educators judge the quality of the books.[7] In 1964 the government passed the Nepali Language Publication Corporation

[7]National Education Commission, *Report of the National Education Commission* (Kathmandu, 1961), pp. 15–16. (Trans. by Regmi Research Project.)

Act to expedite the work of producing educational materials in Nepali. Although materials in Nepali are now being produced by the government, no effective system of distribution has yet been devised. Private book publishers, spurred by the profit motive, have been more successful in distributing their own books but, without the educational expertise of the government publishers, the books produced by private publishers have tended to be inferior translations of Hindi and English books, which often reflect the political and cultural values of the latter.

Nepali-language textbooks are now being used extensively in the high schools of the tarai, but apparently this textbook policy has not yet been fully implemented in the colleges of the tarai or indeed elsewhere in Nepal. The problem is a familiar one to educators in many developing countries. The Nepali language does not have the vocabulary needed for translation of many college-level textbooks, particularly those in the scientific fields, because the language is a product of a culture which has had no technological orientation until recently.

The effectiveness of the language policy in the tarai naturally depends to a large extent on the language proficiency of the teachers. In the absence of specific data about the proficiency of teachers, only limited assumptions can be made in this regard, on the basis of information about the cultural backgrounds of teachers. The following data were collected about 214 teachers in 21 high schools of 5 tarai towns: 51 percent of them were hill people, and the remaining 49 percent plains people. Nineteen percent of all the teachers in the survey were plains people born in the tarai and 30 percent of the total were plains people born in India. It is unlikely that any of the plains people born in India speak enough Nepali to use it for teaching purposes, because most, if not all, of them were educated in India and had little contact with Nepali until they were hired as teachers. The same may even be true of many of the teachers of plains origin born in the tarai. Between 30 and 49 percent of the teachers in the survey probably had little or no knowledge of Nepali.[8]

The data for college teachers present a somewhat different picture. Of the sixty teachers in four colleges, only 27 percent were of hill origin. Among the teachers of plains origin, 28 percent were born in

[8]The data were collected during 1966 and 1967 from two high schools in Bhadrapur, Jhapa district; twelve in Biratnagar, Morang district; four in Rajbiraj, Saptari district; one in Malangwa, Sarlahi district; and two in Taulihawa, Kapilabastu District. The twenty-one high schools were all the high schools in the five towns at the time of the survey.

the tarai and 45 percent in India. Again, assuming that most of the teachers of plains origin born in the tarai could speak Nepali, still about half of the college teachers probably had little or no knowledge of Nepali.[9] Thus, there is a much higher percentage of hill people among high-school teachers than among college teachers—51 percent of the former compared with 27 percent of the latter. Fewer hill people have the advanced degrees needed for teaching at the college level, and those who are qualified prefer to teach in Kathmandu. For this reason, colleges in the tarai more than high schools find it necessary to recruit teachers from India. The greater number of Nepali-speaking teachers and the greater accessibility of Nepali-language textbooks in the high schools indicate that students of plains origin have more contact with the hill culture at the high-school level than at any other.

It is at the primary-school level that the government encounters the greatest difficulty. This is verified by the following data about 96 teachers in the primary schools of the eighty-one villages surveyed in 1967 and 1968. Of these, 87 percent were plains people, most of whom received their education in India or the high schools of the tarai before the new language policy was implemented. Consequently, few of them can speak Nepali. Although this situation will begin to change as graduates from high schools with the new Nepali curriculum become primary-school teachers, it will take considerably more time before enough primary-school teachers familiar with Nepali will be available to make an impact at this level.

The progress being made at the high-school and college level is reinforced by the rapid increase in the percentage of students of hill origin enrolled. The following data were collected from the twenty-one high schools and four colleges already mentioned: 43 percent of the high-school students and 51 percent of the college students are now of hill origin.[10] The percentage of students of hill origin is much higher in both the high schools and colleges than the percentage of hill people in the tarai population, a little more than the 8 percent recorded in the 1961 census of Nepal.

Because of the Nepali-language curriculum, children of upper- and business-caste plains people, who represented the large majority

[9]The data were collected in 1966 from one college in each of the following towns: Bhadrapur, Biratnagar, Rajbiraj, and Janakpur, all in the eastern tarai. They were the only colleges in these towns at the time of the survey.

[10]These data were gathered from the registration books in these institutions. Principals, headmasters, and teachers assisted with the caste identifications in doubtful cases.

of students in these institutions during the 1950s, are now enrolling in institutions across the border in India. This exodus is explained by the fact that they find it much easier to study in institutions that use their mother tongues as the medium of instruction. For example, large numbers of students from the Maithili-speaking subregion of the tarai enroll in northern Bihar colleges at Madhuwani, Darbhanga, Muzaffarpur, Sitamarhi, Motihari, and Jaynagar, where Hindi is the medium of instruction and where some subjects can be studied in Maithili. In the recently established college at Jaynagar, an Indian railhead south of Mahottari district, about 50 percent of the students come from Mahottari and adjacent tarai districts. A college established at Bhadrapur in Jhapa district has been struggling to survive because most of the college-bound students of the district are Bengali-speakers and find it easier to study in the colleges of West Bengal.

On the other hand, the children of Nepali-speaking hill people, mostly urbanized hill Brahmins, Chetris, and Newars in government service and business, now find the curriculum in the tarai high schools and colleges easier. These three groups are predominantly middle class in orientation and place a high value on education as a means of obtaining economic resources and social status. Now, instead of being sent to Kathmandu to live with relatives while obtaining their education, children from these groups are being enrolled in local institutions. Because of the increased numbers of Nepali-speaking students, the use of Nepali in the classroom and in nonclassroom-related activities is encouraged, and this in turn discourages the enrollment of students who speak Hindi and other plains languages. Evidently, the education system has become an effective instrument for Nepalization of the tarai.

Chapter VIII

POLITICS IN THE NEPALESE TRADITION

In the course of the past several hundred years, Nepal has experienced a succession of political systems: a monarchy under the Shah kings (1769–1846), an oligarchy under the Rana prime ministers (1846–1951), an uncertain period of government shared by the monarchy and various political parties (1951–59), a parliamentary system (1959–60), and reestablishment of absolute monarchy (since 1960). Notwithstanding the variety of governmental forms, many of the same economic and cultural factors have determined the tenor of Nepalese politics throughout. In the following sections of this chapter, the formal structure of the current political system will be analyzed, along with the socioeconomic factors that determine political behavior. This analysis provides the framework for an assessment of the extent to which the population of the tarai is being integrated into the nation's political life.

ORIGIN AND STRUCTURE OF THE PANCHAYAT SYSTEM

King Mahendra, with army support, terminated the Nepali Congress government in December 1960 and established a government under his direct control. This represented "an authoritarian resolution of the basic conflict between two antithetical by-products of the 1950 Revolution,"[1] a reformist, democratically oriented elite and a strong monarch. During the next two years, the King searched for a governmental structure that would include some elements of popular government and yet would insure support for his authoritarian resolution. He appointed a committee to study various political institutional models. "The results of these and other inquiries, as formalized in the Constitution King Mahendra bestowed on the country on December 16, 1962, was a rather odd but ingenious combination of

[1] Bhuwan Lal Joshi and Leo E. Rose, *Democratic Innovations in Nepal* (Berkeley, 1966), p. 392.

certain features of the 'National Guidance' system in Egypt and Indonesia, the 'Basic Democracy' system in Pakistan, the 'Class Organization' system in Egypt and Yugoslavia, and the panchayat system in operation in several Indian states."[2] In the Royal Proclamation promulgating the new Constitution, King Mahendra inferred that the parliamentary system, being a foreign creation, was not as much in "step with the history and traditions of the country"[3] as the panchayat system.

Panchayat means council or assembly. Ever since the caste system took hold in the villages of India and Nepal, each caste group has formed its own panchayat or council of elders. These may include the caste members of only one village or a number of neighboring villages. When problems involving the relationship between individuals from different caste groups arise in a village, the elders of the different castes in that village gather in an informal body, the village panchayat, to solve these problems. There is no evidence that any of the previous governments in Nepal's history attempted to systematize or formalize these local bodies and, to the extent that the current system above the village level is an adaptation of Indian, Pakistani, Indonesian, Egyptian, and Yugoslavian systems, one wonders how much more Nepalese it is than the parliamentary system borrowed from the British. Nevertheless, by suggesting that the panchayat system had its roots deep in Nepal's history, the King was able to tap an essential source of support in the vital stirrings of nascent Nepalese nationalism.

The panchayat system, as set out in the 1962 Constitution, appears in diagram 1. Since the Constitution was written, zonal panchayats have been eliminated and a few other lesser modifications in the system have also been made. However, its basic structure remains the same, with the King at the top, supported by two separate four-tiered structures, one for class organizations and one for panchayats. The government has had difficulty activating the class organizations at all levels, but particularly below the district level, primarily because the classes as listed in the Constitution, i.e., peasants, youth, women, industrial laborers, ex-servicemen, and college graduates, bear little resemblance to the real class structure of Nepalese society. The economic classes are based chiefly on ownership of land, and the cultural classes are those of the caste system. To the extent that the class

[2]*Ibid.*, p. 396.
[3]*Proclamations, Speeches and Messages of H. M. King Mahendra Bir Bikram Shah Deva*, vol. II (Kathmandu, 1967), p. 149.

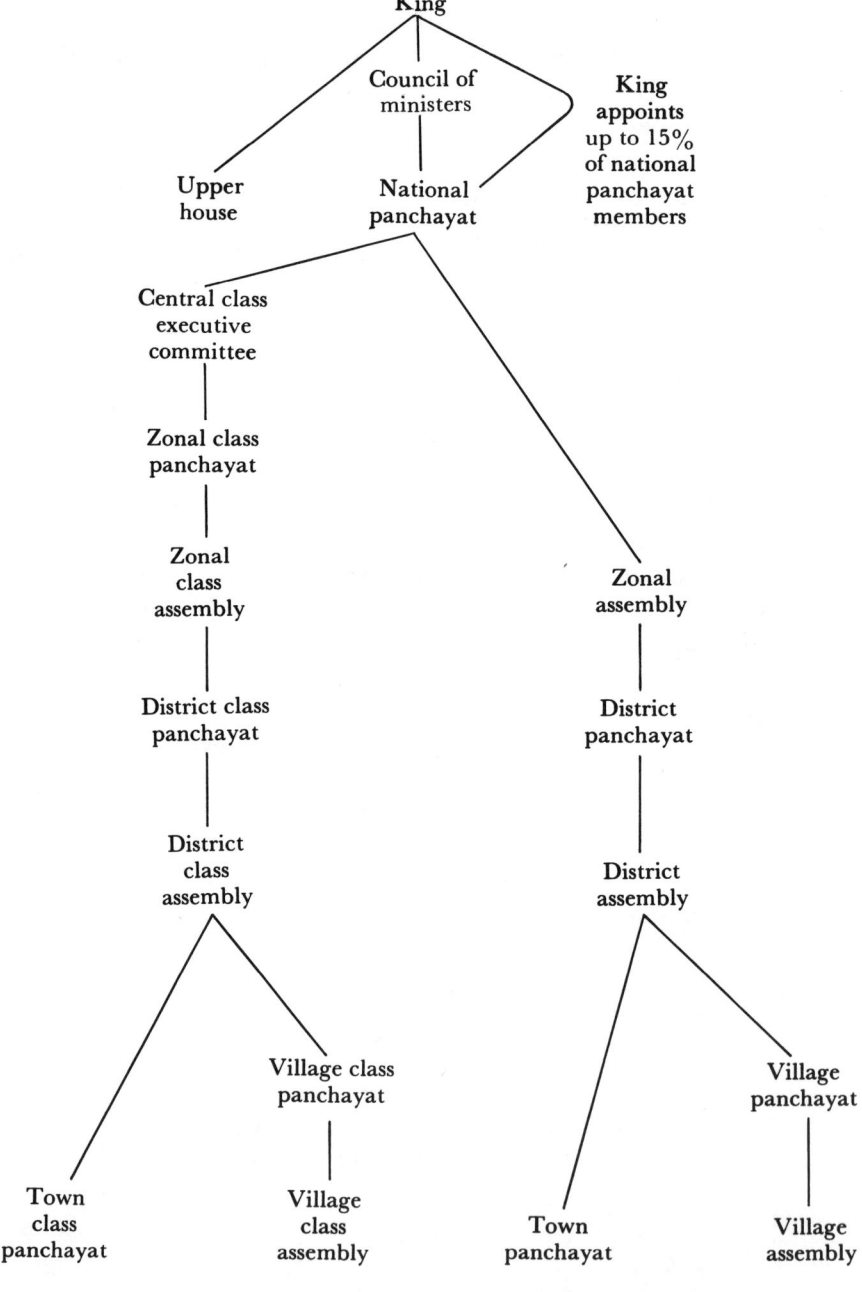

DIAGRAM 1
NEPAL'S PANCHAYAT SYSTEM

organizations operate, they are in the hands of the economic and cultural classes that have dominated previous Nepalese political systems, the large landowners, most of them of the Brahmin and Chetri castes.

The four tiers of panchayats have now been functioning since 1962. Anyone aspiring to win a seat in the National Panchayat must win a series of four elections. He must first be elected as a representative to the village panchayat from the ward or subdivision of his village. The average ward has about 500 people living in it. Next, he must be elected from the 9-member village panchayat to the district assembly. The average district, at least in the tarai region, has about 500 village panchayats and thus an assembly of about 500 representatives. In the third election, the district assembly must elect him to 1 of 11 seats in the district panchayat. Nepal is divided for administrative purposes into 14 zones and subdivided into 75 districts, each zone including 4 to 7 districts. The district-panchayat members from each district in the zone make up the membership of each zonal assembly and, in the fourth election, the zonal assembly elects 1 and, in some cases, 2 representatives from each district panchayat in the zone to the National Panchayat. Under this system, the aspirant needs to win votes from only a small number of voters at any one time, approximately 500 in the ward and district-assembly elections, 9 in the village-panchayat election and 44 to 77 in the zonal assembly election.

The vote block one needs to control in the zonal assembly is actually much smaller than the majority of assembly members. A rule handed down by the election commissioner, just before the zonal elections were held in 1967, stipulated that the nomination and second for any candidate for a National Panchayat seat must come from his own district panchayat, rather than from the entire zonal assembly membership. This means that an influential district-panchayat member, who can gain the backing of 8 of the other 10 district panchayat members, will be able to run unopposed in the election from the zonal assembly to the National Panchayat. In contrast, under the parliamentary system, a candidate for Parliament was elected directly by the voters of his district constituency. If the district were heavily populated, this meant approximately 20,000 voters. With the small electorate of the present system, wealth and political leverage can be concentrated much more effectively to determine the results of the election.

TABLE 12
National Panchayat Electorate

National Panchayat representatives	Electors	Position of electors
90	825 [a]	Members of district councils
15	75 [b]	Members of national councils of class organizations
16	1 [c]	King
4	5,400	Graduates
125	6,301 total electorate	

[a] 11 members of 75 development districts = 825 electors.
[b] 15 members of 5 central class executive committees = 75 electors.
[c] Strictly speaking, the King is not an elector, but he appoints 16 members.

A further illustration: although Nepal is a nation of approximately 11 million people, the size of the electorate responsible for sending 125 representatives to the National Panchayat is 6,301, as detailed in table 12. Approximately 5,400 Nepalis with B.A.'s or more advanced degrees registered to vote in the graduate-constituency election of 1967. The number of registered graduates has undoubtedly increased considerably since then. The graduate constituency elects 4 members through the only direct, nation-wide election from the villages and towns to the National Panchayat. It provides an opportunity for the educated elite to participate in national politicking and serves as a kind of political safety valve.

If we leave aside the graduates who, after all, elect only 4 representatives (3 percent of the National Panchayat membership), the King, his ministers, advisors, and administrators need to exercise their formidable influence, if they so wish, on only 950 electors in order to obtain a National Panchayat body that will be sympathetic to legislation drawn up in the Palace Secretariat and the Central Secretariat. The panchayat system therefore presents the King with a much more manageable political process than did the parliamentary system.

The King appoints 15 percent of the National Panchayat representatives. He appoints his ministers from among National Panchayat members, and can dismiss ministers without reference to the opinion of that body. His ministers introduce legislation, and his veto of legislation cannot be challenged. Under certain conditions he can enact legislation without National Panchayat approval. Meetings of the body are held *in camera*, and political alignment among members has been at least partly circumvented by the abolition of political parties. "By and large, therefore, the National Panchayat has more the character of a consultative body whose opinion is solicited by the king and his ministers than a real legislature."[4]

With the termination of the parliamentary system, therefore, power has shifted from the legislature to the Palace Secretariat and the Central Secretariat, where it was located in the pre-1951 governments. The role of the army in the events of December 1960 also demonstrated that it is a locus of power, latent but nevertheless real and capable of being a determining factor in Nepal's political system.

POLITICS AT THE VILLAGE LEVEL

This discussion of village politics and the discussion of district level politics that follows are focused on the tarai. However, patterns that determine political behavior in the tarai are similar to those that are evident in the villages of northern India and in the hill villages of Nepal. The interaction between regionally distinctive hill and plains groups, occasionally in unmasked competition, is the distinguishing factor of politics in the tarai. Traditionally, politics at all levels in Nepal has been determined primarily by the factors of landownership and caste status. In an almost totally agrarian society, wealth is produced by the land and, of course, wealth plays a key role in politics. Landowners' resources are translatable into influence and into the time needed to invest in political activity. A few politically important individuals, particularly among the Newars, have their wealth rooted in family business and, as Nepal begins to modernize, a few individuals from other groups are now beginning to invest wealth generated by their agricultural resources in commercial and industrial activity. At the village level, however, landownership remains almost exclusively the measure of wealth. There are a few large landowners of low-caste status. They occasionally play important roles in politics as caste status is not usually as decisive a factor in politics as landownership. However, high-caste status is always an advantage, and a close correlation exists between control of land, high-caste status, and political influence.

[4]Leo E. Rose and Margaret W. Fisher, *The Politics of Nepal* (Ithaca, 1970), p. 57.

In each of the tarai districts there appear to be a few very large landowners, individuals who own thousands of acres and often play key roles in district as well as village politics, but in most villages there are no landowners with such extensive resources. In many villages the largest landowners control no more than one or two hundred acres, sometimes considerably less. Although some of them become important at the district level, the influence of most does not extend beyond their villages. Like their fathers, and perhaps many generations of predecessors, these landowners of more modest means have been sitting in the informal councils of village elders to deal with problems that affect their villages. If the impact of the panchayat system is to be assessed properly, we must attempt to measure the extent to which these landowners have transferred their participation from the traditional councils to the new village panchayat organizations. In an attempt to make this assessment, the headmen of each of the 81 villages in the 1967–68 field survey were asked whether the largest landowner in the village was a member of the village panchayat.[5] In the sample villages of Jhapa district, 40 percent of the largest landowners were panchayat members. In Mahottari-Dhanusha, Bara, Kapilabastu, and Kailali, the percentages were 42, 20, 40, and 38 respectively. The conclusions drawn from these data must be qualified. An unknown percentage of the biggest landowners are absentee, living in other villages, in tarai towns or, in the case of some wealthy landowners of hill origin, in Kathmandu. Some of them may be members of other village panchayats. Nevertheless, the data indicate that over the four or five years between the establishment of the village panchayats and the time the data were collected, perhaps as many as half of the largest landowners actually living in the villages were elected to the panchayats.

It is extremely difficult to judge the extent to which the panchayats are active and decisions are made within them. The most important decisions are still probably made outside the panchayat framework. An example drawn from the survey in Bara district may be representative. In a village in the southern part of the district, the biggest landowner is a hill Brahmin who resides in Kathmandu most of the year. He is a descendant of a former Raj Guru, the principal religious advisor in the Palace. Many years ago, this landowner's family had

[5]It was impossible to obtain information about the size of individual land holdings, because villagers wanted to conceal these facts from tax collectors and land-reform officials.

received a small gift of tax-free land in the village area, but the Brahmin has no interest in the politics of the village, only in collecting rent from his tenants. The next-largest landowner is an Ahir who lives permanently in the village. The majority of the villagers are Ahirs, and he is the most influential man in the village. He has chosen not to become a panchayat member, because he is suspicious of the hill people who are district-level police and administrative officials, people he might have to deal with if he were a panchayat member, particularly if he were panchayat chairman. Therefore, he selected the trusted Kalwar shopkeeper of the village to be chairman of the panchayat, and the Kalwar was subsequently elected to that post by the Ahir majority.

Because the Kalwar is a businessman, transporting goods to his shop from across the border, he has frequent contact with government officials and finds it much easier than the influential Ahir, who speaks no Nepali, to represent the village when such contacts are necessary. But the Ahir continues to wield a decisive influence, playing a key role in settling village disputes in counsel with other village elders, only a few of whom are panchayat members. When recognized village leaders such as this Ahir associate themselves directly with their panchayats, the panchayats become more than a facade for village government. It is likely that more of these leaders will be willing to play an active role in their panchayats if funds are put at the disposal of the panchayats for village-development projects. This is not the place to debate the pros and cons of entrusting development funds to the traditional elite groups, but there is no doubt that this would stimulate their interest in the panchayat system.

Drawing the traditional elite into the panchayat system would activate the system, giving it substance in the eyes of the population. However, this in itself would cause no change in the traditional socio-economic structure of village society. To establish the groundwork for any kind of fundamental change, the panchayat system must provide those who have not heretofore shared in the decision-making process an opportunity to share authority with those who have maintained exclusive control over that process. Let us look at a few selected statistics for villages in the districts of the 1967–68 field survey. Seventeen percent of the people living in the sample villages of Kapilabastu are members of various untouchable castes among the plains Hindus; 5 percent of all village-panchayat members in the district in 1967 were also members of these untouchable castes. Twenty-eight percent of the population in the sample villages of Bara are plains Hindu untouchables and 10 percent of all village-panchayat members in 1967 were included in this untouchable category. In Mahottari-Dhanusha, 21 percent of the sample population falls into this category and 14 percent of all village-panchayat members in the same year.[6] Most of these untouchables are elected to the panchayats from wards that are composed exclusively of these groups, wards in which they do not have to compete with more-privileged caste groups. This explains the mechanism that operates to place them in the panchayats.

Considering that members of these castes have been among the most economically destitute and have generally been excluded from decision-making in their villages, the fact that a number of them now sit together with members of other caste groups in the new panchayats is remarkable. However, it is necessary to observe that many of the panchayats are inactive and most of those that function are dominated by members of the traditional elite. The Nepalese government has not yet found a way to provide the village panchayats with a *raison d'être*, other than that of springboard for individuals who have political ambitions at the district and national levels.

Two positions in the village panchayat can have political and monetary value. The first is that of representative to the district assembly, because from the district assembly one has the opportunity to be elected to the district panchayat and then on to the National Panchayat. The position of village panchayat chairman can also be rewarding, because the chairman can often make considerable profit from monetary gifts received from villagers for support in presenting occasional problems to district administrators. The need to obtain a citizenship certificate is an example of such a problem. These positions are generally held by members of the landed upper castes, except in those villages that are inhabited exclusively by lower-caste or tribal groups.

POLITICS AT THE DISTRICT LEVEL

Before the Shah kings consolidated the tarai under their control in the 1770s, the region was ruled by a number of petty chieftains, some of whom owed no more than nominal allegiance to the pre-Shah rulers. These petty chieftains were generally Rajputs, members of

[6]These data were collected from the records of the Chief Development Officer in each district surveyed. The C.D.O.'s assistants helped make caste identifications.

the warrior caste of northern India, but there were also some large landowners among the "yeoman farmer" castes—Ahirs in the eastern tarai, Kurmis and a few middle-caste Muslims in the mid-western tarai. Even after the Shahs and Ranas had established some semblance of systematic administration in the tarai, the largest landowners continued to operate as feudal lords. They gave obeisance to Kathmandu, but local law was their law. They maintained private "police" forces to protect the people in their villages from bands of marauding criminals and to enforce their will in these villages. There were conflicts among them for control of land, conflicts that occasionally turned into small-scale wars. The government in Kathmandu appointed district commissioners to oversee local administration, to collect taxes and maintain law and order. When district commissioners were strong, the landowners lost much of their former influence, but when district commissioners were weak or the districts were particularly isolated from Kathmandu, the large landowners retained much of their feudal status. Over the past two decades, the government has improved its administration of the tarai and tightened its control over locally powerful families. Nevertheless, administrative control is not yet complete, and the region retains much of its character as an open frontier, with rapid in-migration, clearing of land, and settlement, along with the presence of rice barons, outlaws with local reputations, and vigilante law.

Since 1951, politics in the tarai districts have continued to be dominated by the largest landowners and district administrators. Many district-level officials, especially those with a high degree of education and a spirit of nationalism, have been striving for the past several decades to implement development plans and to reform local administrative procedures. In this they have often been opposed by the traditional elite, who prefer to retain the status quo.

On the other hand, there are frequent reports of government officials less than dedicated to the welfare of the total community. The relationship between district administrators and large landowners is often less one of antagonism than cooperation to the mutual advantage of both. Some officials allegedly receive payments from landowners to overlook land holdings in excess of the 40-acre ceiling established by the 1964 Land Reform Act.[7] Occasionally they take sides in factional disputes, for example, assisting a representative of one local landlord faction to win an election over the representative

[7]*Gorkhapatra*, June 24, 1969.

of an opposing faction. According to the press, this is accomplished in various ways: intimidation of voters, stuffing of ballot boxes, preventing candidates who are out of favor from filling the necessary preelection campaign forms, or even arresting them before the election.[8]

Caste is as important a factor in district-level politics as it is at other levels. For example, during the period preceding Nepal's only national election, the hirelings of a powerful Rajput killed two leading Ahirs in Saptari district. A few Rajput families control much of the land in the district, but the Ahirs make up the largest caste group there and can be described as an aggressive, upward-mobile caste. Some Ahirs have been gaining considerable economic and political importance in Saptari, challenging the position of the Rajputs. In this case the Rajput was reported to be a local Nepali Congress leader and the Ahirs to be organizers for the Communist Party, although members of these caste groups are found in both parties, and the communists have not been reluctant to resort to the same violent tactics against Nepali Congress workers.

Another factor in district-level politics in the tarai, perhaps the only factor not also present in the politics of the hill districts, is that of regionalism. The Shah kings and Rana prime ministers over the past several hundred years have given away large tracts of tarai forest land as tax-free grants to family members, advisors, and retainers. Grants of forest land, no longer tax-free, are still being made by the Palace Secretariat to prominent people in Kathmandu. Gradually, as these lands have been cleared and settled, the recipients of the land, mostly Chetris but also hill Brahmins and Newars, have become among the most influential landowners in the region. These powerful hill people become involved in district politics, and occasionally factionalism arises along regional lines, the landowners of hill origin opposed to the landowners of plains origin. Most of the district administrators are hill people of the Brahmin, Chetri, and Newar groups and there is a natural cultural ground for communication and cooperation between the landowners and officials of hill origin. Indeed, they sometimes come from the same extended families.

Although no data could be collected to document the number of landowners of hill origin at the district level, data collected at the village level are reflective of the district-level situation. Hill people

[8]See, for example, *Naya Samaj*, Jan. 27, Mar. 18, 1969; *Jagriti Weekly*, Feb. 18, 1969; *Naya Nepal*, Jan. 27, 1969; *New Herald*, May 14, 15, 1969; *Samiksha Weekly*, July 13, 1969; *Matribhumi Weekly*, Oct. 7, 1969.

represent 16 percent of the population in the sample villages of Jhapa district; in 30 percent of the sample villages, a hill person was the largest landowner. The corresponding statistics for Kailali are 10 percent of the sample population and 38 percent of the largest landowners; in Mahottari-Dhanusha, 14 percent of the sample population and 40 percent of the largest landowners; in Kapilabastu, 9 percent of the population and 20 percent of the largest landowners. In Bara, the most extreme example of the disproportionate number of hill people in the landowning category, they represent 2 percent of the sample population and 25 percent of the largest landowners in the sample villages.[9]

The following data document the predominance of hill people in the district administration. In late 1967 and early 1968, 82 percent of the gazetted officers posted in four districts, Jhapa, Bara, Kapilabastu, and Kailali, were hill people, 80 percent of all these officers were hill Brahmins, Chetris and Newars, and 2 percent of them hill tribals.[10] Eighty-one percent of the senior-ranking police officers posted in the same four districts were hill people during the same period, 56 percent of them hill Brahmins, Chetris, and Newars and 25 percent hill tribals.[11] Eighteen percent of the gazetted officers and 19 percent of the ranking police officers were plains people, among them several plains Brahmins and Kayasthas, a Bhumihar, a Rajput, an Ahir, and a Rajbanshi.

Because large landowners and government officials play key roles in district politics, and because of the disproportionate number of hill people among the landowners and government officials in the tarai districts, it is clear that hill people have a decisive impact upon politics in the tarai. As they exert their influence, they challenge the position of the landowners of plains origin who have controlled much of the region for generations. As pointed out previously, politics at the village level operate only partly within the panchayat framework. This is true at the district level as well. Data on participation in the panchayat system are available, and they provide an insight into the competition between representatives of the regional groups within the tarai population. For these data, see tables 13 through 17.

[9]These data were collected as part of the 1967–68 field survey.

[10]These data were assembled during interviews with chief development officers and other administrators in each district. Time limitations did not permit the collection of such data for Mahottari-Dhanusha.

[11]These data were obtained during interviews with leading police officials in each district. The ranks included in the data are superintendent, deputy superintendent, inspector, and subinspector.

TABLE 14
Mahottari-Dhanusha District: Participation in Village- and District-Level Panchayat Bodies, by Caste, Tribal, and Regional Affiliation[a]

Regional and communal groupings	Village sample of population[b]	Village panchayat				District assembly		District panchayat	
		Members 1962	Members 1967	Chairmen 1962	Chairmen 1967	Members 1962	Members 1967	Members 1962	Members 1967
Hill castes	6.4		8.2	18.4	19.1	17.9	18.8	21.7	34.8
Hill tribals	7.4		2.6	1.6	1.6	1.6	3.1	4.3	
Hill people, subtotal	13.8	Data not available	10.8	20.0	20.7	19.5	21.9	26.0	34.8
Plains Hindus	77.9		81.5	75.3	72.7	74.2	74.0	73.9	65.2
Muslims	7.1		5.9	2.1	4.9	4.2	2.6		
Plains tribals	1.2		1.7	2.6	1.6	7.1	1.6		
Plains people, subtotal	86.2		89.1	80.0	79.2	80.5	78.1	73.9	65.2
Position vacant									
Caste not identified									
Total	100.0		100.0	100.0	100.0	100.0	100.0	100.0	100.0

[a] Data collected from the records of the Chief Development officer in Mahottari-Dhanusha district.
[b] Data collected from field survey of twenty-four villages in Mahottari-Dhanusha, 1967–68.

TABLE 13
Jhapa District: Participation in Village- and District-Level Panchayat Bodies, by Caste, Tribal, and Regional Affiliation[a]

Regional and communal groupings	Village sample of population[b]	Village panchayat				District assembly		District panchayat	
		Members 1962	Members 1967	Chairmen 1962	Chairmen 1967	Members 1962	Members 1967	Members 1962	Members 1967
Hill castes	14.1		32.4	51.2	41.9	57.8	55.6	72.7	54.6
Hill tribals	2.0		2.1		4.6		4.4		
Hill people, subtotal	16.1	Data not available	34.5	51.2	46.5	57.8	60.0	72.7	54.6
Plains Hindus	18.1		3.2	2.3	2.3	2.2	2.2		
Muslims	4.3		2.8			2.2			
Plains tribals	56.2		59.5	46.5	51.2	37.8	37.8	18.2	45.4
Plains people, subtotal	78.6		65.5	48.8	53.5	42.2	40.0	18.2	45.4
Position vacant								9.1	
Caste not identified	5.3								
Total	100.0		100.0	100.0	100.0	100.0	100.0	100.0	100.0

[a] Data collected from the records of the Chief Development Officer in Jhapa district.
[b] Data collected from field survey of ten villages in Jhapa district, 1967–68.

TABLE 15

Bara District: Participation in Village- and District-Level Panchayat Bodies, by Caste, Tribal, and Regional Affiliation[a]

Regional and communal groupings	Village sample of population[b]	Village panchayat					District assembly		District panchayat	
		Members 1964	Members 1967	Chairmen 1962	Chairmen 1967		Members 1962	Members 1967	Members 1962	Members 1967
Hill castes	1.2	3.7		8.9	7.4			12.2	27.3	18.2
Hill tribes	.4	.8								
Hill people, subtotal	1.6	4.5		8.9	7.4			12.2	27.3	18.2
Plains Hindus	79.4	57.4	Data not available	56.3	56.5	Data not available		64.5	54.5	81.8
Muslims	13.7	13.8		7.1	6.5			1.9		
Plains tribals	5.4	14.6		13.4	21.3			14.9	18.2	
Plains people, subtotal	98.5	85.8		76.8	84.3			81.3	72.7	81.8
Position vacant										
Caste not identified		9.7		14.3	8.3			6.5		
Total	100.0	100.0		100.0	100.0			100.0	100.0	100.0

[a] Data collected from the records of the Chief Development Officer in Bara district.
[b] Data collected from field survey of twenty villages in Bara district, 1967–68.

TABLE 16

Kapilabastu District: Participation in Village- and District-Level Panchayat Bodies, by Caste, Tribal, and Regional Affiliation[a]

Regional and communal groupings	Village sample of population[b]	Village panchayat				District assembly		District panchayat	
		Members 1962	Members 1967	Chairmen 1962	Chairmen 1967	Members 1962	Members 1967	Members 1962	Members 1967
Hill castes	8.5	Data not available	5.2	8.6	14.8	18.5	13.6	36.4	25.0
Hill tribals	.5					1.2		9.1	
Hill people, subtotal	9.0		5.2	8.6	14.8	19.7	13.6	45.5	25.0
Plains Hindus	66.4		59.3	65.4	55.6	62.0	67.9	45.4	66.7
Muslims	18.0		19.1	16.1	18.5	9.9	12.3		
Plains tribals	6.6		12.7	9.9	11.1	7.4	6.2	9.1	8.3
Plains people, subtotal	91.0		91.0	91.4	85.2	80.3	86.4	54.5	75.0
Position vacant			1.6						
Caste not identified			2.2						
Total	100.0		100.0	100.0	100.0	100.0	100.0	100.0	100.0

[a] Data collected from the records of the Chief Development Officer in Kapilabastu district.
[b] Data collected from field survey of nineteen villages in Kapilabastu district, 1967–68.

TABLE 17

Kailali District: Participation in Village- and District-Level Panchayat Bodies, by Caste, Tribal, and Regional Affiliation[a]

Regional and communal groupings	Village sample of population[b]	Village panchayat				District assembly		District panchayat	
		Members 1962	Members 1967	Chairmen 1962	Chairmen 1967	Members 1962	Members 1967	Members 1962	Members 1967
Hill castes	9.6	15.3	14.9	61.9	52.4	59.5	59.5	54.5	54.5
Hill tribals		.3	.2						
Hill people, subtotal	9.6	15.6	15.1	61.9	52.4	59.5	59.5	54.5	54.5
Plains Hindus	.9	.8	.2						
Muslims	1.2	.3							
Plains tribals	88.3	80.4	73.6	38.1	47.6	40.5	40.5	45.5	45.5
Plains people, subtotal	90.4	81.5	73.8	38.1	47.6	40.5	40.5	45.5	45.5
Position vacant		.5	9.5						
Caste not identified		2.4	1.5						
Total	100.0	100.0	100.0	100.0	100.0	100.0	100.0	100.0	100.0

[a]Data collected from the records of the Chief Development Officer in Kailali district.
[b]Data collected from field survey of eight villages in Kailali district, 1967–68.

Analysis of these tables should be prefaced with a word of caution. The village sample of population is included in each table to give the reader a base for comparison of other data in the table. It must be remembered that the small sample results in some minor distortions of the real village population of these districts.[12]

Looking at the tables, one is struck by the continually larger percentage of positions in panchayat bodies that the hill people obtain as they move up the panchayat ladder. In all five districts, hill people constitute a larger percentage of village-panchayat members than percentage of villagers and a larger percentage of village-panchayat chairmen than panchayat members. This is most pronounced in Kailali, where in 1967 hill people were 10 percent of the village sample, 15 percent of village-panchayat members, and 62 percent of panchayat chairmen.

In the districts of Mahottari-Dhanusha, Bara and Jhapa in 1967, the percentage of hill people serving as village representatives to district assemblies was even higher than their percentage of village-panchayat chairmen. The increase was particularly high in Jhapa. Hill people represented 16 percent of the village sample, 35 percent of village-panchayat members, 47 percent of panchayat chairmen, and 60 percent of representatives to the district assembly.

Moving a rung higher up the panchayat ladder from the district assembly to the district panchayat, one again finds a continually larger percentage of hill people represented in three of the five districts, Mahottari-Dhanusha, Bara, and Kapilabastu. In 1967, the largest percentage increase was in Mahottari-Dhanusha, from 22 percent of the district-assembly membership to 35 percent of the district-panchayat membership. In both Jhapa and Kailali, the hill people suffered five percentage-point declines while moving up this rung of the panchayat ladder. It is interesting that the decline in representation took place in the two districts that have majorities of tribal people. This is an exception to the general pattern of political behavior evident in the tables, as the plains tribals usually encounter considerable difficulty attempting to assert themselves in the face of competition from high-caste groups.

Among both the hill and plains people, the upper castes predominate in representation over the lower-caste and tribal people. This may

[12]The distortions can be identified in table 4 of ch. I, where sample and census data are compared.

be illustrated by using caste data not included in the tables.[13] As already mentioned, the untouchable castes among the plains people have been able to find some representation in the village panchayats, although they seldom reach a higher rung on the panchayat ladder. For example, in Kapilabastu district, Chamars, an untouchable caste found throughout India and the tarai, were 8 percent of the village sample and in 1967, they were able to obtain 1 percent of the village-panchayat seats in the district.[14] However, no Chamar has reached a district-level body in Kapilabastu, and this has been the pattern experienced by most other low-caste groups. There are some exceptions, particularly evident in Mahottari-Dhanusha, where Sudis, Telis, and Dhanuks, all untouchables, have been elected to the district panchayat. Some of the untouchables, particularly the Sudis and Telis, have turned from their traditional caste occupations and have become wealthy businessmen. The Sudis are a remarkable example of successful upward mobility. Although they constituted only 2 percent of the village sample in Mahottari-Dhanusha, 3 of the 23 district-panchayat members in 1967 were Sudis. Nevertheless, even in this district, among the plains people, Brahmins and Rajputs continued to win election to panchayat bodies out of all proportion to their numbers in the population.

The hill Brahmins, Chetris, and Newars continue to prevail over the lower-caste and tribal people of hill origin. Among the hill people who were elected to the district panchayats of the five selected tarai districts in 1962 and 1967, only two, a wealthy Thakali merchant from the town of Taulihawa in Kapilabastu district in 1962, and a member of the prominent Giri family of Mahottari-Dhanusha in 1967, were not members of these three groups. The Giris belong to a small upper-caste group of Sanyasis among the hill people. Despite the example of the Sudis and the Thakali, politics within the panchayat system follows closely the pattern of traditional political behavior. This is as true in the hill region as in the tarai. A 1967 survey of village and district-level leadership in the eastern hills published by the Panchayat Ministry admits this. Authors of the survey state:

> ... the new order [the panchayat system] does not seem to have made any significant impact on the content and composition of the traditional leadership. The latter, in fact, reflects strongly the socioeconomic

[13]These were collected during the 1967–68 field survey, but the data for each caste were too extensive to be included here.
[14]One Chamar was even elected chairman of a village panchayat in 1962.

realities of our rural setting and is basically geared to the traditional power-structure and relationship of production. This is manifested in greater magnitude in the case of village Panchayat Chairmen. In a country where the per capita income is Rs. 419, the fact that a predominantly large section of our respondents registered their annual income to be falling within the brackets of Rs. 3,000 to Rs. 4,999 and Rs. 5,000 and above, amply illustrated this point. Besides, most of them happened to be the descendants or relatives of old mukhiyas, talukadars and jimmawals, i.e., the traditional offices of local power.[15]

An additional observation about the data in the tables needs to be made here. Despite the disproportionate representation of hill people at each panchayat level in both 1962 and 1967, except in Mahottari-Dhanusha, their representation was less in 1967 than it was in 1962. In Kapilabastu, for example, the percentage of hill people in the district panchayat dropped from 46 percent in 1962 to 25 percent in 1967. In Bara it dropped from 27 percent to 18 percent over the same period. This can be explained at least in part by the reaction among politically active plains people to the royal coup of 1960. A great many of these people had committed themselves to the Nepali Congress or other political parties during the 1950s. They tended to be confused and alienated by the abrupt termination of the party system and refused to participate in the first panchayat elections in 1962. This afforded many hill people who had not invested so heavily in the party system an opportunity to participate in local politics.

Some leaders among the plains people were still refusing to become involved in the panchayat system in 1967. However, it appears from the data that many had set their suspicions aside by then and were taking their places in the system, in the process crowding out of office some of the less influential hill people. Comparable data from a later election would be needed for verification. If this is a continuing trend, it would indicate that the new political system is finding acceptance in the tarai, and this would be an important step in the integration process, drawing more of the plains people into the national political sphere. On the other hand, it would become more difficult for hill people to maintain their hold on elective offices in the villages and districts of the tarai, and this would impede the Nepalization process.

---

[15] Pashupati Shamshere and Mohammad Mohsin, *A Study Report on the Pattern of Emerging Leadership in Panchayats* (Kathmandu, 1967), p. 32.

We have seen how the percentage of elected officials among hill people increases from the village to the district level of the panchayat system. This trend continues at the national level. In 1967, eight National Panchayat representatives were elected from the five tarai districts selected for study. Four were elected from the densely populated Mahottari-Dhanusha district,[16] and one from each of the other four. Of the eight representatives, five were hill people: three hill Brahmins, one Chetri, and one Sanyasi (Giri). The other three were plains people: one plains Brahmin, one Rajput, and one Marwari. Thus, although the hill people account for not more than 10 percent of the population in the five districts combined, in 1967 they held 63 percent of National Panchayat seats from these districts.

In addition to administrative support for candidates of hill origin, a major reason for the increase in the percentage of hill people elected to the National Panchayat over the percentage in the district panchayats is to be found in the structure and function of the panchayat system at the zonal level.

To understand the function of the zonal units, it is necessary to examine the way in which the zonal concept evolved in the minds of those who established the system. In 1961, when King Mahendra appointed a committee to draw up the Panchayat Constitution, he also appointed a committee to reorganize the country's administrative units, to make the units compatible at least in part with the panchayat structure formulated in the Constitution. The committee, in its final report, emphasized economic integration. It stressed the fact that the hill region could not be developed without tapping the resources of the tarai, and pointed out the basic need for transportation and communication systems to tie the two regions together. The committee also touched on the problem of political integration, the need to develop a sense of unity among the people living in the two regions.[17]

The Demarcation Committee was successful for the most part in creating zonal units that included both hill and tarai districts. Of

[16]In 1962, Mahottari was divided into two administrative units (Mahottari and Dhanusha) but, in order to compare census data for the single pre-1962 Mahottari district unit with data obtained for the two districts since then, the two new districts were studied as a single unit.

[17]Nepal, Ministry of National Guidance, *Report of the Development Districts and Zones Demarcation Committee* (Kathmandu, 1961), pp. 4–5. (Trans. by Regmi Research Project.)

the fourteen zones created, the two far-western zones and the four easternmost zones actually run from the Tibetan border to the Indian border. Four zones, although not stretching the full width of the country, include both tarai and hill districts. In only four zones was the committee unable to follow through with its plan for regional integration.

The Demarcation Committee envisaged the creation of zonal panchayats with extensive administrative powers over the district units within the zones. However, the 1962 Constitution did not specify the functions to be invested in the panchayats at the zonal, district, or village levels. Although the 1963 Zonal Panchayat Act delegated numerous functions to zonal bodies, by the time the Act was amended in 1964, the concept of the zonal panchayat's functions had undergone radical change. The amended Act assigned only two basic functions to the zonal bodies. The first is a publicity function, to create national unity by encouraging the use of the Nepali language and by encouraging the adoption of the national "culture" and "character".[18] The second function is political, to elect representatives to the National Panchayat, and is accomplished in zonal assemblies that include the district-panchayat members from each of the districts in the zone. These bodies elect one or, in some cases, two members from each district panchayat to the National Panchayat.

Whatever the intent, the effect of the elective function of the zonal assemblies is to put the election of National Panchayat representatives from tarai districts into the hands of hill people, because hill people represent the majority of assembly members in all but one zone. In six of the nine zones that include tarai districts, one or two tarai districts are grouped with three or four hill districts. Because there is an equal number of district-panchayat members for each district, the representatives from hill districts form a majority in each of the six zones. In two other zones, the tarai districts are grouped together with equal numbers of hill districts but, as pointed out in the last section of this chapter, some hill people are also elected to the tarai district panchayats and, therefore, hill people also form majorities in the assemblies of these two zones. In only one zone, Narayani, which includes Bara district, is the number of tarai districts greater than the number of

---

[18]See Zonal Panchayat Act 1963, *Nepal Gazette*, vol. XII, Extraordinary Issue No. 31A, Jan. 16, 1963, and Zonal Panchayat (Amendment) Act 1964, *Nepal Gazette*, vol. XIV, Extraordinary Issue No. 18B, Nov. 16, 1964.

hill districts, and the people of plains origin are therefore probably a majority of the Narayani Zonal Assembly.[19]

Seventy-five percent of the Kapilabastu District Panchayat members were plains people in 1967, but they were a minority in the Lumbini Zonal Assembly. This explains at least in part the election of a hill Brahmin, a very large landowner with Palace connections, as the Kapilabastu representative to the National Panchayat in that year. In Mahottari-Dhanusha, 65 percent of the panchayat members[20] were plains people, and yet they represented a minority in the Janakpur Zonal Assembly. In 1967, two of the four National Panchayat representatives from Mahottari-Dhanusha elected by this zonal assembly were hill people. In 1965, a Marwari, a member of the important business caste among the plains people, was elected from the Narayani Zonal Assembly to represent Bara district. This is the one zone in which the plains people appear to represent a majority of the zonal-assembly membership, and this is likely to be a key factor in the election of this Marwari.

There is no evidence that zonal organizations are fulfilling their publicity functions, so that the zones are left with their elective function alone. Since the inauguration of the panchayat system, a number of voices have been raised in criticism of this function. Suggestions have been made that the zonal assemblies be abolished and that the district assemblies or district panchayats elect their own National Panchayat representatives. This suggested method of a more direct way of electing representatives would avoid the disadvantage experienced by the plains people in zonal-assembly elections. Because the zonal assemblies meet only at intervals of several years, the government could abolish them with little disruption to the political process. The fact that this has not been done seems to indicate that the government prefers the more indirect system with the checks it maintains on the representation of plains people at the national level.

POLITICS AT THE NATIONAL LEVEL

Control of land and high-caste status are decisive factors in politics at the national level, as at other levels. Although control of land is

[19] Whether the plains people are, in fact, a majority depends upon the number of hill people elected from the three tarai districts and the two inner-tarai districts of the zone. The inner-tarai districts are heavily populated by Tharus.

[20] Actually there are separate panchayats for Mahottari and Dhanusha, but for reasons explained in footnote 16 of this chapter, the two districts are being studied as a single unit.

generally the more important of the two, high-caste status has always been a prerequisite for leadership in traditional Hindu society and, despite the challenge of modernization to such traditional Hindu axioms, it remains an important advantage. Two additional determinants of success in national politics have gained importance since the 1951 revolution. The first is identification with the hill culture. Since 1951, groups that lack the cultural characteristics of the hill people have been introduced into national politics through the party system. With the arrival in Kathmandu of plains people seeking political influence, the distinction between the national hill culture and the regional plains culture took on a significance it had not had before.

The other determinant that became important after 1951 is education. Although the Brahmins have pursued their Sanskrit education in Kathmandu for countless generations, only the termination of Rana rule, with its opposition to modern education, opened the educational floodgates. Since then, there has been a rapid growth in the number of schools and colleges in Nepal and in the number of Nepalis who have received B.A.'s and other advanced degrees. Education is becoming an increasingly important qualification for leadership. It provides an aspiring Nepalese politician with ability to deal more adequately with the complex problems faced by his village and his nation in the modern world. Caste is a traditional status symbol, and education has become a modern one. B.A. and M.A. designations are in frequent use as suffixes to names. Occasionally, as a gesture of repudiating the traditional social structure, individuals will substitute these degree suffixes for last names that disclose caste identification. Thus, education not only enables many young Nepalis to compete in economic and political spheres, even in the absence of more traditional qualifications, but it also signifies the the declining importance of caste, at least among the urbanized elite. The changing importance of these two factors makes it necessary to preface observations about the dynamics of national politics with a word of caution. The following observations are tentative, and allowances need to be made for exceptions and for corrections based on further investigation.

Only two groups, the hill Brahmins and Chetris, possess all four of the prerequisites for successful participation in Nepalese national politics: control of economic resources, high-caste status, identification with the hill culture, and a high level of educational attainment.

Ever since Prithvi Narayan Shah defeated the Newar kings of Kathmandu Valley in 1769, the Chetris have held the reins of power in the Palace and the army. Prithvi Narayan Shah brought Brahmin clerks, advisors, and priests with him to Kathmandu. Together, the Chetris and the Brahmins have controlled the most important government positions since then.

Only one group, the Newars, falls into the next category, those who possess three of the four prerequisites mentioned above: control of economic resources, identification with the hill culture, and education. The Newars have evolved their own unique social system, a complex, dual-caste system with one set of castes for the Hindu half of the Newar population and another set for the Buddhist half.[21] The Newars who stand high within their own caste system are by no means regarded as outcastes by orthodox Hindus. However, in pre-revolution Nepalese society, individuals' relationships were determined more completely by the ascriptive characteristics of the caste system than is true today, and the Newars found their cultural differences a handicap in competing with the Brahmins and Chetris.

Kathmandu Valley has been the center of the rich Newar culture from time immemorial. The Newars' proximity to the seat of power is an important reason why, despite their cultural differences, they have gradually become the third group in the ruling coalition. Yet, despite their proximity to the Chetri rulers and Brahmin advisors, the Newars would not be as important today if it were not for the combination of characteristics they exhibit as a group: cultural adaptability, artistic and technical skills, commercial acumen, and a high level of education. These characteristics have made it possible for the Newars to seize more readily than other groups the opportunities presented by modernization. For centuries, the Newars have played key roles in the commercial and artistic life of Tibet as well as Kathmandu Valley. Over the past several hundred years, they have been migrating from Kathmandu Valley into the hills,[22] where they have established trading centers and have become the most important business community throughout the hill region. More recently, they have migrated into the tarai, where they are now businessmen, landowners, and political leaders. Newars have been elected to a number

[21]See Gopal Singh Nepali, *The Newars* (Bombay, 1965), ch. 6, and Colin Rosser, "Social Mobility in the Newar Caste System," in *Caste and Kin in Nepal, India and Ceylon*, ed. by C. von Fürer-Haimendorf (New York, 1966), pp. 68 ff.
[22]Dor Bahadur Bista, *The People of Nepal* (Kathmandu, 1967), pp. 16–17.

of town panchayats in the tarai. In 1967, 11 Newars represented hill districts in the National Panchayat and 2 represented tarai districts. Newars share with Brahmins a keen awareness of the benefits education can provide. Of the 5,500 Nepalis who registered as voters in the 1967 graduate constituency election,[23] 36 percent were hill Brahmins and 28 percent Newars. Only 12 percent were Chetris.[24]

The historical events that have shaped Nepalese society since Prithvi Narayan Shah conquered the Valley from Newar kings have created considerable rivalry between the hill Brahmins and Newars. Gradually since the late eighteenth century the Shah kings and later the Rana prime ministers, all Chetris, began appointing Newars to positions previously held by Brahmins, first chiefly clerical positions but later more senior administrative positions. Although the Chetris have continued to rule, to dominate the officer corps of the army, and to hold many of the highest administrative positions, the Brahmins and Newars have competed for other positions. The result has been the emergence of an occasionally intense rivalry between Newar and Brahmin factions in the Central Secretariat, with the Chetris holding the balance. Since the revolution, Tribhuvan University and the various colleges associated with it have become foci for factionalism, because education has become a critical factor in upward mobility for both Brahmins and Newars. The majority of faculty members and students are drawn from these two groups. In academic politics, although Brahmin-Newar coalitions form occasionally, the competition for important administrative and departmental posts and even for student-government offices is often shaped by this rivalry.

Some Newars feel that Brahmins have used the caste system to limit upward mobility among non-Brahmins. On the other hand, some Brahmins view the upward movement of Newars as evidence that the traditional social order is declining. Indeed, it appears that modernization has adversely affected the position of some of the more traditional Brahmins who live in urban settings. For example, the Raj

[23]Only those with B.A.'s, the traditional Shastri degree equivalents, or more advanced degrees qualify as graduates.

[24]This caste breakdown was made from Nepal, Election Commission, *Snatak Pratinidhitwa-Rashtriya Panchayat ko Nirwachan ko Matadata Namavali* [Voters List for the National Panchayat Election: The Graduate Constituency]. (Kathmandu, 1967.) Informed observers estimate that approximately 10,000 Nepalis were eligible to vote in this election, but only about half of them registered. There were 868 caste Hindus of plains origin and Muslims registered. Another 329 voters could not be identified by caste, although many of them appear to be of plains origin.

Guru, the royal preceptor and guardian of Hindu orthodoxy, once a powerful Brahmin responsible for upholding the observances of the caste system, has lost much of the influence he once wielded. However, because the Brahmins have proven themselves capable of exploiting the advantages of modern education, there is little likelihood that they will suffer greatly in competition with other groups. The fact that the Brahmins' preeminence no longer goes unchallenged does not mean that the caste system is losing its significance in Nepalese society, but it does indicate that a few of those who previously were politically disinherited can now compete for influence.

Beyond the Chetri-Brahmin-Newar "establishment," other groups in Nepal's population remain uninvolved in national politics or at best involved in only token ways. Because the census of Nepal furnishes no caste data, it is impossible to calculate the size of many nonparticipating groups, but it appears that they represent a large majority of the population. These groups can be categorized on the basis of the the four prerequisites for successful participation in national politics. Into one category fall the low-caste hill people such as the Ghartis, Sarkis, Kamis, and Damais, and also the hill-tribal people such as the Magars, Gurungs, Tamangs, Rais, Limbus, and Sherpas. With a few individual exceptions, these groups lack three of the prerequisites: economic resources, high-caste status, and education. They possess only identification with the hill culture. Among the hill tribals, a few Sherpas and Thakalis have accumulated considerable wealth through trading, and a few members of other tribal groups have retained control over large ancestral land holdings. Those tribal people who have enlisted in the British and Indian armies have acquired some education and some economic benefits. On the whole, the hill tribals do not suffer as many disadvantages as the low-caste hill people, and a few representatives of hill tribes find their way into Kathmandu's political circles. For example, in the constantly shifting cabinet membership of the 1960s, two hill tribals have generally been included as ministers of junior rank, one usually representing a tribal group from the western hills and the other a tribal group from the eastern hills. On the whole, however, the percentage of both hill-tribal and low-caste hill people in influential political positions has been far less than their percentage of the total population.

The upper- and business-caste plains people can be placed in another category. They possess three of the prerequisites, economic resources, high-caste status, and education, but lack the fourth, identification with the hill culture. This category includes the plains Brahmins, Bhumihars, Rajputs, Kayasthas, and some of the business-oriented groups such as the Marwaris. A few Muslims would also find their place in this category. An occasional individual from groups in this category attains prominence and is appointed to a judgeship or a ministerial post. Lack of identification with the hill culture nevertheless remains a formidable barrier to their successful participation in national politics and, in proportion to their numbers in the total population, they are poorly represented in Kathmandu.

The last category includes the low-caste Hindus of plains origin, most Muslim groups, and the plains tribals such as the Tharus, Rajbanshis, Tajpurias, Mechis, and Gangais. These groups lack all four of the prerequisites for participation in national politics and frequently find themselves excluded even from local politics. A few individuals from the Tharu, Rajbanshi, and Tajpuria tribes have been able to retain control of large ancestral land holdings and have become key figures in local politics. Indeed, several Tharus attained national recognition during the period of party politics. Nevertheless, these groups carry with them the largest economic and cultural deficits as they attempt to move into the sphere of national politics.

The foregoing observations about advantaged and disadvantaged groups in national politics can be substantiated by reference to data available on communal representation in politically important national bodies. A comparison of membership in two elective bodies, the 1959 Parliament and the 1967 National Panchayat, is instructive. As table 18 indicates, there was an increase in the representation of hill people from 82 percent in the Parliament to 90 percent in the National Panchayat and a corresponding decrease for plains people from 18 to 10 percent.

Among the hill people, the Chetris and Newars gained most in representation from the change in governments. The Chetris increased their numbers by 10 percent and the Newars by over 7 percent. For the Newars this meant an increase of almost threefold. The hill Brahmin group was the one group in the ruling coalition to suffer a decline in representation. It is axiomatic that one of the three groups will experience a decline in influence when the other two increase their strength. This is particularly the case with regard to the Brahmin-Newar equation. Until recently, most Chetris have put less emphasis on education than have the Brahmins. It appears now, however, that the Chetris are less dependent on the Brahmins,

TABLE 18
Regional and Communal Groups within the 1959 Parliament
and the 1967 National Panchayat[a]

Regional and communal groupings of representatives	1959 Parliament No. of reps.	Percent of total	1969 Nat. Panchayat No. of reps.	Percent of total
Hill Brahmins	31	28.4	30	24.0
Chetris	30	27.5	47	37.6
Newars	5	4.6	15	12.0
Low-caste hill people	1	.9	1	.8
Hill tribals	22	20.2	19	15.2
Hill people, subtotal	89	81.7	112	89.6
Caste Hindus and Muslims from the plains	13	11.9	11	8.8
Plains tribals	7	6.4	2	1.6
Plains people, subtotal	20	18.4	13	10.4
Total of all representatives	109	100.0	125	100.0

[a]Caste identifications made from lists of members of 1959 Parliament and 1967 National Panchayat.

their traditional advisors. The Chetris are beginning to send their sons for advanced education, and these young men are taking a more active role in politics at all levels.

Low-caste hill people were represented by only a single individual in both the Parliament and the 1967 National Panchayat. The hill-tribal people suffered a 5-percent decline in representation, the largest of any category under discussion. The caste Hindus of plains origin and the Muslims experienced a 2-percent decline in representation, and the plains tribals declined in the same proportions as the hill tribals.

Despite the government's current administrative-decentralization efforts, political leaders at the village and district levels have been unable to exert as much influence in Kathmandu since the introduction of the current indirect-election system as they were able to exert during the brief direct-election period. The current Palace-oriented system has returned the political advantage to those who live closest to the source of power in Kathmandu. Although the data in the table substantiate the fact that nonestablishment groups now have more difficulty entering the national political sphere, the change in the political system is only one of the factors that inhibit more proportional representation. Another is the head start—what might be called political momentum—that Nepalese history has given to the groups in the ruling coalition, providing them with advantages in any political system that might evolve.

Since the National Panchayat is in reality no more than a consultative body, it is perhaps more profitable to look at the representation of various groups in national institutions that are the real centers of power in the present system: the Palace, the Central Secretariat, and the army. In 1960 the primary center of power shifted from Parliament to the Palace. In the Palace, the Chetris and the Newars are the two key groups. The King is a Chetri, and in 1967, except for King Mahendra's press secretary, who was a Brahmin, all of his secretaries, including nine "personal" secretaries, three "principal" secretaries, four "private" secretaries, and his chief private secretary, were Newars. There is evidence that King Birendra, as he fashions his own Palace Secretariat, may change its composition and bring in a group of younger and less traditional advisors from various cultural backgrounds. For generations, however, Shah kings have apparently felt less vulnerable to conspiracy when surrounded by Newar rather than Brahmin secretaries. During the 1960s, with the increased importance of the Palace Secretariat as King Mahendra's administrative and policy-making body, his Newar secretaries inevitably acquired increased influence. Because the King is the single major source of power in Nepal today, the influence of others is determined to a large extent by their ability to gain access to him and obtain his support. King Mahendra's secretaries were the filters through which he viewed much of the world beyond the Palace walls. They controlled much of the information that reached him and determined in many cases who obtained access to him. If political-behavior patterns in Nepal follow those of other countries, it is logical to assume that family members, friends, and associates of these royal secretaries have found access to the King easier than have many others. Unquestionably, the position of the Newars as a group has been enhanced by their role in the Palace administration.

The Central Secretariat is a secondary center of power, responsible for the implementation of governmental decisions. Although much of the crucial decision-making takes place in the Palace, a great many less important decisions are made in the Central Secretariat. It is a much larger, more loosely organized and diverse body than the Palace Secretariat and, among the administrators working there, at least a few are representatives of groups traditionally unrepresented or underrepresented in the centers of power. In table 19, data from 1854 and 1950 are compared with data for 1965. It is impossible to judge how closely the individuals included in the 1854 and 1950 data are comparable in their administrative functions to the Central Secretariat administrators. For this reason, any conclusion drawn must be tentative. A further limitation of these data results from the fact that it was not possible to obtain a caste breakdown that included a distinction between hill and plains Brahmins or between members of the warrior caste of hills origin (Chetris) and plains origin (generally called Rajputs in the tarai). Nevertheless, there is some comparability, and the historical perspective provided by the table is interesting.

TABLE 19
Regional and Communal Distribution of National-Level Administrators

Regional and communal groupings	1854[a]		1950[b]		1965[c]	
	No.	Percent	No.	Percent	No.	percent
Hill and plains Brahmins	31	40.3	19	38.0	68	40.0
Chetris and Rajputs	22	28.6	5	10.0	52	30.6
Newars	22	28.6	26	52.0	34	20.0
Hill tribals					9	5.3
Low-caste hill people					1	.6
Caste Hindus (except Rajputs and Brahmins), Muslims from plains	2	2.6			5	2.9
Plains tribals					1	.6
Total	77	100.0	50	100.0	170	100.0

[a]List of signatories to the first code of laws (Muluki Ain), 1854. Reprinted by the Law Book Committee, Singha Darbar, Kathmandu, 1963.

[b]List of signatories to the 1950 statement denouncing King Tribhuvan's escape to India. See K. B. Devkota, *Nepal ko Rajnaitik Darpan* (Kathmandu, 1959), pp. 29–33.

[c]The 170 individuals include Special Class, Class I, and Class II gazetted officers from the following services: Administrative, Foreign, Agriculture, Education, Engineering, Forestry, General, Health, Panchayat, and Land Reform.

Aside from the first three groups listed in the table, almost no others were represented in the national administration before the 1951 revolution. A few individuals from other groups were brought into lower administrative positions during the 1950s and 1960s. Although 1967 data are not included in the table, these data indicate a significant increase of nonestablishment groups over 1965. In 1967, there were ten hill tribals and eight middle- and low-caste Hindus of plains origin serving as land-reform officers in the upper ranks of the administration.[25] The significant increase in the hiring of these groups occurred with the expansion of the land-reform program. This may have been the result of the need for better communication between the government and these groups during the period in which the complex land-reform program was being implemented.

Although the Brahmin and Chetri categories are not broken down by region of origin in table 19, it is unlikely that more than one or two Brahmins of plains origin were among the Brahmins included in the 1854 and 1950 columns, and it is highly unlikely that any Rajputs were present. By 1965, however, a few plains Brahmins and Rajputs were present among administrators at the upper levels, and it is likely that the number has increased since then.

TABLE 20
Caste Breakdown of Senior Army Officers, 1967

Caste	Number	Percent of total
Chetri	137	74.0
Hill Brahmin	12	6.5
Newar	12	6.5
Gurung	12	6.5
Sanyasi (Giri)	2	1.1
Rai	2	1.1
Tamang	2	1.1
Magar	1	.5
Kayastha	1	.5
Unknown	4	2.2
Total	185	100.0

[25]In Administrative Class II or higher.

The third center of power in Kathmandu is the army. Traditionally, high-ranking officers in the Nepalese Army have been Chetris. This is understandable, as Chetris are soldiers by caste and the history of Nepal, at least in the modern period, has been dominated by Chetri kings, generals, and courtiers. Since the revolution, however, the caste distribution of army officers has changed somewhat, with hill Brahmins and Newars beginning to obtain a few higher-ranking positions, although usually in such noncombat commands as the medical and signal corps. Table 20 provides a caste breakdown of all officers with a rank of captain or higher who were stationed in Kathmandu Valley in 1967. All the generals posted in Kathmandu Valley in 1967 were Chetris.[26] Given the martial tradition of the hill tribes, it is surprising that they are not better represented; only the Gurungs appear to be successful in the competition for higher ranks. Only one individual of plains origin appears in these data, a Kayastha captain in the field-ambulance corps.[27]

Royal power rests to a large extent upon the loyalty of the army. To insure its loyalty, King Mahendra retired a number of the Chetri generals of the rival Rana clan and has promoted Chetris of his own Thakuri clan and other Chetri clans such as the Mallas, Thapas, and Basnyets.[28] Among King Mahendra's key generals in the late 1960s were two Thakuris, Commander-in-Chief General Surendra Bahadur Shah and Lt. General Ranga Bikram Shah, officer in charge of the Royal Guard. Although most public attention is focused on politics within the Palace and Central Secretariats, political activity within the army could determine Nepal's future. Thus far, army officers evidence few political inclinations. So long as they remain politically passive and loyal to King Birendra, he will be provided with a secure base of support.

Thus, in the three centers of power, the ruling coalition of Chetris, hill Brahmins, and Newars continues much as it did before the revolution. In recent years, representatives of groups that constitute the

---

[26]No data were available for officers posted outside the Valley, and it is not known whether any generals may have been posted elsewhere in Nepal.

[27]Names of four officers could not be identified by caste, but their caste names appear similar to those of Chetris and hill tribals.

[28]There has been a great deal of intermarriage among Chetri clans, particularly between the royal branch of the Thakuri clan and the Shamsher branch of the Rana clan. The young King Birendra, his father, and his grandfather were all married to Shamsher Rana women. Therefore, it is likely that most of the Thakuri generals have Rana family ties.

majority of the nation's population, plains people and low-caste and tribal people of hill origin, have begun to make their presence felt in the Central Secretariat. By 1967, representatives of these groups were 12 percent of senior administrators in the Central Secretariat. In that year, they also accounted for 13 percent of ranking army officers. However, members of these groups had not yet been appointed to key administrative positions in the Palace Secretariat. The plains people, taken separately from other underrepresented categories, had obtained significant representation only in the Central Secretariat, where they accounted for 7 percent of its senior administrators by 1967.

In elective politics, where one's success is determined by support from below rather than appointment from above, non-Chetri-hill-Brahmin-Newar groups have fared better, gaining 26 percent of the seats in the 1967 National Panchayat. Plains people held 10 percent of those seats. However, with the shift in power from Parliament to the Palace in 1960, membership in legislative bodies since then has signified little in terms of real political influence. Among most low-caste and tribal people of both the hill and plains regions, there is still little political consciousness and little demand for admission into the centers of power. But the more affluent and better-educated upper-caste people of the tarai are aware of the extent to which they remain excluded from Kathmandu's inner sanctum and from the administration of government in the districts of their own region. The result is a sense of alienation from those who control the government in Kathmandu and from the hill-culture-oriented nationalism that they espouse. As has been documented in this chapter, the introduction of the panchayat system, with its indirect-election procedure, has increased the problems encountered by plains people in their efforts to gain representation in Kathmandu. This has reinforced their sense of alienation.

It is perhaps true that all innovative political systems, in order to be accepted, must incorporate elements of more traditional politics. The key question about the panchayat system is whether it has brought about the type of change in traditional Kathmandu-oriented politics needed to move the nation ahead more rapidly toward political integration than did the political-party system. Because the panchayat system has failed to bring about the participation of those groups that have composed the traditionally underrepresented majority, the question must be answered in the negative. Perhaps during the 1970s, under the new leadership of King Birendra, the panchayat system can be modified to include broader national participation.

Undoubtedly, King Mahendra hoped that the panchayat system would somehow operate to broaden the national political base, because he must have realized that he needed to mobilize the support of diverse groups in order to push ahead with the nation-building process. Nevertheless, his desire to establish the new system was motivated chiefly by a more immediate concern, to maintain royal power. Because the panchayat system has been designed primarily to preserve the source of traditional power at the national level, it is understandable that it can not challenge traditional politics at other levels.

Chapter IX

OPPOSITIONAL POLITICS IN THE TARAI

Among the tarai inhabitants who resent Nepalese government policies are villagers with little or no land. They form a large segment of the tarai population, and their resentment stems mainly from the government's economic policies. A much smaller but more influential element of alienated people are the relatively affluent and better educated who live in the tarai towns. For the most part, their resentment is a reaction to the government's policies that discriminate against plains people. The few landowners who fall into this category are most often discontented because local-government officials have taken sides against them in conflicts involving other landowner factions.

THE LAND-REFORM PROGRAM AND DISCONTENT IN THE RURAL AREAS

Discontent among the economically disadvantaged rural population results primarily from economic problems, hence it is useful to evaluate briefly the land-reform program upon which the government bases much of its agricultural-development program. As might be expected, a government founded on a traditionalist solution to conflict between modernizing and traditional elites would find it difficult to formulate and implement economic reforms that undercut the power base of the traditional elite. What, then, was the motivation behind the land-reform program? It is clear that King Mahendra, like other ruling monarchs, wished to appear to be a modernizer, even though he was prepared for only the most cautious steps in that direction. His speeches were couched in the modern idiom, but the spirit was "dharmashastric in its fundamentals."[1] It also appears that at least a few influential government officials entertained hopes that the land-reform program could be used as a vehicle for transferring to hill people the

[1] Leo E. Rose, "Secularization of a Traditional Hindu Polity: The Case of Nepal" (unpublished manuscript, University of California, July 1971), p. 21.

landholdings of plains people. Inasmuch as more than 50 percent of the rich tarai lands are held by large landowners of plains origin, such a transfer would have reaped handsome benefits for the hill people with influence in Kathmandu. Whatever the original intentions of some officials, during the 1963–64 period when the land-reform legislation was being drawn up, the Indian government made it clear that it would not tolerate the dispossession of the tarai plains people in this manner.

The pressure for reforms applied by aid-giving nations was another factor. Among the development agencies that have used the most pressure are the U.S. Agency for International Development and the Ford Foundation. In 1962, Wolf Ladejinsky, Consultant for the Ford Foundation, wrote a report to King Mahendra in which he inferred that foreign aid was a futile gesture if not accompanied by land reform.[2] In an article two years later, Ladejinsky stated his message more emphatically: "Important though the other ingredients [technical assistance, cooperatives, credit, etc.] are, unless those who work the land own it, or are at least secure on the land as tenants, all the rest is likely to be writ in water."[3] This message was not lost on the Nepalese government. It needed to attract foreign aid and, therefore, it went through the motions of enacting land-reform legislation. The result was a product of expediency rather than a commitment to fundamental change.

The commitment to reform and the long-range educational value of foreign advisors like Ladejinsky are beyond question, but the experiences of these advisors were often far removed from the Nepalese context. They tended to bring to Nepal preconceived ideas about the kinds of reforms that could be implemented, and to estimate unrealistically the administrative capabilities of those at the local level who would be responsible for implementing reforms. In addition, because they often had an inadequate understanding of the dynamics of Nepalese politics, they sought to persuade those who controlled policy-making in Kathmandu in the 1960s to implement reforms that would transfer land resources, the basis of wealth and power in Nepal's agrarian society, from family members, relatives, retainers, and other traditional allies to those segments of the population over whom this landed elite has ruled.

[2]Letter addressed to H. M. King Mahendra, dated Feb. 15, 1962, Kathmandu, mimeographed for public distribution.
[3]Wolf Ladejinsky, "Agrarian Reform in Asia," *Foreign Affairs*, XLII (April 1964), 446.

As might be expected under the circumstances, the 1964 land-reform laws did little to alter the status quo. In fact, the laws simply formalized much of the existing landholding system. Few large landholdings exist in the hill region. Large landholdings and extensive use of tenant labor and daily-wage labor have prevailed only in the tarai. Therefore, the land-reform program has been focused primarily on the tarai, but control of land in the tarai and elsewhere in the country has generally remained in the same hands. Land-reform laws permit a landowner in the tarai to retain 25 bighas (approximately 40 acres) of land and to transfer the same amount to each son over sixteen years of age and each unmarried daughter over thirty-five years of age. The 40-acre ceiling is a high one in view of the high man–land ratio in Nepal. Perhaps no more than 7 or 8 percent of the cultivable land in the tarai exceeded this ceiling when the Lands Act came into force in 1964[4] and, in the hills, landholdings that exceeded the ceiling were few. In addition, the right to transfer land to family members represented a convenient loophole in the law. Furthermore, some land-reform officials proved unable to implement the law, permitting landowners to transfer land titles to individuals not eligible under the law, relatives and family friends who hold titles for the original owners. In some cases, records have been falsified and officials paid to overlook irregularities. As a result, by mid-1968, only 146,000 acres of excess land had been acquired by the government.[5] And of the land acquired, by mid-1972, only 56,000 acres had been redistributed.[6] Nor did the reforms abolish the widespread institution of the absentee landlord. If land had been transferred to the hands of those who actually worked the land, the high landholding ceiling notwithstanding, the reforms would have represented a step in a more progressive direction.

The essential conservatism of the land-reform program was underscored by the government's willingness to sanction high rent ceilings. With regard to rent rates, one Nepalese scholar observed that the 1964 Lands Act "has given formal recognition to a practice prevalent over a large part of the country, and might possibly even aggravate the situation for tenants, particularly those on newly reclaimed lands. The general practice is to share only the main crop, but the act entitles the landowner to claim half of each crop and subsidiary produce grown

[4]B. P. Shrestha, "Current Land Reform Programme in Nepal," *Nepalese Perspective*, II, No. 45 (1966), 14.
[5]*Gorkhapatra*, Apr. 30, 1968.
[6]*Ibid.*, May 31, 1972.

throughout the year."⁷ Thus, in some instances, this aspect of the reforms meant only further burdens to tenants, and landowners found no reason to complain. In 1970, the government revised its rent-ceiling policy, returning to the prereform rate of 50 percent of the main crop only. If officials are able to enforce the revised policy, this will ease the tenants' burdens.

One of the most unfortunate consequences of the land-reform program has been the eviction of many tenant families from land they had been cultivating. At the time the reforms were enacted, there was a rash of land-title transfers. Some of these resulted in the replacement of tenants by owner-cultivators. This type of transfer is illustrated by the example of Kushmaha village, where Tharu tenants were replaced by hill-Brahmin owner-cultivators.⁸ Many transfers resulted in the replacement of tenants by laborers paid on a daily basis, individuals without even the minimum security that tradition has provided for tenants. This type of transfer occurred frequently in the mid-western tarai and was commented upon in chapter V in connection with the Ukhada land reforms and citizenship problems.

Legal actions initiated by landowners and government officials threatened many tenants, leading to an outburst of violence in Nawal Parasi district in September 1966, around the district's administrative center in the village of Parasi. A crowd estimated at 4,000 rioted and threatened the lives of government officials. According to official reports, 9 persons were killed and 12 others wounded in the police firings that resulted.⁹ The publicly released version of the report contained no explanation of the riot, and the doors were closed to unofficial investigations. Nevertheless, the *Gorkhapatra*, the government's Nepali-language daily, suggested that "certain elements had misguided the peasants on the issue of land reform, and they should not be left unpunished."¹⁰ The government-sponsored Peasants Organization expressed the view that the disturbance was at least partly the result of citizenship problems arising from the abolition of the Ukhada land-tenure system, especially in Nawal Parasi and Rupandehi districts.¹¹

---

⁷Mahesh C. Regmi, *Land Tenure and Taxation in Nepal*, vol. IV (Berkeley, 1968), p. 138.
⁸See the section on caste and communal characteristics of migrants in ch. IV.
⁹*Nepal Gazette*, vol. XVI, Extraordinary Issue No. 29, Oct. 14, 1966.
¹⁰*Gorkhapatra*, Sept. 19, 1966.
¹¹*Jana Awaz Weekly*, Oct. 1, 15, 1966.

The compulsory-savings scheme, initiated in 1965, is yet another aspect of the land-reform program that caused widespread resentment in the large rural segment of the tarai population. Progressive in concept, the scheme was designed to generate capital reserves for investment in agricultural improvements and in small-scale industry, and would stimulate economic development if it could be implemented. But it was unrealistic to assume that 32,000 compulsory-savings village ward committees could be created, each committee with 3 members, and that these 96,000 villagers would somehow grasp novel ledger, account, and investment concepts and at the same time forsake local politics and self-interest in order to promote something called "the well-being of the community."

According to the blueprints of the scheme, every farmer was required to deposit a small percentage of his crops with the government each year, and the capital acquired in this way would be loaned back to villagers who needed it for investment purposes. Most farmers looked upon the scheme as simply another form of taxation, despite the government's promise to return their deposits with interest at the end of five years. Many farmers made the required deposits during the first several years of the scheme's operation, but many others, particularly landowners with the power to resist, avoided making deposits. During 1967 and 1968, the Nepalese press reported frequently that ward committees were not keeping adequate records of savings collected, that committee members and other locally influential people were misappropriating the savings, and that resistance to payment was growing. Finally, in April 1969, protests against the scheme turned to violence.

The trouble reportedly began in Taulihawa, the administrative center of Kapilabastu district, when a crowd of village women surrounded and attacked officials attempting to collect compulsory savings.[12] Violence quickly spread across Kapilabastu district and into Rupandehi district. Looting and police firings occurred in a thirty-village area over a three-week period. During this period, at least twenty-three persons lost their lives, hundreds were wounded, and many others arrested. Compulsory-savings depots and private homes were looted and burned.[13]

During this second major outburst of violence in the 1960s, the government again suppressed information, thereby encouraging the

[12]*Samaj*, Apr. 3, 1966; *New Herald*, Apr. 3, 1969.
[13]*Gorkhapatra*, May 5, 1969.

press to issue speculative and often irresponsible analyses of the problems involved. When one sifts through the press reports, a series of interrelated problems emerge. One problem was the government's inability to administrate the compulsory-savings scheme properly because collection procedures were too complex for the Nepalese village context. Savings were reportedly being collected by intimidation from villagers living at a subsistence or near-subsistence level. For some villagers, the payments were apparently difficult to make, and for others, who were aware that some savings were being misappropriated, the collections were intolerable.

The government was naturally anxious to prove that outside agitators rather than its own policies produced the violence. The government reported that among the sixty-four persons arrested by April 14, thirty-two were Indians. Local-government officials claimed at the time that "some Indians who have been trying to settle down in Nepal and some Indian dacoits [bandits] are responsible for these disturbances."[14] Thus, the second interrelated problem was citizenship. It is not clear whether the "Indians" were actually bandits, political organizers, or simply villagers of plains origin who had not been able to obtain citizenship certificates. Without dismissing the possibility that bandits or political organizers were involved, it is reasonable to assume that most of the "Indians" were tenants and landless laborers, perhaps some of them recent settlers in the tarai, perhaps some alienated earlier by land-reform measures that resulted in their evictions from tenancy holdings. Many fled from the troubled area to India, and this was used as evidence by some observers in Kathmandu that they were Indians,[15] despite the fact that this appears to have been the sensible thing to do, given the virtual state of anarchy.

A third interrelated factor may have been antigovernment political organization. The Kathmandu press claimed that Nepali Congress and Communist organizers had encouraged the violence. This possibility can not be disregarded, for some evidence of underground party organization in the mid-western tarai has come to light. The fires of violent protest, once ignited, often envelop those who are the objects of other grievances. In this case, latent Hindu-Muslim tension was brought to the surface, and became a fourth interrelated problem. Kapilabastu and Rupandehi districts have larger concentrations of Muslims than most other tarai districts. Muslims and Hindus apparent-

[14]*Ibid.*, Apr. 15, 1969.
[15]*New Herald,* May 1, 1969.

ly directed some of their frustrations against each other, and one ultranationalist Kathmandu newspaper charged that exiled Nepali Congress workers were facilitating the "infiltration of a large number of Indian Muslims and other Indians into this region of Nepal to create disturbances."[16] Although the validity of this charge is doubtful, it is evidence of the "specter of migration" fear.

The violence forced the government to suspend collection of savings throughout the country. Suspension of the scheme left the government with a welter of problems: organization and, in some cases, reconstruction of ward-committee records, retrieval of misappropriated savings, and repayment of savings along with the interest originally promised. Because some of the savings were never invested, they have not been generating interest, and it will be difficult for the government to make good its promise to repay the farmers. On the other hand, the government's credibility would be seriously undermined if it defaulted on payments, hence government spokesmen have continued to insist that payments are forthcoming. By 1972, three years after the scheme was suspended, the government reported that most of the accounts had been audited, that misappropriations were not as widespread as supposed, and that the scheme may be tried again, this time exempting small farmers and tenants from collections.[17]

The villagers' resentment of the government's land-reform program is compounded by economic and administrative problems over which the government has little or no control. Economic problems result to a large extent from the limited resources available for development purposes, resources without which it is difficult to push ahead vigorously with programs to relieve poverty. Inadequate local administrative talent is another handicap. Regardless of the form of government or its ideological orientation, it would be difficult to supply rural areas across the country with a large number of administrators who understand how to guide the complex process of economic development and who are willing to put the nation's goals ahead of self-interest. To create a corps of enlightened administrators at both the national and local levels is one of the keys to modernization.

In 1967 the government inaugurated the "Back to the Village Campaign" in an attempt to mobilize support for its programs and to neutralize the influence of the underground political parties in the rural areas. In a speech to the National Panchayat in May 1967,

[16]*Dainik Nirnaya*, Apr. 8, 1969.
[17]*Gorkhapatra*, Mar. 13, 1972.

King Mahendra introduced the campaign as follows:

> The majority of the people of the country live in the villages. Accordingly, we must go back to the villages to achieve the fundamental objectives of the [panchayat] system. The apathy persistent in our rural society for hundreds of years has not yet disappeared, and consciousness of rights and duties has not yet been aroused among our village people to the extent desired. Ignorance, disease and poverty are still deep-rooted in the villages. Although we have made progress toward the infusion of consciousness and dynamism among the rural people as a result of development programs launched under the present system, and also as a result of the land reform program introduced as an integral part of the system, yet we have to accelerate the pace of our progress.[18]

He went on to say:

> The problem is complicated because educated people who provide leadership have the tendency to leave the villages. This tendency is unfortunate. Now everyone should concentrate his entire attention upon village activities in order to fulfill the objectives of the system as soon as possible. These objectives are difficult to fulfill, and they can be achieved only through cultivation of the qualities of nationalism, patriotism, honesty, discipline, and diligence. Since it has become imperative that the nation's entire energy be organized and mobilized in a single powerful national campaign to attain these objectives, and everyone should make the necessary sacrifices and contribute their strength to implement this campaign ... I ... call upon all Nepali people to participate in the "Back to the Village National Campaign" in a disciplined and carefully guided manner.[19]

The King then outlined ten specific objectives to be implemented at the village level through the medium of the campaign. They are interesting because they represented his interests and his aspirations.

> 1. Consolidation and expansion of the spirit of nationalism and national unity.
> 2. Dissemination of the fact that the nation needs the partyless panchayat democracy, the fact that it has no alternative in Nepal, and the fact that "partyless feeling" should be developed.
> 3. Cultivation of behavior in accordance with Nepal's nonaligned foreign policy.

[18]*Ibid.*, Oct. 1, 1967.
[19]*Ibid.*

4. Introduction of a campaign to eliminate corruption, injustice, oppression, and unnecessary administrative inefficiency.
5. Infusion of consciousness and dynamism in the village society.
6. Further strengthening the implementation of the land-reform program, the new legal code, social welfare programs, and nationwide reconstruction activities.
7. Propagation and extension of cooperative programs and feelings.
8. Imparting of knowledge about the significance of forest and wild-life protection and afforestation.
9. Emphasis on agricultural production.
10. Arousing of consciousness regarding the need for cottage industries.[20]

As part of the campaign, all educated people were to spend some time in the villages to do the following: teach villagers about the history and heroes of Nepal; encourage the use of the Nepali language and literature; distribute replicas of the national flag and other national emblems; stress the fact that the existence of political parties causes national disintegration and that the current partyless system is more appropriate to the spirit and traditions of the Nepalese people, etc. Mandatory periods of time to be spent in the villages were set for government officials and those elected to various levels of the panchayat system; others were encouraged to follow their example.

It may not have been coincidental that the campaign was conceived about the time the Nepalese government was experiencing some confrontations with Chinese officials in Nepal. The cultural revolution was still in full swing in China, and Chinese officials seemed particularly belligerent. The "Back to the Village Campaign" has certain undeniable similarities to the cultural revolution. The outline of campaign plans sounded less like a public-works program than a religious crusade. There were no quotas of wells to be dug, trees to be planted, or roads to be built. Instead, there were admonitions about eschewing pomp and luxury, corruption, and class consciousness. There were also directions for all citizens to study and discuss together liturgies such as the following:

1. My Nepali nation is lofty and sacred. My prime objective is to achieve the all-around development of the country and the people. I am performing these duties inspired by the desire to serve the nation. I live and protect my nation as a staunch nationalist.

[20] *Ibid.*

2. Faith in the Crown and its leadership are providing me with constant enthusiasm and support. Accordingly, I am undaunted and determined, and am never tired of performing any work which benefits Nepal and the Nepali people. To no one at any time do I express feelings of despair with respect to the panchayat system. I make myself always responsible to the panchayat system.

3. After finishing my work in the evenings, I shall pass my leisure hours participating only in national music and art programs and in the cultural programs appropriate to the system.[21]

Early in 1967, buttons with Mao's profile began to circulate in Nepal and were worn by some students. By mid-1967, two or three kinds of buttons with King Mahendra's picture were circulated and considerable pressure to wear them was applied to government officials and elected panchayat members. The little red books of Mao's thoughts, printed in both Nepali and English, were available in the marketplace; following inauguration of the "Back to the Village Campaign," a book of King Mahendra's thoughts was also published.

The formal launching of the campaign on December 15, 1967 was followed by a wave of enthusiastic speeches by officials and panchayat members. But gradually the speeches began to sound stale, and they decreased in number. Many officials put off their compulsory visits to the villages until the last possible date. There were no concrete plans for village-development work and no clear directives for village workers to follow. Initial enthusiasm faded, mobilization of the urban elite did not take place, and the villagers remained as isolated from the mainstream of national affairs as they had been previously. Although the campaign has not been officially terminated, little has been heard about it since 1969, and it is clear that the campaign has not achieved its objectives.

Thus far, urban-oriented opposition groups have also shown only limited ability to establish communication with the villages,[22] but the possibility of more effective oppositional organizations in the villages raises a potentially serious problem for the government. Perhaps for this reason, following King Birendra's assumption of power, there has been some talk in the Palace of revising and revitalizing the campaign.

[21]*Ibid.*
[22]L. S. Baral, "Opposition Groups in Nepal, 1960–70," *India Quarterly*, vol. XXVIII (January–March 1972), 39.

OPPOSITION PARTIES

Although the two major political parties, the Nepali Congress and the Communist Party of Nepal, make their presence felt in both Kathmandu Valley and the tarai, they tend to operate more openly in the tarai. This is due partly to the fact that the government is better organized to detect and suppress antigovernment activity in the Valley and partly to its ability to siphon off through the offer of government employment many of the potentially disaffected in the Valley. In addition, party activists in the tarai have Indian territory to use as sanctuary, if needed. Both parties also have a larger number of alienated people to draw upon for support in the tarai, people who feel not only physical but cultural distance from those who govern in Kathmandu; these are the plains people who feel threatened by the government's efforts to Nepalize the region.

There is little open opposition to the government in the tarai. Nevertheless, considerable effort is being made by Nepali Congress and Communist Party workers to organize support in the towns and villages of the region. Competition between the two parties for support has become particularly keen since Nepali Congress leaders were released from jail in the fall of 1968 and others were allowed to return from exile in India. Let us look at the activities of the two parties and the competition between them.

The Communist Party of Nepal was established in 1949. During the 1950s, as the party grew, revolutionary and moderate factions emerged, the former led by Pushpa Lal Shrestha, and the latter by Keshar Jang Rayamajhi. Pushpa Lal's was the minority faction, drawing its strength primarily from Kathmandu Valley and the eastern tarai. In the parliamentary elections of 1959, the Communist Party ran candidates in 46 of the 109 constituencies and won 4 seats, 2 in Rautahat district of the eastern tarai, 1 in Palpa district of the western hills, and 1 in Kathmandu Valley. It also received strong support in other eastern-tarai constituencies, notably in Saptari district, and in other constituencies of Kathmandu Valley.[23] Compared with the Nepali Congress victory in 74 constituencies, however, the Communist Party looked weak.

[23]Leo E. Rose, "Communism Under High Atmospheric Conditions: The Party in Nepal," in *The Communist Revolution in Asia*, ed. by R. A. Scalapino, 2d ed. (Englewood Cliffs, N. J., 1969), pp. 365, 369, 373, 383. The party was established in Calcutta because political organization in Nepal at the time was suppressed by the Rana regime in power.

The royal coup precipitated a split between the Pushpa Lal and the Rayamajhi factions. Pushpa Lal fled to India to organize opposition to King Mahendra's government, whereas Rayamajhi remained in Kathmandu to support the King. Pushpa Lal's revolutionary efforts foundered in 1962 as a result of the Sino-Indian conflict and the Nepali Congress decision to terminate its rebel activities. Members of the Rayamajhi faction, on the other hand, were having some success in panchayat elections. It was in a position to elect eighteen party members to the National Panchayat in the 1963 elections, a considerable improvement, compared with the 4 members elected to the Parliament four years earlier.[24]

Immediately after the coup, the King attempted to suppress the Nepali Congress, which he viewed as the party most threatening to his position. The Rayamajhi faction claimed at the same time that it had disbanded the Communist Party in order to comply with the King's ban on all political parties. With all national and local Nepali Congress leaders either in jail or in exile, the moderate communists were able to organize without competition, not only where they had been strong in 1959, but also in some regions where they had previously been weak. Rayamajhi himself was appointed to the Council of State, an essentially honorary body, and Communist Party members or sympathizers have been included in a number of ministries since 1963.[25] As one observer of Nepal's political scene commented in the late 1960s: "Rayamajhi's tactics have gained tangible benefits for his small group of adherents as well as a degree of viability for his Party within Nepal. However, this has been achieved at the cost of the modicum of public support the Party once enjoyed, particularly among students."[26] In both Kathmandu Valley and the tarai, support for the party's antimonarchical faction appears to be growing, particularly among student groups in the urban centers.

There are two India-based communist movements that have reportedly reinforced oppositional politics in the tarai, the Naxalites in the eastern tarai and the Tarai Liberation Front in the midwestern tarai. In 1967, when the extremist wing of the Communist Party in India gained temporary control of some villages in the Naxalbari

---

[24]*Ibid.*, pp. 373–377, 379–380, 384. Candidates for panchayat positions run without party labels. Nevertheless, in the rather intimate small-town political atmosphere of Kathmandu, the informal party affiliations of politically important people are usually known.
[25]*Ibid.*, pp. 377–378, 380.
[26]*Ibid.*, pp. 380–381.

region of Darjeeling district of West Bengal, bordering the far-eastern tarai, the Indian press claimed that the extremists, later termed Naxalites, were using the tarai as a base of operations and a sanctuary. Fears were expressed in Bhadrapur, the administrative center of Jhapa district, that the terrorist tactics of the Naxalites would be used in the district.[27] Although this has not occurred as yet, there have been occasional claims in both the Indian and Nepalese press that the Naxalites are involved in organizational activities in the tarai.

Information about the Tarai Liberation Front is less speculative. At the time that the Nepali Congress rebels were operating along the India-Nepal border in 1961–62, the Tarai Liberation Front was established to press the demands of the plains people living in Nepal. According to the Nepalese government, one of the Front leaders, Ramji Mishra, was killed by Nepalese police in June 1963.[28] Although the government claimed that Mishra was a "notorious dacoit," *The Hindustan Times*[29] called him the leader of a movement for the liberation of Indian settlers living in the western tarai. It was reported that the Nepalese Army had also killed the head of the Front, Raghu Nath Rai, about the same time. According to *The Statesman*,[30] Rai had been kidnapped from Nautanwa, an Indian border town opposite Bhairawa in Rupandehi district, and then killed in Nepalese territory.

Some time in early August 1967, one of the Indian newspapers carried an article by Raghu Nath Thakur, who called himself a leader of the Tarai Liberation Front. He claimed that "thousands of persons in the tarai had fallen victim to oppression," and were being driven off the land so that it could be resettled by hill people. The substance of Thakur's article appeared in a letter to the *Gorkhapatra*,[31] by three panchayat members form Jhapa district who denied Thakur's charges. At the end of August, the Nepalese government reported that the "self-styled President" of the Front, Satyadeo Mani Tripathi, had been killed and two companions injured in a clash between Tripathi's group and a "rival" group in Nautanwa.[32] Observers in Kathmandu surmised that the "rival" group in this case consisted of hirelings of local Nepalese-government officials.

[27]*Swatantra Samachar*, June 27, 1967; *Nepal Samachar*, June 28, 1967; *Samaj*, June 27, 1967.
[28]*Gorkhapatra*, June 19, 1963.
[29]*Hindustan Times* (New Delhi), June 18, 1963, p. 1.
[30]*Statesman*, Aug. 28, 1967, p. 5.
[31]*Gorkhapatra*, Aug. 13, 1967.
[32]*Rising Nepal*, Aug. 30, 1967.

During 1967, there were reports of tension between the Communist and Nepali Congress factions in the large Nepalese student community at Banaras Hindu University. Congress supporters gained control of the Nepalese student organization in Banaras. Pushpa Lal, whose main support came from students, was forced to move to Darbhanga, 200 miles northeast of Banaras. In early 1968, there was speculation that an armed antigovernment camp had been established in Darbhanga,[33] adding support for the possibility that Pushpa Lal's group might be associated with the Tarai Liberation Front. Whether such a camp existed is impossible to prove from information available. If it did exist, it never became effective as a center for launching armed attacks upon Nepalese border posts.

In April 1969, violence erupted in the mid-western tarai, and the *New Herald* reported: "The Pushpa Lal group of the banned Nepal Communist Party is reported to be very active in Gorakhpur in India. The group has also extended its activities to the Gurkha Recruitment Depot in Kunraghat. It is being given unrestricted freedom to make propaganda against the panchayat system and engage in other subversive activities against Nepal from Gorakhpur."[34]

In May, after the violence had subsided, the newly appointed Prime Minister, Kirtinidhi Bista, toured the riot-torn area, and according to the *Motherland*:

> His Majesty's Government has conveyed Nepal's concern to India over the presence of armed gangs of politically active persons on the Indian side of the Nepal-India border. These gangs have been active for some months now and the Indian authorities have been unable to bring them under control. These gangs are working under various names, but all of them claim allegiance to the revolutionary views of the extreme leftists. One of them is led by a person called Vishwa Nath Tiwari. It consists of 40 or 50 armed men, who operate mostly in the Lakhimpur-Kheri area.[35]

Man Mohan Adhikari, one of the most important leaders of the left wing of the Communist Party of Nepal and one of the few Communist leaders jailed at the time of the royal coup, was released from jail in February 1969, only three months after the release of

---

[33]*Gorkhapatra*, Jan. 1, 1968.

[34]*New Herald*, Apr. 18, 1969. Both Gorakhpur and Nautanwa are situated in Gorakhpur district in Uttar Pradesh, just south of Rupandehi district in Nepal.

[35]*Motherland*, May 19, 1969. Lakhimpur-Kheri district of Uttar Pradesh in India borders on Kailali district of the far-western Nepal tarai.

Nepali Congress leaders. Soon afterward, he became the main spokesman for the left-communists in Nepal, issuing frequent statements criticizing the Prime Minister and his associates, but at the same time carefully avoiding any direct criticism of the King. In August 1972, Adhikari even ventured to call upon his countrymen to unite for the purpose of bringing about the downfall of the Council of Ministers.[36] Two months later, he was reported to have reached an agreement with Pushpa Lal to cooperate in organizing the left wing of the party. According to the report, Adhikari would be responsible for political organizing inside Nepal and Pushpa Lal outside, but they agreed to refrain from launching guerrilla-type activities from Indian territory[37]

The Nepalese press is able to provide only limited coverage of events occurring outside Kathmandu Valley, because newspapers do not assign reporters to rural areas and the government restricts information about political unrest. Therefore, it is difficult to assess the strength of extremist communist groups such as the Naxalities, the Tarai Liberation Front, or the Pushpa Lal faction of the Communist Party of Nepal, and it is also difficult to know what relationship, if any, exists among these groups or between these groups and the Chinese embassies in Kathmandu and New Delhi.

The Nepalese government has seldom reacted publicly to the activities of these groups, but Nepali Congress leaders have repeatedly stated their concern. On May 15, 1968, when Subarna Shamsher, acting President of the Nepali Congress government-in-exile, offered reconciliation with King Mahendra, he cited the threat of the "forces of subversion" as one of the reasons the Nepali Congress had decided to cooperate with the King. When asked to elaborate, he named the Nepalese Communists as these "forces of subversion" that "were threatening the basic fabric and values of the Nepalese national life."[38]

Soon after B.P. Koirala, Ganesh Man Singh, and other Nepali Congress leaders were released from jail in late October 1968, Ganesh Man, in blunt statements reminiscent of his political style of a decade earlier, emphasized Subarna's concern about the headway the communists were making in Nepal. In the course of several speeches delivered at Birganj in Bara district in December, he contended that "The

---

[36]*Ibid.*, Aug. 30, 1972.
[37]*Naya Sandesh Weekly*, Oct. 6, 1972.
[38]*Statesman* (Calcutta), May 16, 1968, p. 7.

release of B.P. Koirala and the pardon granted to Subarna Shamsher and his associates were the result of foreign pressure and the realization of the growing communist danger faced by Nepal."[39]

In the following months, Koirala himself sounded an anticommunist note, but in less alarming tones. He expressed the view that there exist only two political systems, democratic and undemocratic, and that it is impossible for the panchayat system to become a third political system compromising between the two, between parliamentary democracy and communism.[10]

By such statements, Nepali Congress leaders furnish evidence of the competition which they feel the communists represent in the struggle to dominate oppositional politics in Nepal. There is no doubt that the communists gained popular support in Nepali Congress strongholds during the years since King Mahendra imprisoned most of the Nepali Congress leaders and particularly after the Indian government called a halt to the armed activities of Nepali Congress rebels in late 1962. Since then, party workers have maintained a series of posts in Indian border towns and have distributed party propaganda in the tarai, but the party has lost its organizational momentum.

When Nepali Congress leaders and workers were released and pardoned in late 1968, Prime Minister Surya Bahadur Thapa, who played a key role in attempting to bring about a rapprochement between the King and Nepali Congress leaders, stated repeatedly that only two alternatives would be open to these leaders. They could either work within the panchayat system, which was his hope, or settle down to nonpolitical lives. Neither has occurred. B.P. Koirala, his brothers, Ganesh Man Singh, and several other leaders have been making speeches designed to attract the following that was previously theirs, particularly among the students, and they have attempted to persuade some of the lesser-known party workers to return to party organizing activities in their local areas.[41]

[39]*Samiksha Weekly*, Jan. 6, 1969.

[40]*Ibid.*, Mar. 29, 1969. Inasmuch as political parties are not supposed to exist in Nepal at present, "democrats" or "democratic forces" are terms used in current Nepalese parlance for supporters of the Nepali Congress, and "Marxists" or "progressives" for Communist Party supporters.

[41]Some leaders, such as Surya Prasad Upadhyaya, and perhaps to some extent Subarna Shamsher, wish to accommodate themselves to the panchayat system and to work for change from within. For a report of the unsuccessful politics of accommodation in 1968–69, see two articles by Frederick H. Gaige, "Nepal: Compromise and Liberalization," *Asian Survey*, IX (February 1969), 94–98, and "Nepal: The Search for a National Consensus," *Asian Survey*, X (February 1970), 100–106.

Both Communist and Nepali Congress workers have been active in distributing antigovernment leaflets throughout the tarai, particularly in 1972 during the months immediately following King Birendra's assumption of power. In August 1972, there was a night raid on a police station in a border village of Saptari district; in the exchange of fire, one policeman was killed. Observers tended to believe that the raid was organized by the Nepali Congress, reminiscent of armed Nepali Congress raids on police stations in the tarai during the 1961–62 period.[42] The day after the raid, Swaran Singh, India's Minister of External Affairs, declared that the Indian government would not allow Indian territory to be used for hostile activities against Nepal. He also disclosed that Nepalese opposition leaders in India had been warned not to attempt to undermine the Indian position.[43]

The most obvious manifestations of competition between the Nepali Congress and Communist parties, but probably the least threatening to the government, occur at Tribhuvan University (on the outskirts of Kathmandu) and in the various university-affiliated colleges in Kathmandu Valley and the tarai. The left-communist or Maoist students tend to dominate politics in the colleges of Patan (in the Valley) and Dharan (in the eastern tarai), but in the university and most of the other colleges, pro-Congress and pro-Maoist student activists seem fairly equally matched, with the control of student unions seesawing from one group to the other. In 1968 and 1970, Maoists controlled the university union and, in 1969 and 1971, the Congressites held the upper hand. When progovernment students have run slates of candidates in university elections, the percentage of votes they have received has been negligible.

Almost every year, there are student disturbances at the university, at Morang College in Biratnagar, and at several other colleges in the tarai. These disturbances often arise out of conflict between rival student groups, but they also involve overt expressions of antigovernment sentiment and, therefore, particularly those in Kathmandu embarrass the government, because they receive considerable domestic and international press coverage.

The most widespread student disturbances in recent years took place in August and September 1972. Agitation began at Morang College in Biratnagar and at Tribhuvan University in opposition to many of the provisions of the government's new education plan. The plan is

[42]*Gorkhapatra*, Aug. 28, 1972.
[43]*Ibid.*, Aug. 30, 1972.

designed to make the educational system more responsive to the manpower needs of a modernizing nation, but many students regard the plan as a threat to their chances to earn college and university degrees.[44] The agitation spread rapidly to most of the colleges and many of the high schools in Kathmandu Valley and the tarai, fanned in mid-August by mass arrests of opposition politicians and the suspension of twelve National Panchayat members[45] who were reported to be Nepali Congress sympathizers. At this point, student leaders escalated their demands to include dismissal of the government headed by Prime Minister Kirtinidhi Bista.[46] The interesting difference between this disturbance and others of the previous few years was the cooperation exhibited among usually competitive student factions. A nine-member action committee composed of equal numbers of representatives from the pro-Nepali Congress and from Maoist and pro-Russian student groups organized the strike within the university.[47]

Political leadership is almost always drawn from the educated upper and middle classes of the urbanized population, and Nepal is no exception in this regard. The university and the colleges are located in urban settings, and within the broader urban context exists the spawning ground for leaders of oppositional parties and much of the financial and logistical support for these parties. Whether from homes in the towns or the villages, those who are educated in the towns usually remain to seek jobs and often to swell the population of unemployed graduates. Some find jobs as school teachers or junior-level government employees, but some remain unemployed for long periods, becoming progressively restless and disaffected. Many, but by no means all, of the opposition-party activists are drawn from among the unemployed. Some are alienated simply because they have time on their hands and their needs have not been recognized by the government. For others, the alienation is reinforced by strong ideological commitments. Among the plains people of the tarai, resentment is compounded by government policies that discriminate against them.

As yet, the tarai's urban centers are few in number and relatively small, and the concentration of police and army units stationed in or near these centers is sufficient to bring rapidly under control all overt expressions of opposition. Then, too, many of the alienated young

[44]*Sahi Awaj Weekly*, Aug. 11, 1972.
[45]*Gorkhapatra*, Aug. 18, 1972.
[46]*Nepal Times*, Aug. 29, 1972.
[47]*Naya Nepal*, Aug. 11, 1972.

urbanites of plains origin are drifting into the cities of India to seek their fortunes, siphoning off potential support for party organizations. Nevertheless, the tarai towns are growing, and with them the number of people responsive to the political parties. The potential for increased opposition is very real in such towns as Bhadrapur, Dharan, Biratnagar, Rajbiraj, Janakpur, Birganj, Bhairawa, and Nepalganj as lower-echelon bureaucrats, small-scale businessmen, industrial laborers, teachers, students, and unemployed graduates become increasingly frustrated by their political impotence in Kathmandu and even in the tarai. During the short period of parliamentary rule, these groups were able to exert influence on the national decision-making process through participation in the political parties. The longer they are denied this opportunity in the present system, the more frustrated and alienated they will become.

The Nepali Congress and the Communist parties are also competing for support in the rural areas of the tarai. Because of poor press coverage and government censorship, it is difficult to assess the impact of party organizing efforts on this traditionally apathetic segment of the population. It appears that village politics remain centered around economic and caste factions, although there is an occasional report of this factionalism taking on the dimensions of party politics. For example, in 1969, candidates with party affiliations were reported contesting the chairmanship of the Bhagwanpur Village Panchayat in Bara district. In this case, and undoubtedly in many others over the past few years, Nepali Congress workers canvassed votes for Nepali Congress candidates.[48] Friction between the hill minority in this large and prosperous village and the plains majority crept into the campaign. It appears that the Nepali Congress workers and their candidate were hill people, and the Communists played upon the consciousness of cultural differences between the minority and majority in order to neutralize Nepali Congress influence. Although both parties receive support from hill as well as plains people, it is evident that local workers from both parties are willing to take advantage of the economic and cultural factions already existing in order to further their causes.

There is evidence that pro-Congress and pro-Communist forces are also beginning to vie for control of district panchayats. Unlike the student politics, this competition, where it exists, is three-sided, with progovernment forces also involved. At the district and national

[48] *Matribhumi Weekly,* June 24, 1969. Bhagwanpur is a center for rice stockists in eastern Bara.

levels, many large landowners are loyal to the present government because they feel that it reinforces their traditional place in the economic and political life of the country. Much of their power is derived from their ability to marshal support for themselves and the panchayat system among those who are economically dependent upon them. During the 1960s, the progovernment landowners controlled the district panchayats. Whether they can maintain their control in the face of Nepali Congress and Communist competition depends to a large extent upon the working relationship between them and the government administrators at the district level. Through these officials, progovernment district-panchayat members must continue to obtain considerable support from Kathmandu. This support has been in the form of pressure on panchayat electors to vote into office those who support the government and also in the form of obstacles to the movement of semidisguised opposition-party members up the panchayat ladder. It is likely that this support will continue. However, as already mentioned, there is evidence of antagonism between some of the better-educated, development-conscious administrators and the more traditionalist landowners, and this antagonism makes analysis of district-level politics complex.

The ideological lines between government administrators and political-party members are not always clear. Just as there are administrators who support more fundamental reforms, there are large landowners associated with the Nepali Congress and even the Communist Party. Landowners have conflicts with each other, sometimes family rivalries dating back many years, and they seek support wherever they can find it. Those who do not obtain support from government officials occasionally turn to one of the political parties. The Nepali Congress has had a particularly close association with many large landowners. An outstanding example of this is the party's long-term association with a group of class-C Ranas.[49] At least in the formative years of the party, these Ranas were more interested in the outcome of their power struggle with the class-A Ranas than in the economic and political ideals of the party.

If the government could mobilize support in the rural population, it might be able to isolate the political parties based in the towns from the mass support they need in order to be a serious challenge to the government. Although villagers are not usually as politically motivated

[49] The Rana clan was divided into classes A, B, and C. The class-A Ranas ruled Nepal and excluded those in the class-C category from the line of succession to power.

as urban dwellers, the two segments of the population share common languages and customs, affording established channels of communication between them, channels which the government, represented primarily by administrators of hill origin, does not have. As yet, there is little evidence that either the government or the political parties have been successful in tapping this source of support, but the villages could hold a key to the dominance of either the government or the parties in the tarai.

SUPPORT IN INDIA FOR OPPOSITION PARTIES

During the 1950–51 revolution and again during the period immediately subsequent to the royal coup, the Nepali Congress received indirect support from the Indian government, if in no other form than Indian government refusal to prevent staging and supplying operations of armed Nepali Congress raids from Indian border towns upon Nepalese government posts in the tarai. The Sino-Indian confrontation in October 1962 forced the Indian government to accept a hard truth, that its security in the Nepalese sector of the Himalayas was more important than the establishment of parliamentary government there. The Nepali Congress had to acquiesce to Indian pressure and call off its raids. Since then, the Indian government has attempted to curb what the Nepalese government calls "antinational" activity on the Indian side of the border.

The Indian government is faced with several problems in its attempt to control this activity. First, the nation has a free press. A number of Indian newspapers have been sympathetic to the Nepali Congress cause because of the party's socialist orientation and its dedication to the principles of parliamentary government. These newspapers have provided the Nepali Congress a hearing among educated Nepalis in the tarai and Kathmandu. The papers remained critical of the King's rule and the panchayat system throughout the 1960s and, although the criticism has been mild by the standards of a free press, it has been bitterly resented in Nepalese-government circles.

Second, India's federal system grants substantial power to the states, including the power to police state borders. Consequently the governments of West Bengal, Bihar, and Uttar Pradesh police their borders with Nepal. Although the central government in New Delhi has urged those state governments to exercise diplomacy in their handling of customs and police problems along the Nepal border, the advice has not always been followed carefully. The Nepali Congress has won considerable sympathy among government officials in those states, particularly in Bihar. Nepalese officials and businessmen crossing into Bihar have been shown little courtesy on a number of occasions.

West Bengal is also a problem in this respect. Although the Communist Party of India has led coalition governments in the state several times, Communist leaders have shown considerable willingness to cooperate with Indian Congress leaders in New Delhi, because of the financial constraints held by the center over the state government. Because of their ideological bonds with Nepalese Communists, however, it would not be difficult for them to overlook activities organized by Nepalese Communists in the border areas of the state. Whether the Government of West Bengal is Communist or Congress-led or under President's rule, the chronic state of unrest often threatens to have its repercussions across the border in the tarai, as was the case during the Naxalbari disturbances.

Third, the Indian government can not prevent Indian political parties and pressure groups from supporting the Nepali Congress and the Communist Party of Nepal. Over the past two decades, sympathizers in India have provided encouragement and financial aid to both the Nepali Congress and the Communist Party of Nepal. For example, Indian socialists have been supportive of the Nepali Congress since the party was founded.[50] The threat of communism articulated in the speeches of Nepali Congress leaders since 1968 may have been partly designed to attract support from anticommunist parties in India or, indeed, from the Indian government itself. Despite the impressive victories of Mrs. Gandhi's Congress Party, India is so splintered politically that it is reasonable to assume that Nepalese opposition parties could find moral support, if not substantial financial support, somewhere in India.

Nevertheless, as long as the Indian government believes that support of the monarchy is the best way to insure stability in the central Himalayas, it is not likely to revert to a policy of indirect support to the Nepali Congress, the type of support the party needed in 1950–51 and 1961–62 in order to mount an effective military and political campaign against the government in Kathmandu. Although the tarai is a natural base of operations for the Nepali Congress or the Communist Party, given the exploitable discontent of the tarai popula-

---

[50]See Bhola Chatterji, *A Study of Recent Nepalese Politics* (Calcutta, 1967).

tion and its location along the Indian border,[51] it is unlikely that without the blessings of the Indian government, opposition parties will be able to mount another serious campaign against the government.

Despite resentment against the Nepalese government's economic policies in the rural areas of the tarai and resentment against the government's efforts at Nepalization in the urban centers, the tarai is not a sea of discontent, ready to drown the government in a high tide of revolution. The government is able to suppress quickly overt opposition, but it appears unable to provide the leadership at local levels that can compete with the opposition parties for support among many segments of the tarai population. Until the government can find a way to counteract the sense of resentment among many tarai people, sporadic agitation is likely to continue, and integration of the region into the national framework is likely to remain an unfulfilled goal.

[51] For example, it would be virtually impossible for the Nepalese Army to trap and destroy rebel units in the tarai if they could make use of sanctuaries close at hand across the border. The hit-and-run tactics of the Nepali Congress rebels against government posts in the tarai were becoming increasingly effective in late 1962, when the Indian government stepped in to discourage further raids.

CHAPTER X

THE PROBLEM OF NATIONAL INTEGRATION

In a number of countries, the problem of national integration has been circumvented by the elimination of minority groups that are difficult to integrate. The bloody histories of such actions are well known. Theoretically, the plains minority in Nepal could be eliminated by forcing all plains people to migrate to India. Despite evidence that Nepal's land-reform program could have been used to transfer large portions of agricultural land from plains people to hill people, effectively dispossessing the plains people, this has not been done to any significant extent, and there is no indication that the Nepalese government plans to attempt mass dislocation and resettlement of its people.

Aside from the administrative difficulties inherent in such an undertaking, several other factors would prevent its implementation. Perhaps the major one is the presence of Nepal's southern neighbor, India, a nation of overwhelming power in comparison with Nepal. In 1971, India was confronted with a massive influx of refugees because of the Bangladesh crisis, and it would do its utmost to prevent the kind of crisis in Nepal that would precipitate another refugee problem. The Indian government might pressure the Nepalese government to resolve such a crisis by lending support to the Nepali Congress, in much the same way that it put pressure on the Pakistani government by lending support to the Bengalis' Mukti Bahini. It could also threaten to force hundreds of thousands of Nepalese settlers in northeastern India to return to Nepal. Or it could simply close the border to trade and thereby prevent essential supplies from reaching Nepal. Any of these alternatives would create a crisis for the Nepalese government, and this prospect limits its options not only with regard to integration of the tarai but also with regard to various other domestic and international issues.

The economic power of the plains people is a second factor. In most developing nations, political and economic power are controlled by the same elite groups. Although the existence of separate politically and economically powerful groups is not peculiar to Nepal, it complicates the process of national integration. The hill majority controls political power in both the hills and the plains through the King, the army, and the administrative service. Of course, the governing elite among the hill people also control many economic resources, but the plains minority controls a large share of Nepal's wealth: much of the best agricultural land in the country, much of the small-scale industry, a significant share of the large-scale industry, and trade between Nepal and the outside world. This economic power gives them the capacity to resist the governing elite, whenever they feel threatened by it. To finance increased oppositional activities by the Nepali Congress and the Communist parties is one obvious way to resist.

Integration of the tarai into the national framework by force is not a viable option for the Nepalese government. A more realistic alternative would be to draw the plains people into the national structure through participation in the nation's political life, through encouragement of the voluntary acceptance of national political and cultural values. This kind of participation would provide the plains people with an investment in the nation's survival and its prosperity.

During the past few centuries, the national culture of Nepal has evolved through the participation of caste and tribal groups in the establishment of various kingdoms in the hill region, the last and most important of these being the kingdom established in Kathmandu in 1769. As has been emphasized throughout this study, the Nepalese national culture is the hill culture of Nepal, the culture dominated by the ruling hill-Brahmin-Chetri-Newar coalition. The Chetris have made the most outstanding contribution to this cultural development. As they migrated into Nepal, they established a number of small kingdoms and, although a relatively small minority of the hill population, they have emerged as rulers throughout the region. They possessed a vitality that gained them leadership among the tribal people and a flexibility that allowed them to assimilate elements of the tribal cultures. Because of their flexibility, the caste system was modified to incorporate the less ritualized, less hierarchically conscious tribal societies. They have been willing, for example, to accept with full equality in the Chetri caste children from marriages not only with Brahmin women but also with tribal women[1] and, therefore, they have determined to a large extent the amalgamation of plains-Hindu and hill-tribal cultural components that today compose the Nepalese national culture.

The Newars have been assimilated into the Chetri-dominated hill culture less completely than the tribal people because the Newar culture is more complex than that of the Chetris, and it is difficult for people of a highly complex culture to accept assimilation into a less complex culture. They have been partially assimilated because the Chetris have allowed them to participate in the governing of Nepal. Gradually, over the generations, the participation of Newars has been extended to all levels of government. As a result, the Newars have invested heavily in the development of the nation.

The Chetris, that is the various lineages of hill kings before the time of Prithvi Narayan Shah and, after him, his successors and Rana prime ministers, developed a close and cooperative arrangement with the Newars and the hill-tribal people. The Chetris needed the business and administrative talents of the Newars and the martial strengths of the tribal people. In addition, of course, they depended on their learned Brahmin advisors as the touchstones of orthodox Hinduism. Despite the economic and political rivalries that have existed among these groups, their mutual interdependence has prevailed and has resulted in the evolution of the unique hill culture.

This process of acculturation did not extend to the people of the tarai, partly because of the country's geography. The tarai people were isolated from the hill people by the dense and malarial forest that separated the two regions of the country. The forest represented a line of defense against attacks by a succession of powers on the plains south of the tarai. Therefore, the hill kings discouraged cutting down of the forest, and this prevented closer contact between the hill people and the people of the plains who lived in the tarai. It was also partly a matter of fear among the hill people that close contact with the plains people might result in the kind of assimilation that would destroy the uniqueness of the hill culture. Although the fear of Indian domination, cultural as well as political, existed before 1951, it has become since then an often-repeated theme in public debate.

If Nepal is to become a nation in a more complete sense than it is now, the plains people must be drawn into the national framework. During

---

[1]Christoph von Fürer-Haimendorf, "Unity and Diversity in the Chetri Caste of Nepal," in *Caste and Kin in Nepal, India and Ceylon,* ed. by C. von Fürer-Haimendorf (New York, 1966), pp. 65–66.

the brief period of party politics in Nepal, the parties served to draw plains people and other minority groups into the political mainstream. Political parties have proven to be effective instruments of national integration in other developing nations. They function as "melting pots," not only for regionally and culturally diverse groups but also for the urban modernizing elite, the traditional rural elite and, indeed, for the large number of nonelite groups as well.[2] Usually they are modern, nonascriptive organizations that encourage participation across the barriers that have previously separated minority groups from each other. They may not create new cultural amalgamations, but they contribute to the breaking down of insularity and suspicion, an essential step in the nation-building process.

Although the traditional ruling elite tends to assert its leadership within a party system as within other governing systems, universal adult franchise forces this elite to reach accommodation with groups that gain power because of the votes they control. Thus, the Nepali Congress and Communist parties, and several other parties as well, sought support from groups that had never participated in the governing process. As was the case during the Shah and Rana periods, the hill Brahmins, Chetris, and Newars dominated party leadership. Nevertheless, for the first time, a number of high-caste plains people rose to leadership rank, and a few low-caste and tribal people also found their way into positions of political prominence. Elimination of the party system since 1960 has returned Nepal to a political system in which the traditional elite can assert its influence more exclusively. Although education has become an increasingly important factor in determining political influence, in the absence of direct elections and of political parties to compete in those elections, landownership and high-caste status, factors monopolized by the traditional elite, remain more decisive in the political process.

Political parties and ruling monarchs have generally coexisted only with considerable tension.[3] When King Mahendra ascended the throne in 1955, Nepal's political system was in a state of flux. The King found himself the most powerful person in the country, but at least temporarily committed to working with an array of political parties. Between 1955 and the time when the first and only elected government took office in 1959, his relationship with the various parties was an

[2]Myron Weiner, *Party Politics in India* (Princeton, N. J., 1957), pp. 230–237.
[3]Samuel P. Huntington, *Political Order in Changing Societies* (New Naven, 1968), pp. 180–185.

uneasy one. Tension increased during the eighteen months of the Nepali Congress government and, in December 1960, the King, supported by the army, overthrew the government and took the reins of power into his own hands.

> Never openly discussed, but certainly one of the most vital considerations leading to the abrogation of parliamentary institutions, was King Mahendra's dissatisfaction with the relegation of the Crown to a comparatively minor role in the governmental structure after the installation of the Nepal Congress government. Another factor may have been King Mahendra's suspicion that the "socialist-oriented" Nepali Congress leaders were plotting the eventual abolition of the monarchy. Certain indiscreet remarks by Nepali Congress leaders alluding to the allegedly obstructionist role played by the King and the 1959 Constitution seemed to add substance to the King's apprehensions.[4]

The control of the traditional elite over the rural areas of Nepal has not yet been challenged. Most of the army officers and many of the bureaucrats are drawn from this elite. Therefore, any government, no matter how progressive the ideology of its leaders, must move ahead slowly and cautiously with reforms.

> A large majority of the landowning and commercial interests in Nepal, for instance, were unalterably opposed to the Nepali Congress government's land and taxation policy. The moderate character of the economic legislation enacted by the Koirala Cabinet did not diminish their apprehensions, since these measures were considered to be merely the first in a series of gradually more drastic changes in the land and taxation system. These vested interest groups, with their close ties to various cliques in the palace, had long since concluded that the King was the last effective barrier to the imposition of fundamental economic reforms, and this attitude was crucial in determining their response to the December *coup*.[5]

The critical dilemma faced by the few remaining ruling monarchs in the world today is whether to opt for political development or for political survival.[6] King Mahendra chose the latter alternative. If he had used his centralized authority to push ahead vigorously with

---

[4]Bhuwan Lal Joshi and Leo E. Rose, *Democratic Innovations in Nepal* (Berkeley, 1966), p. 386.
[5]*Ibid.*, p. 388.
[6]Huntington, *op. cit.*, p. 177.

various fundamental reforms, he might have been successful in moving Nepal more quickly in the direction of a modern nation-state, but he would also have created a stronger and more politically conscious middle class. The middle class would not only demand a share of his power, but it might also work actively to undermine his position. "The ideology and outlook of twentieth-century intellectuals and middle-class groups, however, tends to describe even the most benevolent despotism as a feudal anachronism. Monarchy is simply out of style in middle-class circles."[7] The King was undoubtedly even more mindful of the fact that effective reforms would undermine the position of the traditional elite and would thus alienate those upon whom he depended for support. Such reforms are likely to bring an army-backed coup from the right more rapidly than lack of reforms would bring a revolution organized by political parties on the left and, therefore, the King must have calculated that his family line could remain in power longer with little or no reform.

During the Rana period, Nepal's rulers put off the day when they would be forced to face the dilemma of development or survival by isolating the country from the outside world, preventing the penetration of modernization with its reformist pressures. But during the 1930s and 1940s, the Ranas could no longer maintain this policy effectively and, gradually, modernizing ideologies found their way into Nepal.

During the 1950s and 1960s, as pressure for modernization continued to grow and find expression in political organizations antithetical to the existence of a ruling monarchy, King Mahendra turned for support not only to the traditional elite but also to a number of aid-giving nations. The policy of isolation having become ineffective by the 1950s, the reverse policy, based on the presence in Nepal of representatives of many foreign governments, seemed best designed to insure the monarchy's survival. King Mahendra began implementing this policy in the second half of the 1950s and, throughout the rest of his life, he was most adroit at balancing the influences of foreign powers to insure the nation's independence and his own power. He invited all nations to assist in Nepal's economic development. The assistance of at least four of these, India, the United States, the Soviet Union, and China, was motivated primarily by political considerations, by the big-power struggle among them and by their determination to maintain the monarchy in order to prevent Nepal from falling into

[7] *Ibid.,* p. 163.

the hands of a government that might be unfriendly to one or another of them.⁸

The financial support of the four major aid-giving nations has been accompanied by the rhetoric of change. However, their aid has assisted the monarchy both directly and indirectly to create a better-equipped and better-trained army and to put a large number of potentially restive, educated young men on the bureaucratic payrolls. It is true that aid-giving agencies of several nations have pressed the King for reforms, but aid programs have been maintained despite the continued absence of significant reforms because, for these nations, change had a lower priority than maintenance of the status quo, which they all found to their advantage for different reasons. Thus, in the short run at any rate, foreign assistance has enhanced the monarchy's chances of survival and has inhibited the growth of pressures for fundamental change.⁹ In the long run, however, foreign assistance also creates increasing demands for goods and services that the government will find difficult to satisfy on its own, and it creates channels by which ideas and ideologies inimical to traditionalism are introduced into the country. In the long run, therefore, foreign assistance may encourage change, but perhaps on a time schedule more acceptable to the aid-giving nations.

Along with support from the traditional elite and foreign governments, King Mahendra sought capacity to survive through nationalist fervor based on strong anti-Indian sentiment among the educated Nepalis of hill origin. Although the middle class is the segment of Nepal's population that tends to have the greatest inherent antipathy to the monarchy, it is also the most narrowly nationalistic. By capitalizing upon this nationalism, King Mahendra was able to neutralize at least to some extent the support that the middle class gave to opposition parties.

To understand the strength of anti-Indian feeling in Nepal, it is necessary to understand the identity problems with which many educated Nepalis find themselves encumbered. Although the emphasis throughout this study has been upon the extensive ties between the tarai and India, there are also many economic and cultural ties

⁸Political considerations have dominated the involvement of most other aid-giving nations as well: Pakistan's by its conflict with India, the aid from Israel and the Arab nations by tension in the Middle East, and British assistance by its interest in recruitment of Gurkha troops in Nepal.
⁹E. B. Mihaly, *Foreign Aid and Politics in Nepal* (London, 1965); see especially pp. 122–124 and ch. XIII.

between the hill region and India. In fact, many Nepalis feel that the ties are too numerous. They fear that Nepal could be assimilated into the greater Indian economic, cultural, and political sphere and might lose its national identity. In order to forestall this possibility, from their point of view, Indian influence in all aspects of Nepalese life must be reduced.

During the 1950s and 1960s, efforts to define Nepal's identity were made in terms of the differences between Nepalese and Indian culture. The search for identity was manifest in the dramatic events of December 1960, and King Mahendra gave increased emphasis to the theme of national identity after assuming direct responsibility for the government.[10] He appealed to the middle class for support against the Nepali Congress by alleging that the Congress government had encouraged "antinational elements."[11] He produced no evidence to support this charge, but suggested that the party was not nationalistic, and that it was involved with Indians in some way prejudicial to Nepal's independence. He appealed for support of the panchayat system by claiming that it would better protect and promote Nepalese nationalism. He called the parliamentary system alien to Nepalese life, and declared that "This [panchayat] system bears the stamp of the genius of the Nepalese race."[12]

The King's strong nationalist platform incorporated as a major plank the principle of nonalignment in foreign affairs. During the period of British dominance in India, Nepal was aligned with British India and, although independent India recognized Nepal's independence, in fact Nepal remained aligned with India during the early 1950s. After King Mahendra ascended the throne, nonalignment was proclaimed as Nepal's foreign policy, and this was essentially an assertion of the country's independence from India. Belligerence toward India is sometimes provoked by rather heavy-handed Indian diplomacy, prompted by Indian fears of China and of Chinese-sponsored subversion in Nepal. The Nepalis react strongly against this pressure.[13]

[10]Leo E. Rose discusses Nepal's "identity crisis" in *Nepal: Strategy for Survival* (Berkeley, 1971), pp. 279–282.

[11]*On to a New Era: Some Historic Addresses by His Majesty King Mahendra* (Kathmandu, n.d.), p. 6.

[12]*Proclamations, Speeches, and Messages of H. M. King Mahendra*, vol. II (Kathmandu, 1967), pp. 134–135.

[13]For example, in 1969, when news of a secret arms agreement between India and Nepal was leaked to the Indian press, the Nepalese Prime Minister, Kirtinidhi Bista, publicly repudiated the agreement and demanded the withdrawal of Indian military personnel from the country. *Rising Nepal*, June 25, 1969.

Anti-Indian-oriented nationalism mobilizes support for the government among middle-class hill people, but it also thwarts the process of national integration, because many hill people have difficulty making the distinction between plains people who are Nepalese citizens and those who are Indian citizens, and some anti-Indian sentiment is automatically transferred to the tarai population. Therefore, the problems of national integration and national identity call for contradictory solutions. Although Nepal's leaders earnestly desire to bring all regions of Nepal into a closer relationship in order to strengthen the nation, these leaders tend to view one of the most important of these regions, the tarai, as an extension of the Indian economy and the Indian culture. Many regard the plains people of the tarai as Indian citizens in disguise, more loyal to India than to Nepal. This suspicion has been reinforced by the businessmen and students of plains origin who have held dual citizenship, and by the extensive family and business ties between people living on the two sides of the border. Because of the identity problem and the resulting distrust of plains people, many members of the Kathmandu elite hesitate to encourage the participation of the plains people in national life. They fear this will enhance Indian influence in Nepal.

The plains people of the tarai have their own identity problems, similar to those of people who have emerged from colonial experiences. Neither Nepal's history nor Nepal's hill culture satisfy their identity needs, because they have not been associated with either. National symbols with which the tarai people could easily identify are missing. The Nepali language, perhaps even more than the Crown itself, is a powerful and pervasive symbol of Nepalese nationalism in the hill region. Despite the fact that the language is now being introduced into the secondary schools and colleges of the tarai, Nepali is spoken by relatively few tarai people, even as a second language. Hindi, the *lingua franca* of the region and a significant symbol for many tarai people, has been rejected as a second national language or even one that is recognized for government use at the regional level.

Through the "Back to the Village Campaign," the government sought to make the symbols and values of Nepalese nationalism familiar to villagers in the tarai and elsewhere in the country. The campaign foundered not only because it was complex and difficult to implement but also because villagers remained merely passive recipients of novel concepts. An informational program, even when put into the context of a quasi-religious movement, is no substitute for active participation in the governmental process as a means of encouraging identification with the nation.

The Nepalese government has drawn up no comprehensive plan for national integration. Even if such a plan existed, it would still be difficult for the government to place national integration above national identity as a priority because, in the minds of the Kathmandu elite, the plains people of the tarai are so closely associated with the major power on Nepal's southern border. Nor, as already mentioned, can the government adopt massive dislocation of plains people as a solution to the tarai problem, because of the certainty of India's objection. Some government officials hope that mass migration of hill people into the tarai will make the formulation of a specific plan for national integration unnecessary. But as the data presented in chapter IV indicate, migration will provide a partial solution at best. There are more people migrating into the tarai from India than from the hills of Nepal. Therefore, despite assistance that the government gives to the hill settlers in the tarai and despite the growing economic and political importance of these settlers in the region, migration as a vehicle for Nepalization has its limitations. Nepalization resulting from interaction among settlers from the hills and plains will occur in tarai subregions where migrants from the hills are settling in large numbers, but even in these subregions, the process will take place only slowly over the next several generations. In other sub-regions already settled largely by plains people, hill migrants will have little impact on the predominant plains culture.

If the government relies on migration and on the several other policies discussed in this study, the tarai problem is likely to remain unsolved and a constant irritant for a long time to come. On the other hand, so long as the Indian government continues to support the monarchy and to discourage the operation of antimonarchical forces from across the border, the irritant will be one that the Nepalese government can tolerate.

However, if the government formulates a comprehensive plan for national integration, not only modifying and coordinating current policies, but also implementing a few additional ones, a solution to the tarai problem might not seem so distant. Some policy changes would lessen hostility among the plains people—for example, the removal of clauses in citizenship laws that discriminate against plains people, simplification of procedures for acquisition of citizenship certificates, and ensuring that certificates reach the hands of all tarai inhabitants who qualify for them. The government could also make sure that tarai inhabitants are not denied their source of livelihood because of the citizenship provisions in the land-reform laws. These changes would cause little anxiety, even among ultranationalistic members of the Kathmandu elite. Provision for direct elections from the district panchayats or district assemblies to the National Panchayat in order to obtain better representation of plains people would probably produce only limited opposition. The recognition of Hindi as an associate national language would cause increased identity problems for some people in Kathmandu, but this gesture of good will toward the tarai population would reap compensatory rewards for the government. If the government were willing to implement a policy of hiring larger numbers of plains people as government administrators, police, and army officers—perhaps quotas of 10 or 20 percent of the employees in each of these categories—it would be creating a viable instrument for national integration as a substitute for political parties. Through such a hiring policy, plains people would gain significant representation in the national centers of power. Undoubtedly, this type of radical policy change would prove threatening to many people in Kathmandu, but if the hiring quotas were increased gradually, the policy might have some chance of acceptance.

The monarchy as an institution could be a key force in the national-integration process. The King has the power to effect change by ensuring the inclusion of new groups in the polity. King Mahendra did not choose to facilitate this kind of change. Brought up in the midst of the court intrigue of the Rana period, he tended to be suspicious of other men's politics and to keep the reins of power closely guarded. He lived in quiet isolation and delegated little of his authority. As the architect of a foreign policy that has assured a full measure of independence for Nepal, he made an outstanding contribution. On the other hand, despite the fact that he was willing to encourage whatever modernization did not directly undermine the traditional order, his leadership in formulating and implementing domestic policies was neither forceful nor progressive.

King Mahendra died in early 1972, and now his son Birendra has the same opportunity to use the monarchy to pull disparate groups into a cooperative political community. King Birendra's upbringing and personality differ greatly from those of his father. Birendra was raised in the post-Rana period during a time, particularly in the 1950s, when many new ideas were being openly debated in Nepal.

Unlike his father, he was not educated in the Palace under religiously oriented Brahmin teachers but at Eton and later, for shorter periods, in the United States, Japan, and Israel. He is outgoing by nature and more comfortable than his father with members of the modernizing elite, the more highly educated men of the Central Secretariat and the university who, like himself, have had substantial contact with the world beyond Nepal. Although, at least for the present, he needs to retain the support of the traditional elite upon which his father depended, he is better prepared to extend himself to other segments of the nation's population. If he is willing to do this, he may be able to move Nepal toward the goal of more complete national unity.

APPENDIX

METHODOLOGY OF THE FIELD SURVEY CONDUCTED IN THE TARAI, NOVEMBER 1967–MARCH 1968

In order to gather district- and village-level data for this study, it was necessary to organize a field survey. Tribhuvan University generously awarded me a grant to hire an assistant, who could speak the major tarai languages, Hindi, Maithili, and Bhojpuri, as well as Nepali.

There are 6,258 villages in the tarai, according to village lists compiled by the Central Bureau of Statistics, Government of Nepal. Because it was possible to study only a few of these villages, it was necessary to follow a sampling technique that would make possible generalizations about the tarai as a whole. The first step was to select districts that could be considered representative of subregions of the tarai. Four factors were used to determine whether contiguous districts were similar to each other: language, religion, population density, and the extent of forest cover. Maps were prepared for each of these factors, to show which of the tarai districts were similar to each other. The language and religion factors reflect important cultural differences. Other factors might have been used to indicate economic differences, such as type of land use, size of land holdings or urbanization. However, statistics on such factors were either nonexistent or unreliable.

Map 7[1] shows that there are four linguistically distinct subregions. Only in the far-eastern part of the tarai, in Biratnagar and Jhapa districts, is no one language spoken by the majority of the population.[2] Map 8 presents statistics on the percentage of Muslims in the various tarai districts. Muslims and Hindus being the only two important religious groups in the tarai population, these statistics indicate the religious composition of the districts. Whatever percentage is not Muslim is almost entirely Hindu. There are four fairly distinct subregions, regions in which contiguous districts vary less than 3.5 percent in terms of the number of Muslims living in the districts.[3]

[1]See map 7 on p. 208.
[2]The districts referred to in the appendix are census districts. See map 1 and map 2 in ch. I for names of census districts and overlapping development districts. Biratnagar census district includes approximately the same territory as Morang development district.
[3]See map 8 on p. 209.

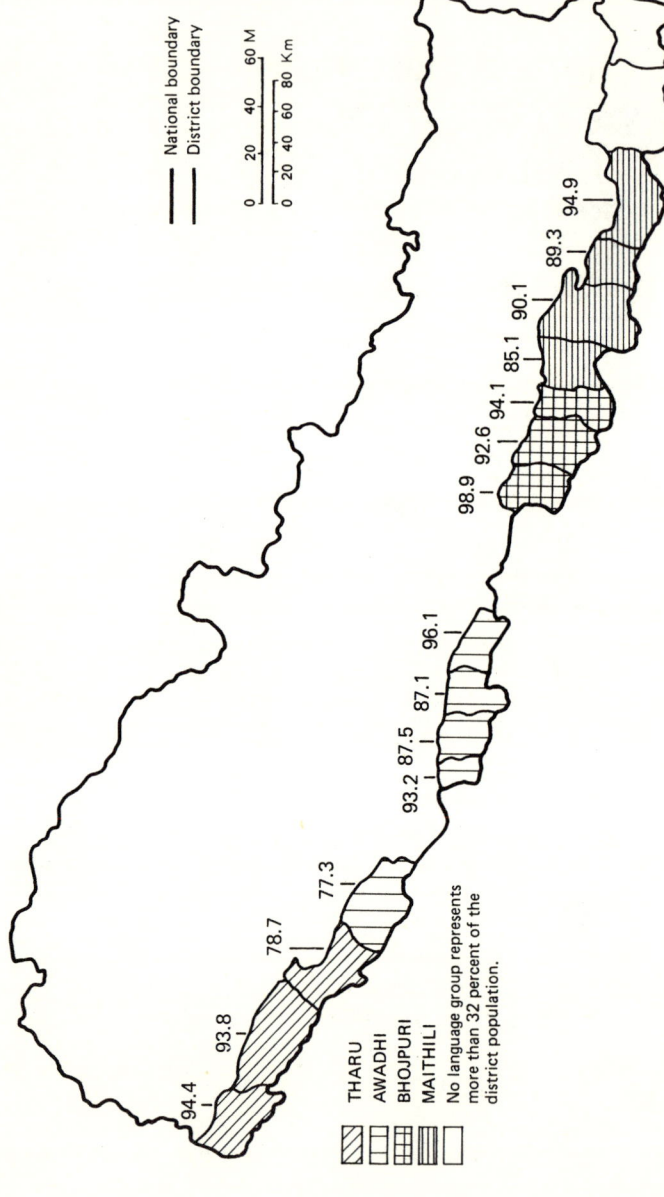

Map 7. Linguistic subregions of the tarai. The percentages given in this map represent the population that speaks various important tarai languages as mother tongues. The data are presented by district for 1961. Example: 77.3 percent of the population in Banke district speaks Awadhi as a mother tongue. Source: *Census of Nepal*, 1961, vol. II, pp. 18–25.

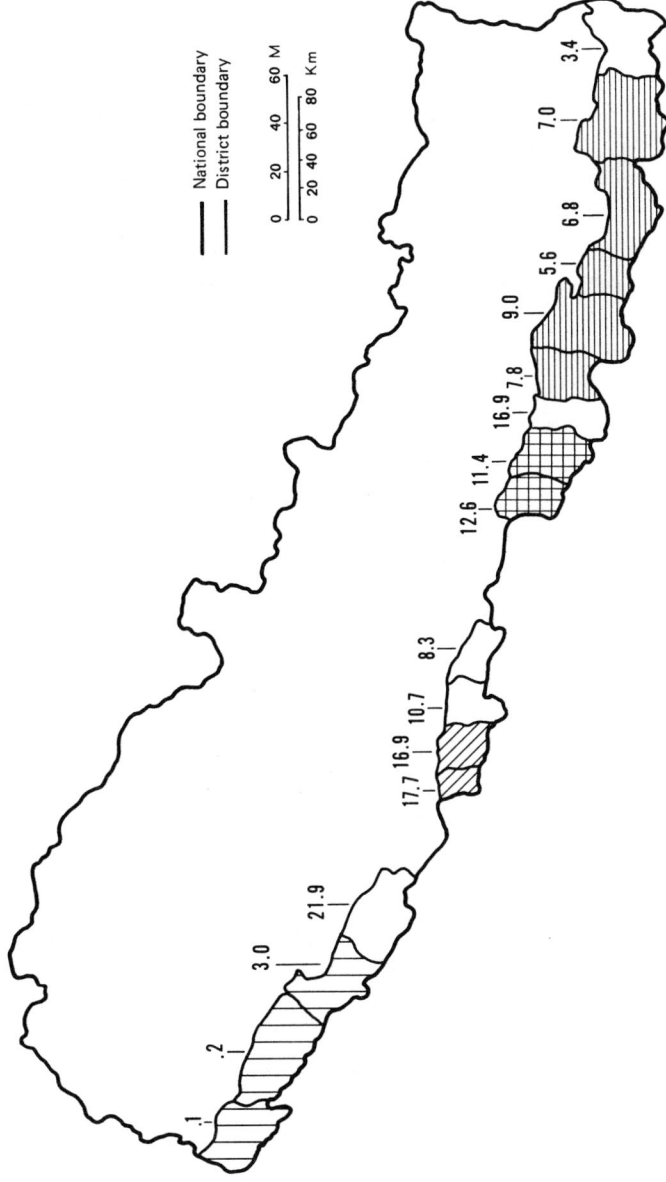

Map 8. Subregions of the tarai having similar religious characteristics. In the tarai districts almost the entire population that is not Hindu is Muslim. Contiguous tarai districts are defined here as sharing similar religious makeup when there is less than 3.5 percent difference in the number of Muslims living in them. Example: 21.9 percent of Banke district is Muslim. Source: *Census of Nepal*, 1961, vol. II, pp. 16–17.

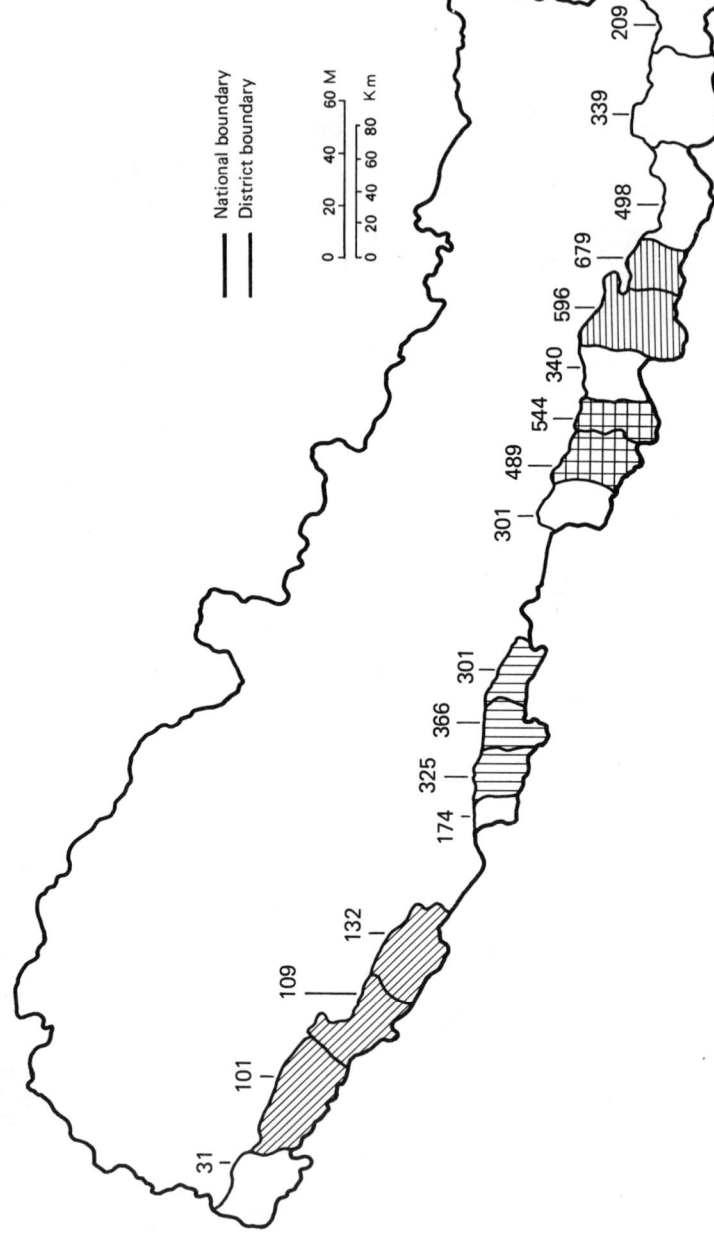

Map 9. Subregions of the tarai having similar population density characteristics. Source: *Census of Nepal*, 1961, vol. II, pp. 1–4.

APPENDIX

Map 9[4] shows that there are four groups of tarai districts with similar population density. Map 6 in chapter IV shows the amount of forest remaining in the tarai. Unfortunately, the data are given by regions delineated by the Forestry Department rather than by census or development districts; nevertheless, from map 6, we can obtain a fairly good idea of the amount of forest cover that still exists in each tarai census district. There are five fairly distinct subregions. The four far-western tarai districts are still heavily forested. In the mid-western tarai, all districts except Palhi have about one-third or less of their area covered by forest. In the central tarai region, nearly half of Parsa, Bara, Rautahat, and Sarlahi districts is still forest-covered. Just to the east of Sarlahi, Mahottari, Siraha and Saptari are almost completely deforested. In the two districts farthest to the east, more forest cover exists than in any of the tarai districts except those of the far west.

Comparison of the four maps indicates that there are four groups of contiguous districts that share common characteristics and can be described as subregions of the tarai. The far-eastern tarai subregion includes Kanchanpur, Kailali, and Bardia. The second subregion consists of the four census districts in the mid-western tarai: Shivaraj, Khajahani, Majkhanda, and Palhi. The third distinguishable subregion includes Parsa, Bara, and Rautahat, and the fourth comprises Sarlahi, Mahottari, Siraha, and Saptari.

From these four subregions, the census districts of Kailali, Kapilabastu-Shivaraj, Bara, and Mahottari were selected for study.[5] The two districts farthest to the east, Biratnagar and Jhapa, do not have enough characteristics in common to form a subregion. Nevertheless, because these two districts include various little-known tribal groups, because there is large-scale migration into these districts, rapid deforestation, and also government-sponsored economic development on a scale more intensive than in other parts of the tarai, these districts are interesting from both the anthropological and the development point of view. Therefore, Jhapa was selected as a fifth district to study.

It was the objective to select twenty villages in each district, although it became necessary to include twenty-four villages in Mahottari-Dhanusha.[6] I decided to use a cluster sample method rather than a purely random selec-

---

[4]See map 9 on p. 210.

[5]The census districts of Kapilabastu and Shivaraj were consolidated into one development district named Kapilabastu. The census district of Mahottari was divided into two development districts named Mahottari and Dhanusha. In Kailali and Bara, the census and development district units cover the same territory.

[6]The lists from which the panchayats were randomly selected were separate for the development districts of Mahottari and Dhanusha. In order to obtain a sampling for the combined Mahottari-Dhanusha census district, three panchayats were selected from the list of each development district, six panchayats in all. Because it was planned to survey four villages in each panchayat, twenty-four villages were selected for Mahottari-Dhanusha.

tion. The latter would have resulted in a wide scattering of villages, some of which would have been difficult to reach because of the lack of roads. The first step of the cluster-selection process was a random selection of five panchayats[7] in each district. An official of the Central Bureau of Statistics, made this selection, using the Bureau's lists of panchayats for each district and Tippett's random tables.

Once the panchayats were selected, they were located on maps. Letters of introduction to district-level officials were obtained from relevant national-level officials. When the headquarters of each district was reached, these letters were presented to the chief district officer with requests for letters of introduction from him to the chairman of each panchayat randomly selected. Several days were spent at each district headquarters going through district records. For each district, I made a caste breakdown of membership in the district assembly and district panchayat for 1962 and 1967, a caste breakdown of the district-level gazetted officers and police officials, and a breakdown of district industry by date established, type of industry, location in the district, and caste of its owner. Whenever possible, I met local political leaders, merchants, and other notables, in order to learn as much as possible about the economy and history of the district.

The second step in the village-selection process was taken upon reaching the panchayats. In all but two cases, the panchayat was named after one of the villages in the panchayat, and I included that village in the survey. While in that village, I sought information about villages in the surrounding area and included three of them in the survey. This was the purposive or nonrandom (cluster) aspect of the selection process. Several criteria were used for the selection. The four villages taken together had to represent as closely as possible the caste make-up of the surrounding village population. For example, if there were some predominantly Muslim villages in the panchayat area, at least one of the four villages had to be a predominantly Muslim village. An effort was made to select both large and small villages, the latter being generally less differentiated in economic terms, e.g., no shops or rice mills. In the few cases where panchayats were located near urbanized district headquarters, an effort was made to survey villages at different distances from that center in order to account for the influence of commercialization.

A schedule was used to gather data, one schedule per village. In each village, an interview was held with the village headman, which usually also included a group of elders as well as a throng of curious onlookers. My assistant acted as a translator and the interviews lasted between two and three hours.

It was impossible to reach all 100 of the cluster sample villages. Unseasonal rain arrived in Kailali district at the same time we did. Kailali was the most remote of the five districts, the sample panchayats were many miles apart,

[7] A panchayat is an administrative unit of one to seven or eight villages with a population of approximately 5,000 inhabitants.

and the jungle trails between them turned to mud. Only 8 villages were surveyed. Nevertheless, because the vast majority of the population in Kailali is Tharu and the villages surveyed were mainly Tharu, the results are probably fairly accurate descriptions of conditions in the district as a whole. In Kapilabastu district, only 19 villages were surveyed. Taulihawa was one of the panchayats randomly selected. However, the village of Taulihawa is the district headquarters, with a population of considerably more than 5,000 and a great deal of commercial activity. It was impossible for the panchayat chairman, his secretary, and the other village leaders to provide detailed information about their village, and the survey of Taulihawa had to be limited to only some general information about education and industry. Because of personal illness in Jhapa, the last district surveyed, the sample had to be limited to 10 villages, only 2 in each randomly selected panchayat. Although the sample is smaller, it is probably still fairly accurate for the district as a whole. All 20 of the sample villages in Bara and all 24 in Mahottari-Dhanusha were surveyed.

Along with the eighty-one cluster-sample villages in the five districts, eighteen recently settled villages of hill people in the five districts were also surveyed. They were studied in order to learn something about the most rapid change occurring in the tarai as a result of the destruction of the forest and rapid population increase. There was no attempt to select these recently established settlements on a random-sample basis. Although information gained from the study of these villages is used in this work, no attempt has been made to draw from the data statistically supportable generalizations. In all, 99 tarai villages, including both the 81 sample and the 18 nonsample villages, were surveyed in 1967–68.

GLOSSARY

Hills: The terms "hills" or "hill region" used throughout this study include all of Nepal from the Siwaliks foothill range north to the Tibetan border. This is a somewhat broader definition than the Nepalis use. The term *pahar* means hill in Nepali and is defined by Nepalis as any mountain that does not have snow on it the year around, i.e., any mountain less than approximately 17,000 feet in elevation. The Nepalis generally do not consider Kathmandu Valley or the three low-lying "inner tarai" valleys as part of the hill region but, in proper geographical terms, they are integral parts of the hill region and are treated as part of the hill region in this study.

Hill people: This term, as used in the study, can be defined in two ways. First, linguistically, i.e., the people whose mother tongue or first language is one that predominates in the hill region of Nepal: Nepali, Newari, Magar, Gurung, Rai, Limbu, Tamang, Sunwar, Thakali, or Sherpa. Second, the term can be defined sociologically, as including those people who belong to the Hindu caste groups found in the hills: hill Brahmin, Chetri, Gharti, Kumhale, Majhi, Kami, Sunar, Damai, and Sarki, as well as the hill-tribal groups: Magar, Gurung, Rai, Limbu, Sunwar, Tamang, Thakali, and Sherpa. The Newars are hill people who do not fit into either the caste-Hindu or tribal category. Many persons in Kathmandu Valley tend to regard *Paharis* or hill people as culturally unsophisticated and, therefore, do not call themselves hill people. There are, in fact, differences in educational attainment and technological sophistication between many Kathmandu Valley dwellers and most of the people living in other parts of the hill region, but in order to make broader cultural comparisons in this study between people of the hill and plains region, Kathmandu Valley dwellers have been included in the more general category of hill people.

Inner tarai: There are three low-lying valleys between the Siwaliks (sometimes called the Churia Range) and the Mahabharat Range: one on the Rapti River in the west, the largest on the Gandak/Narayani River in central Nepal, and the third on the Trijuga River in eastern Nepal. These have been inhabited mainly by Tharus until recently, but now they also contain large numbers of settlers from the hills.

Geographically, economically, and to some extent culturally these valleys are part of the hill region and are not part of the tarai region included in this study.

Mother tongue: This is the "first language" an individual learns to speak, and the language he uses within his family circle. In the study, the terms mother tongue (used by the Nepalese census) and first language are used interchangeably.

Outer tarai: This is the region referred to in the study simply as the tarai. It includes all the territory in Nepal south of the Siwaliks Range. It is the flat plains region of Nepal, the northern fringe of the Gangetic plain that lies within Nepal's national boundaries.

Nepalization: This term has been coined for use in this study to describe the process by which plains people living in Nepal take on the characteristics of the Nepalese culture. The major element of the Nepalization process is the learning of Nepali. However, the adoption of the dress, food, and manners of the hill people is also part of the process.

Plains languages: These are languages spoken by people who live on the Gangetic plain, either on the Indian or Nepalese side of the border. The major languages are Hindi, Urdu, Maithili, Bhojpuri, and Bengali; languages spoken by fewer people include Jhangar, Marwari, Raji, and various dialects of these languages such as Awadhi and the Morang Pradesh dialects.

Plains people: This term, as used in the study, is based on linguistic distinctions. Plains people are those who speak plains languages as their mother tongues or first languages, whether they were born or live in the plains or the hills.

Plains-tribal languages: In Nepal, the Tharus speak principally dialects of Maithili and Bhojpuri. In northern Uttar Pradesh are Tharus who speak dialects of Hindi. The Rajbanshis and Tajpurias speak dialects of Bengali. It is likely that the Mechis, Gangais, and Dhimals also speak Bengali dialects. Santali is a language in its own right; those who speak it are migrants from the Chota Nagpur Plateau in India. Several of the very small tribes such as the Dangars appear to have languages of their own.

Plains tribes: These are groups living chiefly on the plains, which do not fit into the Hindu caste system. A number of these groups are to be found in the tarai. The Tharus are by far the most numerous; others are mentioned above.

SELECTED BIBLIOGRAPHY

I. PUBLICATIONS AND RECORDS OF THE GOVERNMENT OF NEPAL AND ITS AGENCIES

Birch, Gunnar. *Prospects of Industrial Development in Nepal.* Kathmandu: Industrial Promotion and Productivity Centre [1965?].
Bista, Dor Bahadur. *The People of Nepal.* Kathmandu: Ministry of Information and Broadcasting, His Majesty's Government of Nepal, 1967.
Dhital, Bhaarat Prasad. *The Rice Market in Dhangadhi.* Kathmandu: Department of Agriculture, Ministry of Forests, Agriculture and Land Reform, His Majesty's Government of Nepal, 1964. (Tr. by Regmi Research Project, No. 792/65.)
Jha, Vedanand. *Basic Characteristics of Panchayat Democracy.* Kathmandu: Ministry of Information and Broadcasting, His Majesty's Government of Nepal, 1966. (Nepal Today Series, No. 1.)
Lange, Dieter. "General Economic Survey Report of Mahottari and Dhanusha District." Rev. ed. Kathmandu: Nepal Industrial Development Corporation, 1967. (Typescript.)
Mahendra Bir Bikram Shaha Deva, Maharajadhiraja of Nepal. *On to a New Era: Some Historic Addresses by His Majesty King Mahendra.* Kathmandu: National Guidance Ministry, His Majesty's Government of Nepal, n.d.
———. *Proclamations, Speeches, and Messages of H.M. King Mahendra Bir Bikram Shah Deva.* Vol. II: December 1960–1965. Kathmandu: Ministry of Information and Broadcasting, His Majesty's Government of Nepal, 1967.
———. *Pronouncements of King Mahendra on Panchayatcracy: Excerpts from King Mahendra's Proclamations, Speeches and Messages.* Collected and translated by Daman R. Tuladhar. Kathmandu: Sandesh Griha, 1968.
Malhotra, Ram. C. *Decentralization of Public Administration in Nepal.* Kathmandu: Ministry of Information and Broadcasting, His Majesty's Government of Nepal, 1966. (Nepal Today Series, No. 3.)
———. *The System of Panchayat Democracy in Nepal.* Kathmandu: Ministry of Information and Broadcasting, His Majesty's Government of Nepal, 1966. (Nepal Today Series, No. 2.)

Mathema, Pushpa Ram. *Report on Tobacco Marketing in Nepal*. Kathmandu: Department of Agriculture, Ministry of Forests, Agriculture and Land Reform, His Majesty's Government of Nepal, 1966.

Mohsin, Mohammed, and Shumshere, Pashupati, J. B. R. *Some Aspects of Panchayat System in Nepal*. Kathmandu: Ministry of Information and Broadcasting, His Majesty's Government of Nepal, 1966. (Nepal Today Series, No. 5.)

Nepal. Central Bureau of Statistics. *Directory of Manufacturing Establishments*. Kathmandu, 1965.

―――. *Foreign Trade, Fiscal Year* 1962–63. Kathmandu, 1966.

―――. *National Agricultural Census*, 1962. 52 vols. Kathmandu, 1962. (In Nepali.)

―――. *Rashtriya Jana-Ganana*, 2018 [National Census, 1961]. In progress. Kathmandu, 1966–. N.B. Throughout the text, this publication is cited as *Census of Nepal, 1961*.

Nepal. Constitution. *The Constitution of the Kingdom of Nepal* [1959]. Kathmandu: Ministry of Law and Parliamentary Affairs, 1959.

―――. *The Constitution of the Kingdom of Nepal* [1962]. English Translation. Kathmandu: Ministry of Law and Justice, His Majesty's Government of Nepal, 1963.

Nepal. Department of Forests. Forest Resources Survey. *Forest Statistics for the Tarai and Adjoining Regions*, 1967. Kathmandu [1968?].

Nepal. Department of Industrial and Commercial Intelligence. *Brief Report of the Industrial Survey of Butaul*. Kathmandu, 1948. (Trans. by Regmi Research Project, No. C-458.)

―――. *Brief Report of the Industrial Survey of Kailali Kanchanpur*. Kathmandu, 1948. (Trans. by Regmi Research Project, No. C-391.)

―――. *Industrial Survey Report: Banke and Bardia*. Kathmandu, 1948. (Trans. by Regmi Research Project, No. C-243.)

―――. *Industrial Survey Report: Bara, Parsa, Rautahat, Sarlahi, and Mahottari*. Kathmandu, 1949. (Trans. by Regmi Research Project.)

―――. *Industrial Survey Report of Saptari and Biratnagar*. Kathmandu, 1948. (Trans. by Regmi Research Project, No. C-140.)

Nepal. Department of Industries. Unpublished records (Registry of Private and Public Firms), 1944–67.

Nepal. Department of Land Revenue. *Administrative Regulations for Butaul*, 1861. (Trans. by Regmi Research Project, 1967.)

―――. *Administrative Regulations for Tarai Districts*, 1861. 5 vols. (Trans. by Regmi Research Project, 1967.)

Nepal. Department of Statistics. *Census of Population, Nepal, 1952/54 A.D.* Kathmandu, 1958.

―――. *Nepal ko Naksa: Thum/Pargannama Bibhajit Janaganana Jillaharu* [Map of Nepal: Division of Census Districts into Thums/Pargannas]. Kathmandu, 1959.

Nepal. Election Commission. [Results of the First General Election, February–April 1959]. Compilation from official lists, by constituency.
———. *Snatak Pratinidhitwa-Rashtriya Panchayat ko Nirwachan ko Matadata Namavali* [Voters List for the National Panchayat Election: The Graduate Constituency]. Kathmandu, 1967.
Nepal. Hydrological Survey Department. *Compilation of Surface Water Records of Nepal Through December 31, 1965.* Kathmandu: His Majesty's Government of Nepal in cooperation with U.S. Agency for International Development, 1967.
Nepal Industrial Development Corporation. *Investing in Nepal: A Resume of Nepal Laws and Regulations Governing the Establishment and Operation of an Industrial Enterprise.* Kathmandu, 1965.
———. *Report on Jute Production in the Morang Biratnager District.* Kathmandu, 1960.
———. *Statistical Abstract*, 1966–. (Irregular.)
Nepal. Land Reform Commission. *Report on Land Tenure Conditions in the Western Tarai.* Kathmandu, 1953. (Trans. by Regmi Research Project.)
Nepal. Ministry of Economic Planning. *Cereal Grain Production, Consumption and Marketing Patterns, Nepal 1965.* Kathmandu [1966?].
———. *Mobility of Agricultural Labor in Nepal.* Kathmandu, 1967.
———. *Physical Input-Output Characteristics of Cereal Grain Production for Selected Agricultural Areas in Nepal, Crop Year 1965–66.* Kathmandu, 1967.
———. *Third Plan of Nepal, 1965–1970.* Kathmandu, 1965.
Nepal. Ministry of Economic Planning and Ministry of Panchayat. *Guidelines to the Decentralization of Government Functions.* Kathmandu, 1965.
Nepal. Ministry of Finance. *Budget Speech.* Fiscal Years 1965–66, 1966–67, 1967–68. Delivered by the Honourable Finance Minister, Surya Bahadur Thapa. Kathmandu, 1965–67.
Nepal. Ministry of Forests. "National Forest Policy, 1959." (Trans. by Regmi Research Project, No. 505.)
Nepal. Ministry of Forests, Agriculture and Land Reform. Department of Agriculture. *Resettlement Project: Nawalpur.* Kathmandu, 1963.
Nepal. Ministry of Home and Panchayat. *The Panchayat, a Planned Democracy.* Kathmandu, 1967.
Nepal. Ministry of Information and Broadcasting. Department of Publicity. *Nepal in Maps.* Kathmandu, 1966.
Nepal. Ministry of Irrigation and Power. *Meteorological Survey.* Unpublished Records on Rainfall, Humidity and Temperature, 1948–1966.
Nepal. Ministry of National Guidance. Department of Publicity and Broadcasting. *Report of the Development Districts and Zones Demarcation Committee.* Kathmandu, 1961. (Trans. by Regmi Research Project, No. 2426.)

Nepal. Ministry of Panchayats. *An Introduction to Bara Development District*. Kathmandu, 1964. (Trans. by Regmi Research Project, No. 67/65.)

———. *An Introduction to Saptari Development District*. Kathmandu, 1965–66. (Trans. by Regmi Research Project, No. 445/66.)

———. *An Introduction to Sarlahi Development District*. Kathmandu, 1965–66. (Trans. by Regmi Research Project, No. 494/66.)

Nepal. *Muluki Ain,* 1854 [Legal Code]. Kathmandu: reprinted by Law Book Committee, 1963.

Nepal. National Education Commission. *Report of the National Education Commission,* 1961. Bishwa Bandhu Thapa, chairman. Kathmandu, 1961. (Trans. by Regmi Research Project, No. 2324.)

Nepal. National Education Planning Commission. *Education in Nepal: Report of the Nepal National Education Planning Commission*. Prepared by members of the Commission, and edited by Rudra Raj Pandey, Kaisher Bahadur K.C. and Dr. Hugh B. Wood. Kathmandu: College of Education, 1956.

Nepal. National Planning Council. *Draft Five Year Plan* [1957–1962]: *Synopsis.* Kathmandu, 1956.

———. *The Three Year Plan,* 1962–65. Kathmandu, 1963.

Nepal Rastra Bank, *Report of the Board of Directors to His Majesty's Government for the Fiscal Years* 1961/62, 1962/63, 1963/64, 1964/65. Kathmandu, 1966.

Pahadi, Badri Prasad. *Bardia Jilla ma Bhumi Sudhar* [Land Reform in Bardia District]. Kathmandu: Department of Land Reform, His Majesty's Government of Nepal, 1967. (Excerpts translated by Regmi Research Project, No. 2/68.)

Pant, Thakur Nath; Mathema, Ram Bhakta; and Shrestha, Madan Bahadur. *The Ghee Markets of Butaul and Nepalganj*. Kathmandu: Department of Agriculture, Ministry of Forests, Agriculture, and Land Reform, His Majesty's Government of Nepal, 1964. (Trans. by Regmi Research Project, No. 10/65.)

Pradhan, Sagar Bahadur, and Bhattarai, Basent Prasad. *A Study of Nepal's Jute Market*. Kathmandu: Department of Agriculture, Ministry of Forests, Agriculture and Land Reform, His Majesty's Government of Nepal, 1963. (Trans. by Regmi Research Project. No. 951/65.)

Pradhan, Sagar Bahadur, and Shrestha, Madan Bahadur. *A Report on the Study of the Potato Market in Palung and the Orange Market in Dharan*. Kathmandu: Department of Agriculture, Ministry of Forests, Agriculture and Land Reform, His Majesty's Government of Nepal, 1963. (Trans. by Regmi Research Project, No. 951/65.)

"Report of the Commission on Decentralization of Administrative Authority." *Gorkhapatra,* July 18, 1964. (Trans. by Regmi Research Project, No. 867/64.)

Shamshere, Pashupati, J. B. R., and Mohsin, Mohammad. *A Study Report on the Pattern of Emerging Leadership in Panchayats; With Special Reference to District and Village Panchayats of Mechi, Kosi and Sagarmatha Zones.* Kathmandu: Research Division, Home Panchayat Ministry, His Majesty's Government of Nepal, 1967.

Shrestha, Madan Bahadur. *Illam Potato Market.* Kathmandu: Department of Agriculture, Ministry of Forests, Agriculture and Land Reform, His Majesty's Government of Nepal, 1963.

Shrestha, Madan Bahadur, and Maharjan, Bekha Lal. *The Paddy Market of Jhapa.* Kathmandu: Department of Agriculture, Ministry of Forests, Agriculture and Land Reform, His Majesty's Government of Nepal [1967?]. (Trans. by Regmi Research Project, No. 1/67.)

Thapa, Bekh Bahadur. *Planning for Development in Nepal: A Perspective for 1965–80.* Kathmandu: Ministry of Economic Planning, His Majesty's Government of Nepal, n.d. (Ph.D. dissertation, Claremont Graduate Center, 1966.)

II. PUBLICATIONS OF OTHER GOVERNMENTS AND THE UNITED NATIONS

Cool, John C., and Bista, Dor Bahadur. "Some Observations on Tharu Peasant Economy in Nepal." Kathmandu: U.S. Agency for International Development, 1966. (Mimeographed.)

Hasel, A.A. "Forest Survey Plan for Nepal." Kathmandu: U.S. Agency for International Development, 1962. (Mimeographed.)

Imperial Gazetteer of India (Provincial Series), vol. I. Calcutta: Superintendent of Government Printing, 1909. "Nepal," pp. 91–129.

India. Census Commissioner. *Census of India,* 1901. Calcutta: Superintendent of Government Printing, 1903.

India. Foreign Department. *A Collection of Treaties, Engagements and Sanads Relating to India and Neighbouring Countries.* Vol. XIV. Compiled by C.U. Aitchison. Calcutta: Government of India Central Publication Branch, 1929.

India (Republic). Census Commissioner. *Census of India,* 1961. Delhi: Government of India Press, 1961.

Israel. [Nepal Aid Mission.] "Summary of Nepal-Israel Cooperation." Kathmandu, n.d. (Mimeographed.)

Jain, B. L. "A Study of Fluctuations of Exchange Rate in Nepal." Kathmandu: Indian Aid Mission, 1959. (Mimeographed.)

Melford, J. B. "Planning and Implementation of Land Settlement Schemes (Five Year Plan 1965–1970)." Kathmandu: FAO/OPEX, 1965. (Mimeographed.)

Okada, Ferdinand E. "Historical Notes on Local Administration in Nepal." Kathmandu: U.S. Agency for International Development, 1963. (Mimeographed.)

Robbe, Earnest. *Report to the Government of Nepal on Forestry.* Rome: Food and Agriculture Organization of the United Nations, 1954. FAO Report No. 209—54/3/1712.
United Nations. Legal Dept. *Laws Concerning Nationality.* New York, 1954. "Nepal: Citizenship Act of 1952," pp. 320–21.
U.S. Agency for International Development, Nepal. *Economic Data Papers—Nepal*, vols. II–IX, 1960–67.
———. "Ethnic Groups in Nepal." Kathmandu, 1964. (Mimeographed.)
———. *Selected Agricultural Statistics, Nepal.* Kathmandu, 1967. (Mimeographed.)
U.S. Department of Commerce. Bureau of International Commerce. "Basic Data on the Economy of Nepal," prepared by Cherie Loustauanau. *Overseas Business Reports*, September, 1968. OBR 68–86.

III. BOOKS AND PAMPHLETS

Baral, Ishwar. "The Tharu Community and Their Culture." *Nepal* (A Collection of Articles on the History and Culture of Nepal). Kathmandu: Tribhuvan University Cultural Association, 1966. (Trans. by Regmi Research Project, No. 174/66.)
Berreman, Gerald D. *Hindus of the Himalayas.* Berkeley: University of California Press, 1963.
Bhasin, A. S. *Documents on Nepal's Relations with India and China, 1949–66.* Bombay: Academic Books, 1970.
Boulnois, L. and Millot, H. *Bibliographie du Népal.* Paris: Centre National de la Recherche Scientifique, vol. I–, 1969–.
Cammann, Schuyler. *Trade Through the Himalayas: The Early British Attempts to Open Tibet.* Princeton, N.J.: Princeton University Press, 1951.
Caplan, Lionel. *Land and Social Change in East Nepal: A Study of Hindu-Tribal Relations.* Berkeley: University of California Press, 1970.
Centre for Economic Development and Administration, Kathmandu. Occasional Papers, 1969–.
Chatterji, Bhola. *A Study of Recent Nepalese Politics.* Calcutta: World Press, 1967.
Chaudhuri, K.C. *Anglo-Nepalese Relations: From the Earliest Times of the British Rule in India till the Gurkha War.* Calcutta: Modern Book Agency, 1960.
Clark, Thomas Welbourne. *Introduction to Nepali: A First-Year Language Course.* Cambridge: Heffer, 1963.
Davis, Kingsley. *The Population of India and Pakistan.* Princeton, N.J.: Princeton University Press, 1951.
Devkota, Krishna Bahadur. *Nepal ko Rajnaitik Darpan* [Political Mirror of Nepal]. Kathmandu: K. C. Gautam, 1959.
Fisher, Margaret W. *Selected Bibliography of Source Materials for Nepal.* 2d ed.

Berkeley: Institute of International Studies, University of California, 1966.
Fishman, Joshua A., Ferguson, Charles A., and Das Gupta, Jyotirindra, eds. *Language Problems of Developing Nations.* New York: John Wiley, 1968.
Flournoy, Richard W., and Hudson, Manley O., eds. *A Collection of Nationality Laws of Various Countries as Contained in Constitutions, Statutes and Treaties.* New York: Oxford University Press, 1929.
Forum for Social Studies. *Go to Village; National Campaign.* Kathmandu, 1967.
Fürer-Haimendorf, Christoph von, ed. *Caste and Kin in Nepal, India and Ceylon; Anthropological Studies in Hindu-Buddhist Contact Zones.* New York: Asia Publishing House, 1966.
Goodall, Merrill R. "Administrative Change in Nepal," in Braibanti, Ralph J.D., ed. *Asian Bureaucratic Systems Emergent from the British Imperial Tradition.* Durham, N.C.: Duke University Press for Commonwealth Studies Center, 1966.
Goyal, Narendra. *The King and His Constitution.* New Delhi: Nepal Trading Corporation, 1959.
Grierson, George A., ed. *Linguistic Survey of India.* 11 vols. Calcutta: Superintendent of Government Printing, 1903–1928.
Gupta, Anirudha. *Politics in Nepal: A Study of Post-Rana Political Developments and Party Politics.* Bombay: Allied Publishers, 1964.
Hagen, Toni; Wahlen, Friedrich T.; and Corti, Walter R. *Nepal: The Kingdom in the Himalaya.* Berne: Kümmerly Frey, 1961.
Hamilton, Francis (formerly Buchanan). *An Account of the Kingdom of Nepal and of the Territories Annexed to this Dominion by the House of Gorkha.* Edinburgh: Archibald Constable and Co., 1819.
Hodgson, Brian Houghton. *Essays on the Languages, Literature, and Religion of Nepal and Tibet, Together with Further Papers on the Geography, Ethnology, and Commerce of those Countries.* London: Trübner and Co., 1874.
Husain, Asad. *British India's Relations with the Kingdom of Nepal, 1857–1947.* London: Allen and Unwin, 1970.
Husain, Mazhar. *The Law Relating to Foreigners in India and the Citizenship Laws of India and Pakistan.* 3d ed. Lucknow: Eastern Book Company, 1961.
Jain, Girilal. *India Meets China in Nepal.* Bombay: Asia Publishing House, 1959.
Joshi, Bhuwan Lal, and Rose, Leo E. *Democratic Innovations in Nepal: A Case Study of Political Acculturation.* Berkeley: University of California Press, 1966.
Karan, Pradyumna P., and Jenkins, William M., Jr. *The Himalayan Kingdoms: Bhutan, Sikkim, and Nepal.* Princeton, N.J.: D. Van Nostrand, 1963.
———, with the collaboration of Jenkins, William M. *Nepal: A Cultural and Physical Geography.* Lexington, Ky.: University of Kentucky Press, 1960.

Kihara, K., ed. *Peoples of Nepal Himalaya.* Scientific Results of the Japanese Expedition to Nepal Himalaya, 1952–53, vol. III. Kyoto: Kyoto University, 1957.

Kirkpatrick, William. *An Account of the Kingdom of Nepaul, Being the Substance of Observations Made During a Mission to that Country in the Year* 1937. London: William Miller, 1811.

Landon, Perceval. *Nepal.* 2 vols. London: Constable, 1928.

McDougal, Charles. *Village and Household Economy in Far Western Nepal.* Kirtipur, Nepal: Tribhuvan University, 1968.

Mihaly, Eugene Bramer. *Foreign Aid and Politics in Nepal: A Case Study.* London: Oxford University Press, 1965.

Narayan, Shriman. *India and Nepal: An Exercise in Open Diplomacy.* Bombay: Popular Prakashan, 1970.

Nath, Yogi Narahari, ed. *A Collection of Treaties in the Illumination on History.* Published on the occasion of the Spiritual Conference convened at Dang on 2022 B. S. [1966]. (Trans. by Regmi Research Project, 1967.)

Nepal Communist Party. "Chunao Ghoshanapatra" [Election Manifesto]. *Navayug*, Nov. 26, 1958.

Nepal Praja Parishad. *Nepal Praja Parishad ko Ghoshanapatra* [Manifesto of the Nepal Praja Parishad]. Kathmandu, 1956.

Nepal Prajatantrik Mahasabha. *Nepal Prajatantrik Mahasabha ko Abashyakata ra Uddeshya* [Necessity and Objectives of the Nepal Prajatantrik Mahasabha]. Kathmandu, 1958.

Nepal Tarai Congress. *Nepal Tarai Congress ko Ghoshanapatra* [Manifesto of the Nepal Tarai Congress]. Raxaul: Prakash Press, 1957.

Nepali Congress. *Chunao Ghoshanapatra* [Election Manifesto]. Kathmandu: Kalpana Press, 1958.

―――. *Kisan Haru ko Nimti Nepali Congressle ke Garyo?* [What Did the Nepali Congress Do for the Peasants?]. Kathmandu, n.d.

―――. *Shastha Rashtriya Adhibeshan Birganj ko Abasar ma Swikrit Ghoshanapatra* [Manifesto Adopted on the Occasion of the 6th National Conference at Birganj]. Patna: Free Press Ltd., 1956.

Nepali, Gopal Singh. *The Newars: An Ethno-Sociological Study of a Himalayan Community.* Bombay: United Asia Publications, 1965.

Nepali National Congress. *Nepali National Congress ko Ghoshanapatra* [Manifesto of the Nepali National Congress]. Kathmandu, n.d.

Northey, W. Brook, and Morris, C.J. *The Gurkhas: Their Manners, Customs and Country.* London: Bodley Head, 1928.

Ojha, Jagdeesh Chandra, and Rajbahak, Ram Prasad. *Banking and Modern Currency in Nepal.* 2d ed. Kathmandu: Educational Enterprise, 1965.

Pant, Yadav Prasad, and Jain, S. C. *Agricultural Development in Nepal*. Bombay: Vora, 1969.
Pemble, John. *Invasion of Nepal: John Company at War*. New York: Oxford University Press, 1971.
Pokhrel, Balakrishna. *Panch Saya Varsha* [Five Hundred Years]. Kathmandu: Jagadamba Prakashan, 1963. Excerpts on "A Brief History of the Nepali Language." (Trans. by Regmi Research Project, No. 121/68.)
Regmi, Dilli Raman. *Ancient Nepal*. 2d ed. Calcutta: Firma K. L. Mukhopadhyay, 1960.
———. *Modern Nepal: Rise and Growth in the Eighteenth Century*. Calcutta: Firma K. L. Mukhopadhyay, 1961.
Regmi, Mahesh Chandra. *Land Tenure and Taxation in Nepal*. 4 vols. Berkeley: Institute of International Studies, University of California, 1963–68.
Rose, Leo E. "Communism under High Atmospheric Conditions: The Party in Nepal," in Scalapino, Robert A., ed. *The Communist Revolution in Asia*. 2d ed. Englewood Cliffs, N. J.: Prentice Hall, 1969.
Rose, Leo E. *Nepal: Strategy for Survival*. Berkeley: University of California Press, 1971.
Rose, Leo E., and Fisher, Margaret W. *The Politics of Nepal: Persistence and Change in an Asian Monarchy*. Ithaca: Cornell University Press, 1970.
Sanwal, B. D. *Nepal and the East India Company*. Bombay: Asia Publishing House, 1965.
Satish Kumar. *Rana Polity in Nepal: Origin and Growth*. New York: Asia Publishing House, 1967.
Shaha, Rishikesh. *Nepal and the World*. 2d ed. Kathmandu: Nepali Congress, 1955.
Sharma, Balchandra. *Nepal ko Aitihasik Ruprekha* [An Historical Outline of Nepal]. Banaras: Madhav Prasad Sharma, 1951.
Shreshtha, Badri Prasad. *The Economy of Nepal*. Bombay: Vora, 1967.
———. *An Introduction to Nepalese Economy*. 2d ed. Kathmandu: Ratna Pustak Bhandar, 1966.
———. *Monetary Policy in an Emerging Economy: A Case Study of Nepal*. Kathmandu: Ratna Pustak Bhandar, 1965.
Shreshtha, Sharan Hari. *Modern Geography of Nepal; Economic and Regional*. Kathmandu: Educational Enterprise, 1968.
Singh, Lekh Raj. *The Tarai Region of U.P.: A Study in Human Geography*. Allahabad: R. N. L. B. Prasad, 1965.
Spate, O.H.K., and Learmonth, A.T.A. *India and Pakistan: A General and Regional Geography*. 3d ed. London: Methuen, 1967.
Srivastava, S. K. *The Tharus: A Study in Cultural Dynamics*. Agra: Agra University Press, 1958.
Turner, Ralph Lilley. *A Comparative and Etymological Dictionary of the Nepali Language*. London: Routledge, Kegan Paul, 1965. (First pub. in 1931.)

United Democratic Party. *Chunao Ghoshanapatra* [Election Manifesto]. Kathmandu, 1958.

Wright, Daniel, ed. *History of Nepal.* [A Vansalvi] trans. from Nepali by Shew Shunker Singh and Sri Gunanand. 3d ed. Calcutta: Ranjan Gupta, 1966. (First pub. in 1877.)

IV. UNPUBLISHED WORKS

Bista, Dor Bahadur. "Caste and Ethnic Groups [of Nepal]." Kathmandu, 1966. (Mimeographed.)

———. "Padipur: A Central Tarai Village of Nepal, Socio-Economic Survey November–December, 1966." Kathmandu, 1968. (Mimeographed.)

Legris, Pierre. "Report to the Government of Nepal on Forestry." Kathmandu, 1961. (Mimeographed.)

Pradhan, Bijaya Bahadur. "Dual Currency System in Nepal." Kathmandu, n.d. (Mimeographed.)

———. "A Scheme for Currency Unification in Nepal." Kathmandu, n.d. (Mimeographed.)

Regmi, Mahesh Chandra. "Economic Conditions in Morang District During the Early 19th Century." Unpublished manuscript. Kathmandu, Dec. 22, 1966.

———. "Industrial Potential of Nepal." Kathmandu, August 1967. (Mimeographed.)

Shumshere, Pashupati. "Agriculture and Land Utilization." [Kathmandu, 1965?]. (Mimeographed.)

Upreti, Bedh Prakash. "Dhangar Tribe of Janakpur, Dhanukha District." Kathmandu, 1966. (Mimeographed.)

———. "Dhimal Tribe of Jhapa District." Kathmandu, 1966. (Mimeographed.)

———. "Thami Tribe of Dolakha District." Kathmandu, 1966. (Mimeographed.)

V. JOURNAL ARTICLES

Allman, T. D. "Tripping the Himalayan Tightrope," *Far Eastern Economic Review*, LXXVI (April 1, 1972), 16–18.

Acharya, Babu Ram. "A History of Nepali Education," *Navin Siksha*, I, No. 4 (July–August 1957), 5–12; No. 5 (August–September 1957), 5–15; and No. 8 (November–December, 1957), 8–12. (Trans. by Regmi Research Project, No. 214.)

Appadorai, A., and Baral, L. S. "The New Constitution of Nepal," *International Studies*, I (January 1960), 217–247.

"Awakening Nepal: Special Survey of the Emerging Economy of the Himalayan Kingdom Where India and China Meet," *Far Eastern Economic Review*, XXVIII June 2, 1960), 1101–1128.
Baral, L.S. "Opposition Groups in Nepal, 1960–70," *India Quarterly*, XXVIII (January-March 1972), 12–45.
Berreman, Gerald D. "Caste and Economy in the Himalayas," *Economic Development and Cultural Change*, X (July 1962), 386–394.
———. "Peoples and Cultures of the Himalayas," *Asian Survey*, III (June 1963), 289–304.
Consing, Arturo Y. "The Economy of Nepal," *International Monetary Fund Staff Papers*, X (November 1963), 504–530.
Dai, Shen-yu. "Peking, Kathmandu and New Delhi," *China Quarterly*, XVI (October–December 1963), 86–98.
Field, A. R. "Himalayan Salt—A Political Barometer," *Modern Review*, CV (1959), 460–465.
Fürer-Haimendorf, Christoph von. "The Inter-Relations of Castes and Ethnic Groups in Nepal," *Bulletin of the School of Oriental and African Studies*, XX (1957), 243–253.
———. "Status Differences in a High Hindu Caste of Nepal," *Eastern Anthropologist*, XII (1959), 223–233.
Gaborieau, Marc. "Les Musulmans du Népal," *Objets et Mondes*, VI (Summer 1966), 121–132.
Gaige, Frederick H. "Nepal: Compromise and Liberalization," *Asian Survey*, IX (February 1969), 94–98.
———. "Nepal: More Problems with India," *Asian Survey*, XI (February 1971), 172–176.
———. "Nepal: The Search for a National Consensus," *Asian Survey*, X (February 1970), 100–106.
———. "The Role of the Tarai in Nepal's Economic Development," *Vasudha* (Kathmandu), II, No. 7 (1968), 53–61, 71.
Gupta, Anirudha. "A Critical Study of Source Material on Contemporary Nepal, 1950–1960," *International Studies*, III (April 1962), 461–474.
Hitchcock, John T. "Some Effects of Recent Change in Rural Nepal," *Human Organization*, XXII (Spring 1963), 72–82.
Hunt, James B., Jr. "The Effects of Land Reform on Achieving Agricultural Production Targets of the Third Plan," *Economic Affairs Report* (Kathmandu), III, No. 3 (1965), 1–9.
"Indian Currency Receipts and Expenditures," *Economic Affairs Report* (Kathmandu), II, No. 2 (1964), 17–19.
Koirala, Matrika Prasad. "Morang, Ancient and Modern," *Souvenir* (Biratnagar, Nepal), January 1965.
Ladejinsky, Wolf. "Agrarian Reform in Asia," *Foreign Affairs*, XLII (April 1964), 445–460.

Mukerjee, Dilip. "Love-Hate in the Himalayas," *Far Eastern Economic Review*, LXIV (June 26, 1969), 711–713.
Muni, S. D. and Phadnis, Urmila. "Ceylon, Nepal and the Emergence of Bangladesh," *Economic and Political Weekly*, VII (February 19, 1972), 471, 473–476.
Nepali, Chittaranjan. "Nepal ma Kariya Mochan ko Itihas" [History of the Emancipation of Slavery in Nepal], *Nepali*, XX (July-September 1964).
"Observer." "Nepal: Revaluation, but no Re-Evaluation," *Asian Survey*, VII (February 1967), 97–101.
Pant, Yadav Prasad. "Nepal's Recent Trade Policy," *Asian Survey*, IV (July 1964), 947–957.
Pradhan, Manik Lal. "Studies on Soils of Tarai Belt of Nepal," *Nepalese Journal of Agriculture*, I (February 1966), 21–32.
"Problem of Food Distribution in Nepal," *Economic Affairs Report* (Kathmandu), II, No. 3 (1964), 31–35.
Rana, Pashupati Shumshere J. B. "India and Nepal: The Political Economy of a Relationship," *Asian Survey*, XI (July 1971), 645–660.
Ray, H. "Communism in Nepal," *Contemporary Review*, CCXII (January 1968), 25–30.
———. "Communist China's Strategy in the Himalayas: Nepal, A Case Study," *Orbis*, XI (Fall 1967), 826–845.
Regmi, Mahesh Chandra. "Recent Land Reform Programs in Nepal," *Asian Survey*, I (September 1961), 32–37.
"Report on the Successful First Year of Land Reform in Budabari, Jhapa," *Economic Affairs Report* (Kathmandu), III, No. 1 (1965), 1–9.
Rose, Leo E. "Himalayan Border States: Buffers in Transition," *Asian Survey*, III (February 1963), 116–122.
———. "Nepal's Experiment with Traditional Democracy," *Pacific Affairs*, XXXVI (Spring 1963), 16–31.
Rose, Leo E., and Dial, Roger. "Can a Mini-State Find True Happiness in a World Dominated by Protagonist Powers: The Nepal Case," *Annals of the American Academy of Political and Social Science*, vol. 386 (November 1969), 89–101.
Schwartzberg, Joseph E. "The Distribution of Selected Castes in the North Indian Plain," *Geographic Review*, LV (October 1965), 477–495.
Shah, Rishikesh. "Nepal: Reflections on Issues and Events of 1971," *Asian Survey*, XII (February 1972), 116–120.
Shreshtha, Badri Prasad. "Current Land Reform Programme in Nepal," *Nepalese Perspective*, II, No. 45 (1966).
———. "New Strategy of Economic Development in Nepal," *Aarthik Jagat*, I, No. 1 (1966), 1–6.

Shrestha, Swayambhu Lal. "The Satars and Some of Their Social Beliefs," *Ruprekha* (April 1966), 189–197. (Trans. by Regmi Research Project, No. 441/66.)

Sinha, P. K. "Cultural Background of Morang," *Souvenir* (Biratnagar, Nepal), January 1965.

INDEX

Adhikari, Man Mohan, 184–185
Agricultural activity, 24, 26–31, 54, 59–60, 63–64, 95. *See also* Jute, Rice, Timber
Ahirs, 59, 61, 81, 91, 143, 145, 146, 147
Army, Nepalese, 136, 141, 160, 161, 167–169, 183, 188, 195, 198–200, 204
Assam, 63, 77n, 95
Awadhi language, 15–17, 116–118

"Back to the Village Campaign," 177–180, 202–203
Baitadi district, 117
Bangladesh, migration into Nepal from, 106; relations with India, 194
Banke district, 14, 16, 78, 83
Bara district, 14, 16, 20–21, 25, 31–32, 34, 39–40, 48, 58–59, 61, 70–71, 73–74, 76–77, 85, 104, 128, 130, 142, 144, 147, 150, 153, 155, 157–158, 185, 189
Bardia district, 13, 14, 16
Bengali language, 15, 115, 119, 129, 135
Bhadrapur, 51, 61, 133n, 134n, 135, 183, 189
Bhairawa, 35, 49, 183, 189
Bhojpuri language, 15–17, 115–116, 118–119, 127, 129
Bhumihars, 147, 162–163
Bhutan, 3, 68, 94; citizenship legislation in, 106
Bihar, 1, 3, 11–12, 15, 17, 23, 24, 37, 48, 51–52, 58, 102, 106, 110, 135, 191–192
Biratnagar, 37, 51, 111, 112, 133n, 134n, 187, 189
Birganj, 35, 88, 104, 112, 185, 189
Bista, Kirtinidhi, 184, 188, 201n
Brahmins, 12–13, 19, 22–23, 33, 65–66, 74–75, 80–81, 85, 91, 103, 104, 114, 131, 135, 139, 142–143, 146–147, 154, 156, 158, 159–169, 174, 195–197, 205
Britain, 205; citizenship legislation in, 105; Gurkhas in army of, 31, 83–84, 162; economic aid to Nepal, 41, 200n; relations with Nepal, 25, 43, 47, 59–60, 68, 105n, 201
Buddhism, 12–14, 160; birthplace of Buddha, 58
Burma, 42; citizenship legislation in, 89, 93; migration from, 77

Calcutta, 37, 50–51, 101, 129, 181n
Caste system, 13, 17, 19–21, 33, 137, 141, 146, 159–163, 195–196, 215–216
Ceylon, 42; citizenship legislation in, 89, 105–106
Chamaria, Radha Kissen, 37
Chamars, 19, 78, 154
Chaudhari, Parashu Narayan, 91
Chetris, 19, 22–23, 33, 65–66, 74–75, 80–81, 85, 122, 131, 135, 139, 146–147, 154, 156, 159–169, 195–197
China, border with Nepal, 1, 5, 35, 46n, 157; economic aid to Nepal, 50–51, 199–200; relations with Nepal, 1–2, 84–85, 179–180
Churia Range. *See* Siwalik Range
Citizenship, 87–106, 111, 113, 144, 174, 176, 202, 203–204
Class Organizations, 137–139, 140
Communication, 24, 118, 126–135, 156
Communist Party of Nepal, 49, 101, 111, 121, 146, 176, 181–182, 184–190, 192, 195, 197
Compulsory-savings program, 175–177
Constitution of Nepal (1959), 122, 198
Constitution of Nepal (1962), 91–94, 105–107, 124, 136–137, 156–157
Cooperatives, 130–131, 179
Currency, Nepalese, 43–45; revaluation of, 51–52, 54; Indian currency use in Nepal, 43–45

Damais, 65–66, 76, 162
Dandeldhura district, 66, 117
Dhanuks, 154
Dhanusha district. *See* Mahottari and Dhanusha districts
Dharan, 111, 187, 189
District panchayats and assemblies, 138–140, 142, 144–158, 189–190, 204

Ecological balance, 5, 10, 63–64, 179. *See also* Forests and deforestation
Economic aid, 199–200; from Australia, 83–84; from Britain, 41, 200n; from China, 50–51, 199–200; from Colombo Plan, 102; from Ford Foundation, 172; from India, 41,

231

45, 199–200; from Israel, 83–84, 200n; from Pakistan, 200n; from Soviet Union, 41, 50, 199–200; from United States, 41, 45, 68, 172, 199–200; from W.H.O., 68
Education, 102, 108, 110, 124, 132–135, 159, 161; policy, 94, 108–109, 111, 112, 113–114, 124, 132–133, 187–188. *See also* Language policy
English language, 108, 125, 127, 132–133, 180

Forests and deforestation, 2, 4–5, 10, 11, 13–14, 20, 25, 59–61, 63–64, 68–70, 73, 82, 84, 85, 145, 146, 179, 196. *See also* Timber

Gandak River, 47–48, 52
Gangais, 20, 59, 163
Gangetic plain, xiii, 4, 5, 10–11, 15, 25, 59, 62–63, 66, 68, 118
Gaur, 112
General Elections (1959), 90, 100–101, 105, 113, 115, 121
Ghartis, 19, 162
Ghosh, Pashupati Nath, 123
Giri family, 37, 91, 105, 154, 156
Gorkha Parishad, 102
Graduate constituency, 137, 140, 161
Gurkhas in British and Indian armies, 31, 45, 84, 162, 184, 200n; in resettlement projects, 83–84
Gurungs, 20, 63, 76, 162, 167–168; language of, 15, 88, 115

Halwais, 78
Himalayas, xiii, 1–3, 11, 25, 49, 56, 63, 191, 192
Hindi language, 15, 17, 109–125, 127–129, 131, 132, 133, 135, 202, 204
Hinduism, 2, 12–15, 17, 19–20, 23, 159–160, 196, 207, 209

India, citizenship legislation in, 89–90, 92; language controversy in, 116; political system of, 137, 141, 191–192; border with Nepal, 1, 2–3, 24, 46–57, 91, 102, 103, 106, 181, 183–187, 191–193, 194, 203; cultural ties with Nepal, xiii–xiv, 2, 11–15, 17, 19–20, 22, 34, 56, 103, 110, 117–118, 127, 129, 133–135, 196, 200–203; economic aid to Nepal, 41, 45, 199–200; economic ties with Nepal, xiii–xiv, 22, 24–26, 28, 29–31, 34–35, 37–38, 40–45, 49–56, 61–62, 93, 95, 101, 118, 191–192, 194, 200–202; political relations with Nepal, xiii–xiv, 1, 2, 46–57, 82–83, 89–90, 95, 98, 104–107, 172, 184, 186, 187, 191–193, 194, 196, 200–203; political relations with China, 1, 49, 191, 201

Indo-Nepal Friendship Treaty (1950), 95, 98
Indo-Nepal Trade and Transit Treaty, 53–54
Industrial activity, 24, 26–29, 35, 37–40, 53–55, 125, 195. *See also* Jute, Rice, Timber
Islam. *See* Muslims

Janakpur, 37, 49, 58, 61, 91, 112, 134n, 189
Jha, Vedananda, 109, 115–116, 123
Jhapa district, 13, 14, 16, 20–21, 32–34, 39–40, 61, 70–71, 73–74, 76–81, 84, 85, 106, 128, 133n, 135, 142, 147–148, 153, 183
Jute, 28, 29, 31, 37, 51, 53

Kailali district, 13, 14, 16, 20–21, 32–34, 39–40, 61, 64n, 66, 70, 72, 73, 77–81, 126, 128, 142, 147, 152–153
Kalwars, 143
Kamis, 19, 65–66, 76, 162
Kanchanpur district, 13, 14, 16, 66, 68, 78
Kapilabastu district, 20–21, 24–25, 31–32, 34, 39–40, 58, 61, 70–71, 73–75, 77–81, 95, 128, 133n, 142, 143, 147, 151, 153–155, 158, 175–176
Kathmandu, City and Valley, 13, 15, 24, 27, 28, 35, 41, 43, 44, 87, 88, 90, 104, 118, 125n, 132, 160, 168, 182, 187, 188, 215
Kathmandu elites, xiv, 2, 38, 42, 56, 73, 74, 82, 87, 96, 99, 107, 110, 117, 120, 126, 140, 142, 146, 158–170, 171, 179, 180, 188, 190, 191, 195–197, 198, 199, 200, 202, 203, 204, 205
Kayasthas, 103n, 114, 122, 147, 162–163, 167–168
Kohars, 19
Koirala, Bishweshwar Prasad, 91, 185–186, 198
Kumauni language, 117
Kumhales, 19
Kumhars, 19
Kurmis, 62, 81, 145

Land reform, 75, 80, 81, 95–98, 130, 131, 145, 167, 171–177, 178, 179, 194, 204; Ukhada, 75, 95–97, 128, 174
Language policy, 108–114, 122–125, 126–135, 202. *See also* Education
Limbus, 15, 20, 76, 162
Literacy rate, 92, 126
Lohars, 19

Magars, 20, 63–64, 65, 76, 162, 167; language of, 15, 88, 115
Mahabharat Range, 63–64
Mahakali River, 3, 41
Mahottari and Dhanusha districts, 14, 16, 20–21, 25, 31–32, 34, 39–40, 58, 61, 70–71, 73–78, 102, 126, 128, 135, 142, 144, 147, 149, 153–155, 156, 158

INDEX

Maithili language, 15–17, 115–116, 118–119, 127, 129, 135
Malaria, xiii, 2, 59–60, 62, 68, 196; eradication program, 68, 73, 85, 88
Marwaris, 15, 37, 104, 156, 158, 163
Mechi River, 3, 25, 41
Mechis, 20, 59, 163
Migration, 20, 25–26, 58–86, 89, 94, 145, 177, 194–196, 203; from Nepal into India, 63, 64–65, 68, 82–83, 84–85, 95, 98; from India into tarai, 14, 23, 26, 34, 58–62, 66, 73–78, 92–94, 98, 101, 106, 183, 177, 203; from hills into tarai, xiii, 11–12, 22, 23, 62–66, 68, 73–78, 80–86, 110, 114, 146, 160, 203
Mishra, Ram Narayan, 91
Monarchy, 197–200, 203, 204. *See also* Shah, Mahendra
Morang district, 5, 25, 68, 76, 82, 85, 133n
Morang Pradesh dialects, 15, 115–116
Muslims, 13–15, 20–23, 32–34, 40, 61–62, 74, 80–81, 106, 118n, 145, 148–152, 161n, 163, 164, 166; tensions with Hindus, 176–177

National (Central) Secretariat, 140–141, 161, 165–166, 168–169, 204, 205
National Educational Planning Commission, 108–111
National Education Commission, 124, 132
National integration, 23, 194–205; defined, xiv; barriers to, xiv, 2, 11–12, 38, 42, 43, 44, 46, 56, 57, 58, 87, 91, 94, 98–99, 103, 108, 111, 117, 129–132, 146, 158–159, 169, 189, 193, 195, 196, 202; policies to promote, 41, 45, 73–76, 82, 85–86, 112, 126–130, 135, 155–158, 169–170, 195–197, 203–205
Nationalism, xiv, 44, 87, 92, 99, 101, 107, 108–110, 112, 125, 129, 132, 137, 145, 157, 169, 178–180, 200–202, 204
National Panchayat, 138–141, 144, 156, 157–158, 161, 163–165, 169, 177, 182, 188, 204
Nawal Parasi district, 24, 47, 95, 97–98, 174
Naxalbari, unrest in, 182–183, 185, 192
Nepalganj, 189
Nepali Congress Party, 90–91, 101, 105, 107, 111, 113, 121, 122–123, 125, 136, 146, 155, 176–177, 181–193, 194, 195, 197–198, 201
Nepali language, 15, 17, 21n, 22, 63, 88, 92, 94, 108–125, 126–127, 132–133, 180; and nationalism, 108–110, 112, 125, 132, 157, 179, 202; in schools, 108–114, 124, 132–135, 202; use in tarai, 109–111, 114–115, 119–120, 127, 129, 131–135, 143, 202
Nepali National Congress, 113
Nepali Pracharini Sabha, 111–112
Nepal Prajatantrik Mahasabha, 100–101, 121
Nepal Tarai Congress, 109–110, 111, 115, 121–124

Newars, 22, 33, 61, 81, 85, 104, 125, 131, 135, 141, 146–147, 154, 160–169, 195–197; language of, 15, 88, 125, 129
Nidhi, Mahendra Narayan, 123
Nonalignment policy, 106, 178, 199, 201, 204

Pakistan, citizenship legislation in, 89, 92; migration from, 101; political system in, 137; relations with India, 194
Palace Secretariat, 140–141, 146, 165–166, 169
Panchayat system, 130–131, 136–141, 169–170, 178, 186, 197, 201; at village level, 141–144, 148–155; at district level, 142, 144–158, 189–190; at zonal level, 156–158; at national level, 158–170
Parliament (1959–60), 90–91, 113, 122–123, 136, 139, 163–164, 181–182, 197–198
Parsa district, 14, 16, 48, 59, 76, 85, 104
Political parties, role of, 49, 101, 113, 115, 121–122, 136, 155, 159, 163, 169, 176, 179, 181–193, 197–198, 199, 201, 204. *See also* specific parties
Population problems, 20, 62–63, 66–68, 70, 83, 85
Praja Parishad, 111, 113
Public Representation Act (1951), 89–90, 100

Rais, 15, 20, 76, 162, 167
Rajbanshis, 20, 59, 80, 115, 147, 163
Rajbiraj, 112, 133n, 134n, 189
Rajputs, 19, 22, 144, 146, 147, 154, 156, 162–163, 166–167
Rana, Jung Bahadur, 60, 105n
Rana family and regime, 25–26, 37, 43, 45, 60, 89–91, 95, 108, 110, 125n, 130, 136, 145, 146, 159, 161, 168, 181n, 190, 196, 197, 199, 204
Rangeli, 111
Rapti River, 25
Rauniyars, 104
Rautahat district, 14, 16, 48, 49, 76, 78, 85, 104, 181
Rayamajhi, Keshar Jang, 181–182
Re-settlement programs, 82–86, 194. *See also* Migration
Revolution (1950–51), 89–91, 110, 136, 191, 192
Rice, 29–31, 37, 38, 39, 54, 104
Rupandehi district, 24–25, 95, 174, 175, 176, 183

Sanskrit and Sanskritization, 12, 23, 63, 131, 159
Sanyasis, 154, 156, 167
Saptari district, 68, 76, 78, 91, 123, 133n, 146, 181, 187

Sarkis, 19, 65–66, 76, 162
Sarlahi district, 14, 16, 78, 85, 133n
"Save Hindi" Campaign, 111–112, 114, 123
Sen Kings, 24, 59–60
Shah, Birendra Bir Bikram, 165, 168, 169, 180, 187, 204–205
Shah, Mahendra Bir Bikram, 41, 98, 101, 107, 111, 112, 113, 114, 122, 124, 125, 136–137, 156, 165, 168, 170, 171, 172, 178–180, 182, 185, 186, 191, 197–201, 204; Royal Coup (Dec. 1960), 91, 107, 136, 182, 198, 201
Shah, Prithvi Narayan, 24–25, 87–88, 160–161, 196
Shah, Tribhuvan Bir Bikram, 90
Shah family, 25, 37, 50, 60, 110, 136, 144–146, 161, 165, 197
Shamsher, Bir, 76
Shamsher, Chandra, 25
Shamsher, Juddha, 25, 37
Shamsher, Subarna, 91, 185–186
Sherpas, 15, 33, 162
Shrestha, Pushpa Lal, 181–182, 184–185
Shrivastava, Kashi Prasad, 122–123
Sikkim, 46, 63, 68, 77, 94; citizenship legislation in, 93, 106
Simraun Garh, Kingdom of, 58–59
Singh, Ganesh Man, 185–186
Singh, K.I., 49, 111–112, 121–122
Singh, Nageshwar Prasad, 105
Singhania family, 37
Siraha district, 14, 16, 68, 78
Siwalik Range, 3–5, 11, 17, 22, 59, 62, 68, 70
Sonars, 19, 78
Soviet Union, economic aid to Nepal, 41, 50, 199–200; relations with Nepal, 1
Student politics, 182, 184, 186–188, 189
Sudis, 76, 154
Sunars, 19
Sunsari district, 5, 85
Susta Forest dispute, 47–48

Tajpurias, 20, 80, 163
Tamangs, 76, 162, 167; language of, 15, 115
Tarai, Inner, 5, 17, 27–28, 41n, 63n, 78, 83, 158n, 215–216
Tarai, Outer, defined, 2–3; census districts of, 5–7; development districts of, 5, 8–10; history of, 24–25, 43, 47, 50, 58–63, 87–88
Tarai Liberation Front, 182–185
Taulihawa, 133n, 154, 175
Telis, 76, 154
Thakalis, 15, 33, 154, 162
Thapa, Surya Bahadur, 54, 186
Tharus, 14, 20, 59, 61, 75, 78, 80, 81, 91, 158n, 163, 174; languages of, 15–17, 115
Tibetan border. *See* China, border with Nepal
Timber, 5, 25, 26, 27, 29, 37, 38, 39, 60, 76, 82
Transportation, 11, 24, 35–37, 41, 50, 62, 128, 130, 156; East-West highway, 41
Tribhuvan University, 161, 187, 205

United Democratic Front, 112–113
United Democratic Party, 102, 111, 121–123
United States, 205; citizenship legislation in, 105; economic aid to Nepal, 41, 45, 68, 172, 199–200; relations with Nepal, 1
Urdu language, 15, 118
Uttar Pradesh, 1, 3, 11–12, 14–15, 17, 23, 58, 106, 110, 117, 184, 191

Videha, Kingdom of, 58–59
Village panchayats, 138–139, 141–144, 148–155

West Bengal, 1, 3, 51, 63, 77, 95, 106, 135, 183, 191–192

Yadav, Suryanath Das, 91

Zonal panchayats and assemblies, 137–139, 156–158

COMMUNITY
A Trinity of Models